YALE CLASSICAL MONOGRAPHS, 5

GREEK POETIC
SYNTAX
IN THE
CLASSICAL AGE

Victor Bers

YALE UNIVERSITY PRESS
NEW HAVEN AND LONDON

Published with the assistance of the
Frederick W. Hilles Publication Fund of Yale University
and of the foundation established in memory of
James Wesley Cooper of the Class of 1865, Yale College.

Designed by Sally Harris
and set in Times Roman type.
Printed in the United States of America by
Halliday Lithograph, West Hanover, Mass.

Library of Congress Cataloging in Publication Data

Bers, Victor.
Greek poetic syntax in the Classical Age.
(Yale classical monographs; 5)
Bibliography: p.
Includes indexes.
1. Greek language—Syntax. 2. Greek language—
Variation.   I. Title.   II. Series.
PA369.B47   1983   485   82-20309
ISBN 0-300-02812-1

10 9 8 7 6 5 4 3 2 1

For Susie

Contents

Preface

This book aims at finding the precise limits and rationale, whether aesthetic or semantic, of certain syntactical phenomena in classical Greek poetry. I consider also some less strictly genre-conditioned features of syntax said to be "elevated" or "solemn." It is an assumption of my method that syntax is an aspect of language separable from lexicon and morphology at least to a degree sufficient for the purposes of practical criticism.[1] Because syntactical differentiae impinge most directly on the fundamental purpose of language, the communication of meaning, I regard them as the most important of the stylistically motivated deviations from everyday language found in Greek poetry. Some syntactical features, moreover, are more specifically "poetic" than virtually any other formal characteristic of poetic language, as they form a boundary that "poeticizing" prose and versified colloquial speech did not cross; consequently these features may be regarded as "superior" differentiae.

My general approach is to compare the branches and subdivisions of Greek literature, what Gildersleeve, greatest of aesthetic syntacticians, called the "departments." I look for the generic, abandoning from the outset any search for syntax molded by a purely individual vision. By concentrating on the formal, I am bound to attend to the linguistic surface of literary works at the expense of other attributes that might be generically determined. By examining occasional features I overlook the systematic, e.g., the phonological recurrences within complete poems described by Roman Jakobson. My focus on formal aspects that correspond closely to genres and subgenres predisposes me to assume that an utterance takes a particular form simply because it occurs in a particular genre or sub-

---

1. The usage of modern theoretical linguists would require the term *grammar* to describe any syntactical phenomena involving inflectional categories, e.g., case or voice. I have decided to retain *syntax* because to classicists, at least, *grammar* suggests accidence (roughly, the contents of Schwyzer, *Gramm.* 1) as well as syntax (roughly, the contents of *Gramm.* 2), and only the latter is the business of this book.

genre. But predisposition is not stubborn prejudice. Obviously, syntax is only one dimension of any literary utterance, thus a syntactical analysis will never account in full for the beauty felt to reside in that utterance. Obviously, genre is not the sole determinant of syntactical selection: often the language allows no choice, or genre plays no role in that choice. Still, Greek aesthetic sensibility demanded language appropriate to genre. The distribution of many linguistic features demonstrates this perfectly well. And if we interpret a syntactical differentia as serving an autoreferential function in respect of genre, we should understand by that more than "the sign points to itself," or "the text speaks of its own composition." Rather, the pointing of that sign always extends beyond itself to imply an association with some branch of an unsurpassed literature. Consequently, we should feel no embarrassment, as if caught in reductionist crudity, for taking pleasure in the discovery that some component of language is as it is, or better, can be as it is, because of where it is.

The method dictates the period this book surveys, for only the fifth and fourth centuries B.C. produced substantial literary texts, contemporaneous with each other or nearly so, in a variety of prose and verse genres.

"Language," according to Meillet's famous dictum, "is a system where everything is connected." But the system need not be symmetrical throughout and the connections need not be equally visible to students of language. Objective research into language, artistic language above all, cannot cut a series of congruent paths, even if the research is meant to be confined to a single language, a single period, and a single linguistic category. We must study a syntactical feature as we find it, embedded in passages of Greek that vary in all those dimensions that can make any two utterances different from each other in nuance or purport: context, imagery, acoustic properties, recollection of other utterances, and so on. It follows that we can never say of any two passages that they are identical in all other respects but differ in genre conditioning, the element on which this book concentrates.[2] Further, the difficulties in isolating genre conditioning vary from feature to feature. For these reasons there is little uniformity of organization and proportion in the discussion of the differentiae.

Yet in every chapter I have made the facts of distribution my chief business, for I regard it as axiomatic (i.e., unprovable but indispensable to the enterprise) that every author and audience of the classical period recognized all linguistic features of artistic language as constituent ele-

---

2. Demetrius and other Greek literary critics do sometimes offer two versions of an utterance, varying only in the stylistic point under discussion. Unfortunately, they were not interested in the differentiae I have examined.

ments of the established and developing literary genres. I also believe, but cannot prove, that insofar as content does not determine the syntax an author will use to express an idea as much as it determines his lexicon, syntax has relatively greater force in drawing the lines of genre distinctiveness where those lines are sharpest. Further, artistic judgment may falter, even in masters like Pindar, Euripides, Isocrates, and Plato. These authors must have sometimes regretted a stylistic decision. But the Greeks of the period were quick to form a canon of authors,[3] and they had the keenest interest in matters of style. Consequently, they would, I believe, make all the stylistic choices of the most admired writers into significant aesthetic facts. By "aesthetic facts" I mean aspects of style that enjoy normative status, practices to copy or avoid, as the case may be, in the creation of new works contributed to an established genre.

For their generous assistance I am grateful to Paula Arnold, Amy Bernstein, Kevin M. Crotty, Sir Kenneth Dover, Victor Erlich, John H. Finley, Jr., Herbert Golder, Justina Winston Gregory, C. John Herington, Kathleen Hughes, Daniel Kinney, Nita Krevans, Mary Kuntz, Brook Manville, Glenn Most, Sheila Murnaghan, Gregory Nagy, Alan Nussbaum, Lionel Pearson, Rolly Phillips, Adele Scafuro, Alexander Schenker, Daniel Tompkins, Gordon Williams, John Winkler, and several anonymous referees. I have been stubborn on many points, so it is no mere topos of prefatory acknowledgments to exonerate these scholars for any errors in the pages that follow. It is a special pleasure to thank Sharon Slodki of the Yale University Press for her blend of $\dot{\alpha}\varkappa\varrho\iota\beta\varepsilon\iota\alpha$ and good humor. For time off from teaching and for financial assistance in meeting the expenses of preparing my manuscript I record here my gratitude to the Morse Foundation and the Griswold Fund at Yale.

---

3. The clearest example of this tendency is the recognition in Aristophanes' *Frogs* that Aeschylus, Sophocles, and Euripides surpassed all competitors.

Abbreviations

Abbreviations for Greek authors and texts are those used in LSJ[9] and *OCD*[2]. Periodicals are abbreviated as in *L'Année Philologique,* with a few trivial exceptions, e.g., *AJP,* not *AJPh,* for the *American Journal of Philology.*

Amigues, *Subord.*	Suzanne Amigues. *Les subordonées par ΟΠΩΣ en attique classique.* Paris, 1977.
ATL	B. D. Meritt, H. T. Wade-Gery, and M. F. McGregor. *The Athenian Tribute Lists.* 4 vols. Cambridge, Mass., 1939–53.
Bechtel, *Gk. Dial.*	F. B. Bechtel. *Die griechischen Dialekte.* 3 vols. Berlin, 1921–24.
Benveniste, *Prob.*	Emile Benveniste. *Problèmes de linguistique générale.* Paris, 1966.
Bers, *Enallage*	Victor Bers. *Enallage and Greek Style. Mnemosyne* supplement 29. Leiden, 1974.
Bishop, "Verbals in -TEO"	C. E. Bishop. "The Greek Verbal in -TEO." *AJP* 20 (1899): 1–21, 121–38.
Björck, *Alpha Imp.*	Gudmund Björck. *Das alpha impurum und die tragische Kunstsprache.* Uppsala, 1950.
Bruhn, *Anhang*	Ewald Bruhn. *Anhang* (vol. 8) to F. W. Schneidewin and August Nauck, *Sophokles.* Berlin, 1899.
Campbell, "Lang. Soph."	Lewis Campbell. "Essay on the Language of Sophocles." In *Sophocles: The Plays and Fragments,* vol. 1. Oxford, 1871–81.

Campbell, *Lyr. Poetry*

David Campbell. *Greek Lyric Poetry.* London, 1967.

Chantraine, *Hom.*

Pierre Chantraine. *Grammaire homérique,* vol. 1: *Syntaxe.* Paris, 1953.

Chantraine, "Stylistique"

"La stylistique grecque." In *Proceedings of the First Congress of the International Federation of Classical Studies.* Paris, 1951.

Cucuel, *Antiph.*

Charles Cucuel. *Essai sur la langue et le style de l'orateur Antiphon.* Paris, 1886.

Cuny, *Nombre Duel*

Albert Cuny. *Le nombre duel en grec.* Paris, 1906.

Cyranka, *Orat. Thuc.*

L. A. Cyranka. *De orationum Thucydidearum elocutione cum tragicis comparata.* Dissertation, Breslau, 1875.

Denniston, *Part.*

J. D. Denniston. *The Greek Particles.* 2d ed., rev. K. J. Dover. Oxford, 1954.

Denniston, *Prose Style*

J. D. Denniston. *Greek Prose Style.* Oxford, 1952.

Dornseiff, *Pindars Stil*

Franz Dornseiff. *Pindars Stil.* Berlin, 1921.

Dover, *Lysias*

K. J. Dover. *Lysias and the Corpus Lysiacum.* Berkeley and Los Angeles, 1968.

Dover, "stile Aristof."

K. J. Dover. "Lo stile di Aristofane." *QUCS* 9 (1970): 7–23.

Dover, "Stil Aristoph."

"Der Stil des Aristophanes." Translation of the preceding by F. Regen in H.-J. Newiger, *Aristophanes und die Alte Komödie.* Darmstadt, 1975.

Escher, *Acc.*

Eduard Escher. *Der Accusativ bei Sophokles unter Zuziehung desjenigen bei Homer, Aeschylus, Euripides, Aristophanes, Thucydides und Xenophon.* Zurich, 1876.

Fairbanks, "Dative Soph."

Arthur Fairbanks. "The Dative Case in Sophokles." *TAPA* 17 (1886): 78–127.

Favre, *Thes. Verb.*

Christophorus Favre. *Thesaurus verborum, quae in titulis leguntur, cum Herodoteo sermone comparatus.* Heidelberg, 1914.

Garbrah, *Erythrae*

K. A. Garbrah, *A Grammar of the Ionic*

Inscriptions from Erythrae. Beiträge zur
Klass. Phil. 60. Meisenheim, 1978.

Gildersleeve, *Pind.* B. L. Gildersleeve. *Pindar: Olympian and Pythian Odes.* New York, 1890.

Gildersleeve, "Pind. Synt." B. L. Gildersleeve. "Studies in Pindaric Syntax." *AJP* 3 (1882): 434–55.

Gildersleeve, "Probs." B. L. Gildersleeve. "Problems in Greek Syntax." Baltimore, 1903. Reprinted from *AJP* 23 (1902): 1–27, 121–60.

Gildersleeve, *Synt.* B. L. Gildersleeve. *Syntax of Classical Greek.* Vol. 1, New York, 1900. Vol. 2 (with C. W. E. Miller), New York, 1911.

Gonda, *Moods* Jan Gonda. *The Character of the Indo-European Moods.* Wiesbaden, 1956.

Goodwin, *GMT* W. W. Goodwin. *Syntax of the Moods and Tenses of the Greek Verb,* rewritten and enlarged. Boston, 1890.

Guiraud, *Phrase nom.* Charles Guiraud. *La phrase nominale en grec.* Paris, 1962.

Havers, "Bedeut. Pl." Wilhelm Havers. "Zur Bedeutung des Plurals." In *Festschrift für Kretschmer.* Vienna, Leipzig, New York, 1926.

Hirt, *IG* H. H. Hirt. *Indogermanische Grammatik,* vols. 1–7. Heidelberg, 1921–37.

Householder and Nagy, "Greek" Fred Householder and Gregory Nagy. "Greek." *Current Trends in Linguistics* 9 (1972): 735–816.

Humbert, *Synt.* Jean Humbert. *Syntaxe grecque.* 3d ed. Paris, 1960.

Jones, *Poet. Pl.* H. L. Jones. *The Poetic Plural of Greek in the Light of Homeric Usage.* Cornell Studies in Classical Philology 19. Ithaca, 1910.

K–G Raphael Kühner. *Ausführliche Grammatik der griechischen Sprache.* Part 2: *Satzlehre.* 2 vols. 3d ed., rev. Bernard Gerth. Hannover and Leipzig, 1898–1904.

Kluge, *Quaest.* Heinrich Kluge. *Syntaxis Graecae Quaestiones Selectae.* Dissertation, Berlin, 1911.

Krüger, *Att.* K. W. Krüger. *Griechische Sprachlehre*

	für Schulen. Part 1: *Ueber die gewöhnliche vorzugsweise die attische Prosa.* Section 2: *Syntax,* 5th ed. Berlin, 1871.
Krüger, *Poet.*	K. W. Krüger. *Griechische Sprachlehre fü Schulen.* Part 2, section 2: *Poetischdialektische Syntax.* 3d ed. Berlin, 1871.
Lammermann, *Urbanität*	Karl Lammermann. *Von der attischen Urbanität.* Dissertation, Göttingen, 1935.
Langholf, *Syntakt. Hipp.*	Volker Langholf. *Syntaktische Untersuchungen zu Hippokratestexten.* Mainz, 1977.
Lasso de La Vega, "Orac. nom."	José Lasso de La Vega. "Sobre la oracion nominal en attico." *Emerita* 20 (1952): 308–36.
Löfstedt, *Synt.*	Einar Löfstedt. *Syntactica.* 2d ed. 2 vols. Lund, 1956
Long, *Lang. Soph.*	A. A. Long. *Language and Thought in Sophocles.* London, 1968.
LSJ	Henry George Liddell and Robert Scott. *A Greek-English Lexicon.* 9th ed., rev. H. S. Jones. Oxford, 1970.
Maas, "Poet. Pl."	Paul Maas. "Studien zum poetischen Plural bei den Römern." *ALL* 12 (1902): 479–550.
Maas, "rev. Sing."	Paul Maas. Review of K. Witte, *Singular und Plural* (see below). *PhW* 1908, cols. 1406–16.
Meiggs and Lewis, *GHI*	Russell Meiggs and David Lewis. *A Selection of Greek Historical Inscriptions.* Oxford, 1969.
Meillet, *Aperçu*	A. M. Meillet. *Aperçu d'une histoire de la langue grecque.* 7th ed. Paris, 1965.
Meisterhans, *Inschrift.*	K. M. Meisterhans. *Grammatik der attischen Inschriften.* 3d ed., rev. Eduard Schwyzer. Berlin, 1900.
Menge, *Poet. Scaen.*	Paul Menge. *De poetarum scaenicorum graecorum sermone observationes selectae.* Göttingen, 1905.
Mommsen, *Beit. Präp.*	Tycho Mommsen. *Beiträge zur Lehre von den griechischen Präpositionen.* Frankfurt, 1886–95.

Norden, *Kunstprosa*	Eduard Norden. *Die antike Kunstprosa.* 3d ed. 2 vols. Leipzig and Berlin, 1909.
*OCD*²	*Oxford Classical Dictionary.* 2d ed., ed. N. G. L. Hammond and H. H. Scullard. Oxford, 1970.
Palmer, "Hom."	L. R. Palmer. "The Language of Homer." In *A Companion to Homer,* ed. A. J. B. Wace and F. H. Stubbings. London, 1963.
Poultney, *Genitive Aristoph.*	J. W. Poultney. *Syntax of the Genitive Case in Aristophanes.* Baltimore, 1936.
Poultney, "Synt. Comedy"	J. W. Poultney. "Studies in the Syntax of Attic Comedy." *AJP* 84 (1963): 359–76.
Radko, "Synt. Trag."	A. M. Radko. "The Syntax of the Narrative Passages in Greek Tragedy." Dissertation, Johns Hopkins University, 1969.
Rau, *Paratrag.*	Peter Rau. *Paratragodia. Zetemata* 45. Munich, 1967.
Rehdantz, *Gramm. u. lex.*	Carl Rehdantz. *Grammatischer und lexicalischer Index.* In *Demosthenes: Neun Philippische Reden.* 4th ed., rev. Friedrich Blass. Leipzig, 1886.
Riddell, "Plat. Id."	James Riddell. "Digest of Platonic Idioms." In his edition of Plato's *Apology.* Oxford, 1867.
Ruijgh, "*TE épique*"	C. J. Ruijgh. *Autour de "TE épique."* Amsterdam, 1971.
Rutherford, *NP*	W. G. Rutherford. *The New Phrynichus.* London, 1886.
Schmid–Stählin, *Gr. Lit.*	Wilhelm Schmid and Otto Stählin. *Geschichte der griechischen Literatur. Handbuch d. Altertumswissenschaft.* Munich, 1929–48.
Schwyzer, *Dialect. Epigraph.*	Eduard Schwyzer. *Dialectorum Graecarum Exempla Epigraphica Potiora.* 3d ed. Leipzig, 1923.
Schwyzer, *Gramm.*	Eduard Schwyzer. *Griechische Grammatik. Handbuch d. Altertumswissenschaft.* 2 vols. Vol. 1, 4th ed., Munich, 1939; vol. 2 (with A. Debrunner), Munich, 1950.
Schwyzer, "Synt. Arch."	Eduard Schwyzer. "Syntaktische Archa-

	ismen des Attischen." *Abhand. d. Preussischen Akad. d. Wiss.* 7 (1940): 1–15.
Sideras, *Aesch. Hom.*	Alexander Sideras. *Aeschylus Homericus.* Hypomnemata 31. Göttingen, 1971.
Silk, *Interact.*	M. S. Silk. *Interaction in Poetic Imagery.* Cambridge, 1974.
Slotty, *Konj. u. Opt.*	Friedrich Slotty. *Der Gebrauch des Konjunktivs und Optativs in den griechischen Dialekten.* Forschungen zur griech. u. lat. Grammatik 3. Göttingen, 1915.
Slotty, "soz. affekt. Pl."	Friedrich Slotty. "Die Stellung des Griechischen und anderer indogermanischen Sprachen zu dem soziativen und affektischen Gebrauch des Plurals der ersten Person." *IF* 45 (1927): 348–63.
Smyth	H. W. Smyth. *Greek Grammar.* Revised by Gordon Messing. Cambridge, Mass., 1956.
Stahl, *Verb.*	J. M. Stahl. *Kritisch-historische Syntax des griechischen Verbums der klassischen Zeit.* Heidelberg, 1907.
Stevens, *Colloq. Eur.*	P. T. Stevens. *Colloquial Expressions in Euripides.* Hermes Einzelschriften 38. Wiesbaden, 1976.
Thesleff, *Styles*	Holgar Thesleff. *Studies in the Styles of Plato.* Helsinki, 1967.
Veitch, *Grk. Verbs*	William Veitch. *Greek Verbs Irregular and Defective.* Oxford, 1881.
Volp, *Num. Pl.*	Eduard Volp. *De numeri pluralis usu Aeschyleo et Sophocleo.* Marburg, 1888.
Wackernagel, "Gesetz"	Jacob Wackernagel. "Über ein Gesetz der indogermanischen Wortstellung." In his *Kleine Schriften* 1.1–103. Göttingen, 1953.
Wackernagel, *Hom.*	Jacob Wackernagel. *Sprachliche Untersuchungen zu Homer.* Forschungen zur griech. u. lat. Grammatik 4. Göttingen, 1916.
Wackernagel, "Misc."	Jacob Wackernagel. "Miscellen zur griechischen Grammatik." *KZ* 30 (1890): 293–316.

Wackernagel, *Vorl.*

Jacob Wackernagel. *Vorlesungen über Syntax.* 2d ed. Vol. 1, Basel, 1926; vol. 2, Basel, 1928.

White, *Verse*

W. J. White. *The Verse of Greek Comedy.* London, 1912.

Witte, *Sing. u. Pl.*

Kurt Witte. *Singular und Plural.* Leipzig, 1907.

Introduction

Prose, Poetry, and Verse

Modern theorists of poetic language must account for free verse, "prose poems," and even "accidental" poetry.[1] The student of Greek poetic language may cling to meter as a reliable formal distinction between poetry and all other varieties of Greek, literary or colloquial. Even the advent of rhythmic prose did not threaten the criterion of meter: ῥυθμὸν δεῖ ἔχειν τὸν λόγον, μέτρον δὲ μή· ποίημα γὰρ ἔσται.[2] Greek does not have a word for what we may call "verse"—otherwise unremarkable language and "pedestrian" content, fitted to a metrical pattern—and hardly any works of this sort existed (see n. 5). But the Greeks were conscious that the prose-poetry dichotomy was not entirely sufficient.

Theoretical discussion of the difference between poetic and nonpoetic language begins in the period treated by this book, roughly the years between Aeschylus' and Pindar's earliest and Demosthenes' last works.[3] From the outset, the discussion is tainted by polemics. Gorgias, seeking to enhance the prestige of rhetoric, declares that meter, and by implication nothing else, distinguished poetry from prose: τὴν ποίησιν ἅπασαν καὶ νομίζω καὶ ὀνομάζω λόγον [i.e., prose] ἔχοντα μέτρον (D–K 11.9).[4] Presumably this manifesto served to justify the importation of poetic diction into prose, which Aristotle rebukes at Rhet. 1404a24–29:

---

1. Such as "Swamps, marshes, barrowpits and other / Areas of stagnant water serve / As breeding grounds," a typographical rearrangement of the text of a report on mosquito control, printed as "poetry" by the Australian literary journal *Angry Penguins*. Disclosure of the hoax played on him did not diminish the editor's appreciation of the "poem" (see C. C. Bombaugh, *Oddities and Curiosities of Words and Literature*, ed. M. Gardner [New York, 1961], pp. 349–50).
2. Arist. *Rhet.* 3.1408b30–31.
3. The earliest nondiscursive allusion to the difference is probably Solon 1.2 West, κόσμον ἐπέων ᾠδὴν ἀντ᾽ἀγορῆς θέμενος, but text and meaning are not beyond question.
4. Cf. Pl. *Grg.* 502c5 . . . εἴ τις περιέλοι τῆς ποιήσεως πάσης τό τε μέλος καὶ τὸν ῥυθμὸν καὶ μέτρον, ἄλλο τι ἢ λόγοι γίγνονται τὸ λειπόμενον;

1

ἐπεὶ δ' οἱ ποιηταί, λέγοντες εὐήθη, διὰ τὴν λέξιν ἐδόκουν πορίσασ-
θαι τὴν δόξαν, διὰ τοῦτο ποιητικὴ πρώτη ἐγένετο λέξις, οἷον ἡ
Γοργίου, καὶ νῦν ἔτι οἱ πολλοὶ τῶν ἀπαιδεύτων τοὺς τοιούτους
οἴονται διαλέγεσθαι κάλλιστα. τοῦτο δ' οὐκ ἔστιν, ἀλλ' ἑτέρα λόγου
καὶ ποιήσεως λέξις ἐστίν.

Notwithstanding Aristotle's insistence in this passage that the diction
appropriate to poetry is distinct from the diction appropriate to prose,
elsewhere he argues that the fundamental distinction between the two is
teleological, not formal:

. . . οἱ ἄνθρωποί γε συνάπτοντες τῷ μέτρῳ τὸ ποιεῖν ἐλεγειοποιοὺς
τοὺς δὲ ἐποποιοὺς ὀνομάζουσιν, οὐχ ὡς κατὰ τὴν μίμησιν ποιητὰς
ἀλλὰ κοινῇ κατὰ τὸ μέτρον προσαγορεύοντες· καὶ γὰρ ἂν ἰατρικὸν ἢ
φυσικόν τι διὰ τῶν μέτρων ἐκφέρωσιν, οὕτω καλεῖν εἰώθασιν· οὐδὲν
δὲ κοινόν ἐστιν Ὁμήρῳ καὶ Ἐμπεδοκλεῖ πλὴν τὸ μέτρον, διὸ τὸν μὲν
ποιητὴν δίκαιον καλεῖν, τὸν δὲ φυσιολόγον μᾶλλον ἢ ποιητήν·
[Poet. 1447b13–20]

φανερὸν δὲ ἐκ τῶν εἰρημένων καὶ ὅτι οὐ τὸ τὰ γενόμενα λέγειν,
τοῦτο ποιητοῦ ἔργον ἐστίν, ἀλλ' οἷα ἂν γένοιτο καὶ τὰ δυνατὰ κατὰ
τὸ εἰκὸς ἢ τὸ ἀναγκαῖον. ὁ γὰρ ἱστορικὸς καὶ ὁ ποιητὴς οὐ τῷ ἢ
ἔμμετρα λέγειν ἢ ἄμετρα διαφέρουσιν (εἴη γὰρ ἂν τὰ Ἡροδότου εἰς
μέτρα τεθῆναι καὶ οὐδὲν ἧττον ἂν εἴη ἱστορία τις μετὰ μέτρου ἢ ἄνευ
μέτρων)· ἀλλὰ τούτῳ διαφέρει, τῷ τὸν μὲν τὰ γενόμενα λέγειν, τὸν δὲ
οἷα ἂν γένοιτο. [Poet. 1451a36–51b5]

Even if we accept Aristotle's premise, it is a heavy coat of inessential
linguistic features that conceals the proper categorization of the works of
Homer, Empedocles, and Herodotus. The argument would have more
bearing on practical criticism if Empedocles had written didactic poems
totally free of poetic words and conventional epithets familiar from Homer
(e.g., χθών 48 Wright [96 D–K].1, νηλεὲς ἦμαρ 120 Wright [139 D–K].1),
and in his native dialect, Doric, instead of Ionic, and similarly, if someone
had actually versified Herodotus.[5] Aristotle's way of emphasizing what he
regards as the true differences among genres, declaring that his definition
holds even when accidental features are reversed, is much like his essentially economic definition of δημοκρατία: the term would still apply if the
poor people of a city, though a minority, controlled the government. The

5. Euenus and Theodectes wrote handbooks of rhetoric in verse (Pl. *Phdr.* 267a3–5; *Suda*
s.v. Theodectes), but exercises like that could not have had any significant impact on the
notion of genre appropriateness. For other authors (including Plato) said to confound the
prose/poetry division, see E. Norden, *Kunstprosa* 1.73–79, 91–95, 104–13.

poor are, however, almost always in the majority, a fact that saves his definition from embarrassment.[6]

Gorgias' claim implies that the prose writer is entitled to exploit any resource of the poet's language, save meter. In practice, however, Gorgias was not so uninhibited.[7] His artistic descendant, Isocrates, could still complain that the prose writer, even of epideictic, was denied use of poetry's κοσμοί (9.8–11).[8]

The tendency of stylistic features like meter and dialect to adhere to each other makes the present study possible. Though we must concede that the conglomerations of stylistic qualities were not fixed but rather gained and lost elements with the incessant evolution of individual authors and branches of literature (this is a point Aristotle makes against Gorgias), a powerful stylistic conservatism limited the rate of change. Besides, a breakdown in stylistic coherence was not irreversible. Andocides, for instance, uses many stray poetic words—probably less for the sake of experiment than out of sheer incompetence—but later, and better, orators ignore his precedent and revert to the earlier standards. Until Xenophon, gross contamination of genres does not occur except in intentional parody.

The stylistic distinctiveness of various genres is explicitly attested by ancient authorities, but their discussions illuminate only a small part of the terrain. Without question, diction in the narrowest sense, i.e., lexicon, is the aspect most prominent in the Aristotelian account of poetic style: syntax makes very few appearances indeed.[9] It is modern work on texts far more than the testimony of ancient critics which assigns stylistic character to syntactic phenomena. Though little ancient sanction exists for the linguistic category I have chosen to study, the relative silence of Aristotle

6. See G. E. M. de Ste. Croix, *The Class Struggle in the Ancient Greek World* (Ithaca, 1981), pp. 72–73. It should also be noted that Aristotle sometimes takes a quite different attitude to Empedocles, actually criticizing him for poeticisms that diminish his merit as a φυσιολόγος, e.g., the metaphorical description of the sea as "earth's sweat" (*Mete.* 357a24); see M. S. Buhl, "Untersuchungen zu Sprache und Stil des Empedokles" (diss., Heidelberg, 1956), pp. 5–6.

7. Schmid-Stählin, *Gr. Lit.* 7.1.3, p. 62, nn. 7–8. Some see the Gorgianic figures as rooted in a time long antedating the distinction between poetry and prose (e.g., Norden, *Kunstprosa* 1.30–31; E. Wellman, *RE* s.v. Gorgias, col. 1603). When one looks at any poetry of the mid fifth century, one sees much on the linguistic level that Gorgias does not touch, aside from τὸ μέτρον.

8. Not that his complaint is to be taken as entirely justified, for he himself exploits some of the devices from which he says prose writers are barred; see V. Buchheit, *Untersuchungen zur Theories des Genos Epideiktikon von Gorgias bis Aristoteles* (Munich, 1960), pp. 67–68.

9. Viz. the poetic plural (*Rhet.* 1407b32–35) and, if word order is included in syntax, the doubling of the attributive article (*Rhet.* 1407b36–38) and anastrophe of preposition (*Poet.* 1458b36–38). On the primacy of diction as the distinctive feature: Meillet, *Aperçu*, p. 219; Chantraine, "Stylistique," p. 23.

and later critics on syntactical differentiae should not intimidate us. The analytic prerequisites for such a study were in an early stage of development, or lacking entirely, until Hellenistic times. Our earliest systematic list of verbal moods is found in Dionysius Thrax.[10] Even Hellenistic scholars have little to say about genre-conditioned syntax, perhaps because they concentrated on one main division of literature—there were no commentaries on prose authors before Aristarchus—and on the general practice of authors, rather than on occasional deviations (Dionysius Thrax 5.1 Uhl.: Γραμματική ἐστιν ἐμπειρία τῶν παρὰ ποιηταῖς τε καὶ συγγραφεῦσιν ὡς ἐπὶ τὸ πολὺ λεγομένων).[11]

Genre Distinctiveness

Since this study dwells on differentiae—the very term suggests precise boundaries and rigorous taxonomy—it would be worthwhile to consider briefly how strictly Greek writers separated the main divisions of literature and their branches from one another in respect to language. An overview of some aspects of language other than syntax serves two functions: it guides our strategy by pointing to those categories likely to yield a significant distribution of syntactical features, and it helps us form an estimate of the degree to which syntax is like or unlike other elements of language in its susceptibility to genre conditioning.

In his *Griechische Verskunst*[12] Wilamowitz spoke of strict partitions:

> From 800 until 300 the Greeks constructed not one but a number of poetic types, styles, and languages which stand beside each other, fixed in their respective places. Anyone who wants to compose poetry must learn these, and learn which of them can be varied [abtönen]—but varied in such a way that a variation is felt *as such*. He must never mix the poetic types, styles, and languages; he must not introduce into any of them the language he speaks in life or writes in prose. . . . Metrical form and language belong together: epic and elegy demand to be written in Ionic, tragedy and comedy in Attic (but Attic of different sorts); lyrics are to be Doricized.

To be sure, there are linguistic features that show this sort of rigor. Some examples: tragedy's nearly total abstention from the deictic iota,[13] its

10. 47.3 Uhl.
11. R. Pfeiffer, *History of Classical Scholarship* (Oxford, 1968), pp. 224, 268.
12. Berlin, 1921, p. 42.
13. The only exception, if three MSS of Stobaeus can be trusted, is τουτί at Eur. fr. 572.1 N. Another MS has τόδε, and Nauck suggests βροτῷ. Another colloquialism, normally excluded by tragedy, and apparently below the Aristophanic norm as well, is ναίχι. On its single appearance in tragedy, Soph. *OT* 684 lyr. (!), see E. Fraenkel, *Due Seminarii*

meticulous deployment of ᾱ for η deriving from original ᾱ in lyrics and melic anapests,[14] its disdain for diminutives; Old Comedy is a bouillabaisse of styles, yet Aristophanes holds no example of anastrophe with μετά + genitive, even though he wrote that combination 85 times;[15] forensic narrative has been shown to differ from comic narrative in ways that went unrecognized until Dover's research on the Lysianic corpus.[16] Some other differences involve strong tendencies: the omission (or, better, nonexpression) of the definite article in poetry as compared with all varieties of prose,[17] the poets' preference for simplex, the prose authors' preference for compound verbs, and, simultaneously, the poets' love of compound adjectives.

There are also surprises, phenomena that should remind us that intuition is sometimes treacherous. Could anyone have predicted that ἅτε, a word found in Herodotus, Thucydides, Old Comedy, Plato, and orators, would make its occasional appearances on the tragic stage only in lyric, never in dialogue? Denniston, the greatest analyst of Greek style in modern times, found τοί a very strange particle for Antiphon to be using.[18] Examples could easily be multiplied.

Wilamowitz was not so finicky in *praxis*. Consider his remark in Eur. *Ba.* 492, where the apparently colloquial τί τὸ δεινὸν ἐργάσῃ; might be thought to violate his canon:

εἴφ᾽ ὅτι παθεῖν δεῖ· τί με τὸ δεινὸν ἐργάσῃ;

"A pretty example of how vulgarisms mix with archaic, stylized tragedy."[19] If it is considered necessary to reconcile Wilamowitz with himself (not perhaps an urgent project), one might say that here is a variation "felt as such." The colloquialism does not discredit the premise of consistency of style because it is well motivated by context: Dionysus so disdains Pentheus' threats that he will not ask about them in properly tragic language, say, of the sort Euripides gives to Agave at 1288:

λέγ᾽, ὡς τὸ μέλλον καρδία πήδημ᾽ ἔχει.

Romani di Eduard Fraenkel, Premessa di L. E. Rossi (Rome, 1977), p. 52, and K. J. Dover, "The Colloquial Stratum in Classical Attic Prose" in *Classical Contributions: Studies in Honour of Malcolm Francis McGregor,* ed. G. S. Shrimpton and D. J. McCargar (Locust Valley, N.Y., 1981), p. 20, n. 23.

14. Meticulously examined by Björck, *Alpha Imp.*

15. Reported by T. Mommsen, *Beit. Präp.,* p. 63.

16. *Lysias,* pp. 83–86, showing that Aristophanic narrative prefers ἔπειτα, ἔπειτα δέ, κἄπειτα, εἶτα, κᾆτα, forensic narrative δέ with initial participle or subordinate clause.

17. Wackernagel, *Vorl.* 2.147–50.

18. *Part.,* p. lxxx.

19. Ad Aristoph. *Lys.* 366.

Similarly, the colloquialism of χαίρειν λέγω at Eur. *Hipp.* 113, which
Stevens explains as emphasizing "the casual unconcern of Hippolytus in his
ignorance of the imminent vengeance of Aphrodite," is a stylistic crossover
that, I imagine, pleased rather than jarred. I am not as confident that unity
of style is preserved by Euripides at *Med.* 472, where the colloquial εὖ
ἐποίησας stands next to the verb μολών, which is poetic in the simplex
form. Stevens (*Colloq. Eur.*, pp. 2–3: cf. p. 54) maintains that "no special
incongruity need have been felt at the juxtaposition" in view of the
frequent use of ἐλθεῖν and μολεῖν close by each other in tragedy. Medea's
"sarcasm," as Stevens terms it, does not seem to me enhanced by combining the expression with the poetic verb, nor am I convinced that the
juxtaposition of the two verbs of motion makes μολών any less poetic. On
the other hand, 465–74 do not abound in other poetic features: I see only
the omission of the article with ψυχήν (474). δράω (at 470) was said to be
the Doric equivalent of πράττειν by advocates of a Doric origin for tragedy
(Arist. *Poet.* 1448b1), and it is certainly common in tragic dialogue; but it
also occurs in comedy without parodistic intent, e.g., at Aristoph. *Pax* 830.
Perhaps both colloquialism and poeticism are at a low ebb in this passage,
and thus accommodate each other easily.

We may attack the same problem in a slightly different form when
noncolloquial phonology veils an apparent colloquialism. Stevens (*Colloq. Eur.*, p. 41) quotes several comic passages in which τί πράττεις means
"How goes it?" or "How do you do?" A nearly equivalent expression in
American English (if I understand Stevens correctly) is "What's up?" He
argues (p. 3) that when the Attic -ττ- is replaced by -σσ-, "the non-Attic
form would not necessarily deny the colloquial character of the phrase
because the forms in σσ and ρσ were in use in historical prose and must
have been familiar on the lips of foreigners."[20] The phrase occurs at
Eur. *Or.* 732 troch.:

> θᾶσσον ἤ με χρῆν προβαίνων ἱκόμην δι' ἄστεως,
> σύλλογον πόλεως ἀκούσας, τὸν δ' ἰδὼν αὐτὸς σαφῶς,
> ἐπὶ σὲ σύγγονόν τε τὴν σήν, ὡς κτενοῦντας αὐτίκα.
> τί τάδε; πῶς ἔχεις; τί πράσσεις, φίλταθ' ἡλίκων ἐμοὶ   732
> καὶ φίλων καὶ συγγενείας; πάντα γὰρ τάδ' εἶ σύ μοι.

Again, dramatic context seems to me the best index of the expression we
are trying to evaluate. A strong colloquial flavor of the sort suggested by
Stevens's translation, i.e., a tone clearly befitting a casual conversation,
would undercut Pylades' concern for Orestes and Electra. One can also
point to predominantly poetic features in these lines: the simplex ἱκόμην

20. See below, pp. 7–9, on the general problem of Ionic and Attic.

(ἵκω is never compounded in poetry), the adjective σύγγονος, the simplex verb κτείνω, τόν used as a relative pronoun, the expansive vocative phrase beginning φίλταθ', single τε joining words (a usage occurring a few times in Aristophanes but "seldom found in the orators" [Denniston, *Part.*, pp. 498–99]). But these objective style markers are less decisive than the absurdity of putting a phrase like "What's up?" in Pylades' mouth at this moment in the play. This is not to deny that a colloquialism lies behind the phrase τί πράσσεις; The significant point here is that if Euripides had the colloquialism in mind, the phonological mutation from the Attic form signals a change in its stylistic flavor. There was no justification for allowing the unalloyed casual tone of Attic conversation into these lines. The resources of tragic language permit a poetically recast version.

The light Ionicism of tragic dialogue represented by -σσ- touches on a general problem: to what extent did the Ionic dialect sound poetic to the Attic ear? This, in turn, immediately brings in a second question: how far does the answer depend on date and genre? I cannot offer a systematic treatment of the difficulty, only some remarks that may serve to shape our expectations in the area of syntax.

Our evidence for dialects is decidedly imperfect. Between Aristophanes and other comic authors and the body of epigraphical material we can derive a fairly complete picture of Attic. But we have practically nothing to document everyday language in the other dialects: for Doric there are the remnants of Megarian at Aristoph. *Ach.* 729–835, and perhaps Epicharmus and Sophron; for Ionic, a number of inscriptions have some value.[21] Even within *Kunstprosa* our evidence has suffered damage in the course of scribal transmission. The manuscripts of Herodotus show signs of having been copied by men unsure of the dialect (see Meillet, *Aperçu*, p. 13, and L. Palmer, *OCD²* s.v. Greek Dialects §15); it is uncertain how Ionic a language Gorgias wrote (see the note in Diels-Kranz ad fr. 11); the dialect of the Hippocratic corpus is obscured by textual corruption (and, according to Chantraine, by "impurities in the author's language"[22]).

The distribution of particles is instructive, for as the "small change" of language (Benedict Einarson's term) they might indicate the subtler levels of dialect affiliation.[23] We could reason that a writer whose borrowings

21. Conveniently listed by R. Schmitt, *Einführung in die Griechischen Dialekte* (Darmstadt, 1977), p. 98. Laconian is represented by several stretches of Aristophanes' *Lysistrata* (Schmitt, p. 55), and Boeotian (less reliably) at *Acharnians* 860–954 and other passages in comedy (Schmitt, p. 68).

22. See J. Irgoin, "Tradition manuscrite et histoire du texte," in *La collection hippocratique et son rôle dans l'histoire de la médecine.* Colloque de Strasbourg (23–27 Octobre 1972). (Leiden, 1975), pp. 3–18.

23. Unlike most words, they can be given a place in discourse on any subject whatever, since they lack extralinguistic referents. Nouns and verbs, by contrast, can be problematic in stylistic analysis because their occurrence in some texts and absence from others may result

from another dialect are limited—and who might, therefore, *not* be suspected of syntactical borrowings—will maintain the particle usage of his
own dialect. This assumes that dialects show great internal consistency.
The facts are otherwise. "There is not . . . a great deal in common between the Herodotean and Hippocratic uses" (Denniston, *Part.*, p. lxx).
And worse, throughout the list of dialect divergences assembled by Denniston it is apparent that there are no obligatory Ionicisms,[24] nor is there
any principle that would enable us to predict which authors of the "semi-
Ionic" group ("tragedians, Herodotus, Plato, Xenophon, [and sometimes
Thucydides]")[25] will share the use of a particle. For example, a literary
precedent exists for connective καὶ δή in Homer, and the combination
persisted in fifth-century Ionic prose (Herodotus, Hippocrates) and in
Plato (*Part.*, p. lxxi); yet it is virtually excluded from tragedy. Conversely,
tragic poets sometimes use δῆθεν, a particle common in Ionic prose but not
attested in epic or lyric poets (*Part.*, p. 264). Denniston's "pure Attic"
group (Aristophanes and the orators) is also not entirely homogeneous in
its usage. Aristophanes joins Herodotus in using μηδέ after a preceding
positive clause, but in the ten canonical Attic orators there is only one
example of this usage (*Part.*, p. 190; citations from sophistic authors are
given by Dover, "stile Aristof.," pp. 19–20 = "Stil Aristoph.," pp. 138–
39). Connective καὶ δή, however, barely ever seen in the orators, is nearly
as rare in Aristophanes (*Part.*, p. 249). We may conclude that dialect
conditions the lexicon of particles, but weakly; the "pure Attic" group
gives fairly good evidence for taking Aristophanes as representing a type of
language that, by and large, persisted unchanged into the fourth century;
the tragedians, Thucydides, Plato, and Xenophon may have been susceptible to Ionic influence. All this agrees fairly well with other linguistic
features, notably the distribution of -σσ- vs. -ττ- and -ρσ- vs. -ρρ-.

"Susceptible to Ionic influence" suggests a marked split between the two
sister dialects, Attic and Ionic. This notion may be profoundly mistaken on
a broader lexical level, for a small body of lexical and phonological
differences between the dialects does not tell us very much about style.

---

only from the differences in subject matter of the texts, not from any literary difference.
Those particles that Denniston classifies as "adverbial," and especially those expressing
emotional moods and nuances, are most obviously useful in determining the flavor of a
passage. But particles that do not alter the emotional nuance of a passage—Denniston's
"connective" and "preparatory" types—are also worth attention. Though not condiments
with a taste of their own, they often absorb the taste of the words they articulate.

24. I.e., on the lexical level. Phonology is another matter (see, e.g., *Part.* p. 415, n. 1, on
Ionic ὦν for Attic οὖν).

25. It is strange to find Herodotus in this group. Whatever the inadequacies of the
transmitted text and whatever his mixture of older and newer Ionic forms and (perhaps) of
the language of various Ionian cities, he is still to be counted a wholly Ionic author.

K. J. Dover argues that the common lexical ground between Ionic and Attic may have been quite extensive in the fifth century, and he urges caution in pronouncing a word poetic by virtue of its absence from fourth-century prose.[26] As G. Lanata shows, the distinction between the technical and poetical vocabulary may not hold for the fifth century.[27] And in his careful analysis of alleged Herodotean poeticisms and Sophoclean Ionicisms, C. Chiasson demonstrates that there are very few reliable examples of either.[28] To end this pessimistic section, I cite a syntactical feature (not one of my differentiae) that illustrates both the rapidity of linguistic change in the fifth century and its uneven absorption by different genres: colloquial language and elevated poetry sometimes stand together against the practice of *Kunstprosa,* but we must be prepared to find a variety of alliances. A subtle example is the conjoining of μή (rather than the expected οὐ) and nonpredicative participles. This mark of a general development in negative particles is found in Sophocles, Euripides, and Thucydides but not in their near-contemporary Aristophanes or in an earlier tragedian (Aeschylus).[29]

I believe that this glance at some aspects of language and genre that are not my analysanda suggests two things (1) patterns of usage do exist, and (2) no single category—dialectal, lexical, or chronological—stands on its own. We must of course recognize the importance of linguistic change and dialect to the evaluation of syntactical features: genre, including the opposition of poetry and prose, is only one element of the edifice of literary language. But we cannot judge whether a particular variety of syntax is "elevated," or "poetic," by inspecting other formal features of the utterance. Still, our ignorance of many branches of linguistic experience in the classical period, and the complexity of poetic creation in any period, need not overwhelm us. A commonsense appreciation of what is appropriate in the literary presentation of human life is a powerful instrument.

"Problem" Authors: Some Specifics

My discussion of individual differentiae proceeds from a number of assumptions on authenticity, dialect, and relation to poetic language. All are controversial, and for the most part I simply allude to the scholarly opinion to which I subscribe.

---

26. *Thucydides, Greece and Rome: New Surveys in the Classics* 7 (Oxford, 1973), pp. 12–13; "stile Aristof.," pp. 8–9 = "Stil Aristoph.," pp. 125–26.
27. "Linguaggio scientifico e linguaggio poetico. Note al lessico del *de morbo sacro,*" *Quad. Urb. Cult. Class.* 5 (1968): 22–36.
28. "The Question of the Influence of Tragedy on Herodotus" (Ph.D. diss., Yale University, 1980), chap. 3, esp. pp. 17–18.
29. A. C. Moorehouse, "On Negativing Greek Participles Where the Leading Verbs Are of a Type to Require μή," *CQ* 42 (1948): 35–40.

Herodotus

I attribute any feature at variance with colloquial Aristophanes (see below) or Attic prose to the Ionic dialect, not to poeticism, unless stylistic elevation seems appropriate to the passage. On the whole I agree with A. W. Förstemann[30] that speeches are more likely to hold poeticisms than narrative. I doubt that educated Athenians of the period would agree with Hermogenes' generalization: ἡ γὰρ Ἰὰς οὖσα ποιητικὴ φύσει ἐστὶν ἡδεῖα (*De Ideis* 2.319 [p. 336 Rabe].[31] That Ionic was a prestige dialect until quite late in the century is a truism,[32] but Athenians could not have counted every word that fell from the mouth of, say, an Erythrean as pure poesy. (On the whole question see Meillet, *Aperçu*, pp. 232–33 [too suspicious of poeticisms] and C. Chiasson [n. 28]; on the broader question of Ionian prose and its relation to poetry see S. Lilja, "On the Style of the Earliest Greek Prose," *Commentationes Humanarum Litterarum* [Societas Scientiarum Fennica] 41 [Helsinki, 1968].)

Antiphon

I assume that the Athenian Antiphon of Rhamnus wrote both the actual court speeches (1, 5, 6) and the exercises or model speeches known as the *Tetralogies*. The latter are relatively more Ionic for reasons of genre convention alone, not because they were written by an Ionic speaker of the same name (see Meillet, *Aperçu*, chap. 12; G. Zuntz, "Once Again the Antiphontean Tetralogies," *MH* 6 (1949); 100–03; K. J. Dover, "The Chronology of Antiphon's Speeches," *CQ* 44 (1950): 44–60. Poeticisms of lexicon are assembled by Cucuel, *Antiph.*, pp. 22–23, but some of them may have been falsely declared poetic: even φροῦδος might not have sounded like an importation from tragedy.[33] On the other hand, extended vocative phrases like ὦ ἄνδρες ἀνοσίων ἔργων τιμωροί, ὁσίων δὲ διαγνώμονες (6.1, words written for an actual litigant) seem to me a sure index of poetic color. (I plan to defend this view elsewhere.)

Thucydides

My strong impression, derived from a general sense of Thucydides' style and the inspection of some particular features, is that ancients (not, of

---

30. *De vocabulis quae videntur esse apud Herodotum poeticis* (Parthenopolis, 1892), p. 1.

31. In any case, *no* generalization will hold true for all authors or classes or words. Sophocles, for example, was more receptive to Ionicisms than the other tragedians, and Ionic forms in tragic dialogue are thought to owe their presence there to the ancient literary tradition, not to contemporary Ionic (Björck, *Alpha Imp.*, p. 159); but there are exceptions, e.g., δῆθεν (see above, p. 8).

32. The dialect may have remained a doctor's cachet for much longer; see K.-D. Fischer, "Ionicisms—A Trademark of the Ancient Medical Profession?" *Liverpool Classical Monthly* 2 (1977): 185.

33. The word occurs at Aristoph. *Pax* 197, not a clearly paratragic context.

course, Thucydides' contemporaries) and moderns have been too inclined to see poetic touches. Nothing in Thucydides' vocabulary is indubitably poetic: ναυβάτας (1.121.3) is pronounced τραγικώτερον than ναύτας by Pollux and is indeed attested in tragedy, even in lyric; but it is also a Herodotean word and therefore arguably Ionic, but not poetic. κεκμηῶτες (3.59.2) appears in tragedy but also in Plato and Aristotle. A look at Thucydides' use of the article is instructive, for its omission is a mark of all serious poetry familiar to Thucydides: the picture is far from clear. Demosthenes has the article with Ἀμφίπολις 29 times and omits it once (where inclusion would create hiatus); Thucydides omits the article 12 of the 29 times he names the city. But his practice in naming the Piraeus is, so to speak, *more* prosaic than that of the orators: they normally write ὁ Πειραιεύς but omit the article with ἐν and ἐξ (Gildersleeve, *Synt.* §557); Thucydides includes the article with these prepositions (8.92.4, 10). Miller's statistics, which show the preference of various authors for the combination of article, attribute, and noun (Gildersleeve, *Synt.* §609), indicate that Thucydides is very close to Sophocles but almost as close to Herodotus; he differs considerably from Aristophanes and the orators (especially Antiphon, whom he resembles in many aspects[34]) in avoiding the order article–noun–article–attribute. The ratio of ὅπως to ἵνα in Thucydidean purpose clauses is 1:.45, exactly the same as in Sophocles and markedly different from Herodotus (1:8.23), Aristophanes (1:10.16), and Demosthenes (1:18.07). A sign of poeticism, perhaps, but this line of reasoning makes Thucydides more poetic than Euripides, who shows a ratio of 1:3.73.[35] We can apply Schmid-Stählin's remark (*Gr. Lit.* 1.5.184) on Thucydides' morphological choices to his syntax: "Why Thucydides decided in individual cases exclusively or predominantly for this form or that form we do not know." The upshot is that I would not attribute a syntactical feature in Thucydides to a poeticizing motive in the absence of strong contextual probability.[36]

Hippocratic corpus

I have already mentioned the problem of textual corruption and apparently poetic words (p. 7). Other considerations making the corpus a dubious touchstone for stylistic analysis are its chronological status (most of it must postdate our period), its terseness, and at the same time its

---

34. J. Finley, "The Origins of Thucydides' Style," *HSCP* 50 (1939): 35–84, esp. 62–82; Denniston, *Prose Style*, pp. 31–32.
35. See Weber's statistics in Goodwin, *GMT,* appendix III.
36. Cf. Dover, *Thucydides* (n. 26). M. S. Silk, *Interact.*, pp. 215–19, has an excellent discussion of a related problem, Thucydides' reputation among ancient critics for metaphorical expression.

tendency to stylization that is strictly *sui generis* in Greek literature (see Langholf, *Syntakt. Hipp.*, pp. 10–11).

Andocides

It seems fitting that a man easy to despise and distrust is also a slippery linguistic witness. He may be suspected of importing both Ionicisms and poeticisms to make an effect (see MacDowell, "The Style of Andokides," pp. 18–23, in his edition of the *De Mysteriis,* and U. Albini, p. 28, in his edition of the *De Pace*).

Aristophanes

Our greatest opportunity and challenge. It is universally agreed that he attests colloquial Attic usage in the late fifth and early fourth centuries.[37] Of course he also writes high-style lyrics, and parodies many sorts of unconventional language, notably that of older and contemporary trage-dians. As he does not scruple to move quickly from one style to another, one must exercise caution. I make extensive use of two excellent mono-graphs, P. T. Stevens, *Colloquial Expressions in Euripides,* and P. Rau, *Paratragodia.*

Plato

H. Thesleff identifies ten categories of Platonic style. The complexity of his table of "style markers" shows the difficulty of telling what colors Plato was drawing from his palette in any particular passage. For instance, the item "pairs" is appropriate to six of the ten styles (*Styles,* pp. 81–94). A frequent problem is the admixture of possible Ionicisms and other non-Attic features (Thesleff, *Styles,* p. 170; Denniston, *Part.,* pp. lxx–lxxi). I think it significant, however, that in the *locus amoenus* passage at *Phdr.* 230b2–c6, an exquisite piece of writing (part of it metri-cal), frankly poetic syntax is not to be found.[38]

Orators

I have already alluded to Dover's discovery of the different way orators express "and then" in narrative (above, p. 5). This should alert us to the chance that even the orators who have dispensed with Ionic touches may have written court speeches in a language quite alien from everyday Greek, the sort of thing one might have heard in the barber shops. We

37. Two qualifications are necessary: (1) The requirements of versification are bound to have caused at least some divergence from everyday language, but the extent of this divergence cannot be gauged. (2) "Everyday" language is by no means perfectly uniform: it must have varied from deme to deme, year to year, and even in an individual's speech from hour to hour, reflecting differences of (*inter alia*) social context and emotional state.

38. Syntactical differentiae are absent as well from the passages, all of which fall into verse and/or are explicitly denominated ἔπη, assembled by Norden, *Kunstprosa* 1.110–11.

have, on the one hand, the commonplace remarks that imply a special courtroom language, and on the other, Aristotle's statement at *Rhet.* 1413b15, which places great emphasis on oral delivery as the special, "professional" element: οἱ δὲ τῶν ῥητόρων [sc. λόγοι] εὖ λεχθέντες ἰδιωτικοὶ ἐν ταῖς χερσίν. However distant forensic speeches were from colloquial Attic, the differences among the three branches of rhetoric are quite clear (see Dover, *Lysias*). The difference between epideictic and the other subgenres is especially evident, but Dover should be followed in his refusal to equate elevated rhetoric and "the poetic" (*Lysias*, p. 64, n. 7). I have watched as carefully as I could for appearances of the syntactical differentiae in epideictic, but have found virtually nothing.

Xenophon
There are two ways of classifying him, as a writer who deviates from the Attic standard, "ein Halbattiker," as Wackernagel calls him, or as the first great figure in a new movement: "il annonce la κοινή" (Meillet). The important point, however, is to recognize that he is eccentric and unreliable as a guide to Attic prose usage, whether from artistic incapacity or the variety of his linguistic experience as an exile. His free use of σύν where pure Attic demands μετά is an emblem of how far he moved from his native dialect; astonishingly, this feature went unnoticed until T. Mommsen, *Beit. Präp.* For extensive documentation and discussion see L. Gautier, *La langue de Xénophon* (Geneva, 1911), esp. pp. 136–42; H. R. Breitenbach, *RE* IX A. 2, s.v. Xenophon, cols. 1895–1901.

The "Pedestrian Gloss"

It is a premise of this study that the syntactical features here examined are not mere items on a grammarian's list or unsystematic oddities of the Greek high style. Rather, I believe that the Greek audience perceived the differentiae as deviations from a specific form in everyday language. As no part of this formulation is beyond challenge, I will try to elucidate my terms and defend my strategy in some detail.

We can be confident that a grammatical category is not overly abstract and therefore inappropriate to the stylistic analysis of Greek literary texts if a native speaker, hearing the putative differentia, had some consciousness of its functional equivalent in his everyday language.[39] I dub this functional equivalent the "pedestrian gloss." Both the adjective and the noun are used in the normal, nontechnical sense. "Pedestrian" is to be

---

39. By "functional equivalents" I do not, of course, mean perfect synonyms: the difference in provenience alone creates a connotative distinction.

understood as "ordinary, conventional, stylistically unremarkable"; "gloss" means a substituted expression, not a strange word, in the sense that γλῶττα is used by Aristotle. The classification "jussive infinitive," for instance, is usefully applied to stylistic analysis if a Greek speaker could gloss ἀγγέλλειν in the Thermopylae epitaph by ἄγγειλον. This criterion has an important corollary: a category is more reliable the more certain we can be that the original audience was conscious of the functional equivalent in its everyday language. A negative example: for stylistic purposes, the category "ellipsis of ἄπιθι or ἔρρε" in the expression ἐς κόρακας (K–G 2.559) is illusory, because the three-word equivalent (though printed in many old elementary commentaries as a pedagogical aid) was almost certainly not inevitably present in the heads of fifth-century Greeks.

One might object that insofar as the pedestrian gloss was only *potentially* present in the consciousness of the Greek audience, which normally attended to poetry with no intention of performing grammatical analysis, it is a concept irrelevant to stylistic analysis. This objection may be elucidated by considering the analogy of a bilingual speaker. A linguist might draw any number of comparisons between the syntax of the realizations of the same semantic content in the two languages; but the bilingual speaker, even if he is himself linguistically self-conscious and trained in the discipline, will hardly ever make such comparisons when he talks or writes. It would, therefore, be a mistake to think that his linguistic experience necessarily included a persisting sense of specific differences between the language he was using at any moment and the language he could substitute. Similarly, it might be said that an Athenian sitting in the Theater of Dionysus, and hearing a terminal accusative (place-to-which without preposition) would apprehend that feature but not perceive the alleged counterpoint of the pedestrian gloss. To this objection I offer one very brief general answer and a number of observations pertinent only to the audience of Greek literature in the classical period.

We can invoke the general notion of language as a system whose entirety is comprehended at every instant by a competent user of the particular code. Merely to speak of a person as both competent in everyday Attic Greek and accustomed to hear and understand the plain meaning of traditional and contemporary verse is to imply that he knows the relevant significant oppositions. For instance, he understands a subjunctive protasis without ἄν as the correlate, marked for membership in poetic or archaic language, of the subjunctive with ἄν. Those of structuralist persuasion will be impatient with the demand for phenomenological details, for example, did the audience subaudibly gloss in their heads, as some pedants of our own day (I include myself) do at performances of Shakespeare.[40]

Those who are not adherents of structuralist doctrine will demand some ancient evidence for the pedestrian gloss. Obviously, this can only be indirect; even an explicit comment by a classical writer cannot be taken as an authoritative statement on how his contemporaries in general responded to deviant features in literary language. He may even be mistaken about his own unreflective way of taking in poetry.

We begin our survey of the linguistic experience of the period by amplifying a point touched on in the appeal to structuralist dogma: the community that composed the audience was familiar with poetry containing all the syntactical features in question. And since none of these features was ever obligatory in any genre of Greek literature, the audience was accustomed to the coexistence of these features with the standard syntax. The proportion of deviant to normal varies from one feature to another, but in no case does the deviant form approach predominance. The consequence of this distribution, I think, is that the deviations of poetic Greek were not shielded from their correlates in routine Greek to the same extent as correlates in the two languages in which a bilingual person performs are shielded from each other. Or, staying within the realm of verse, we can say that the syntactical deviation is not as much a part of the audience's expectation as metrical structure.[41] It follows, then, that we have more reason to suppose that consciousness of the pedestrian gloss played a part in the mental processing of the deviant form.

Second, to the extent that any member of the fifth-century Athenian audience of tragedy also went to hear Old Comedy, he would be accus-

---

40. "Untutored" appreciation of subtle effects is often defended by the analogy of the nonprofessional's experience of music (see C. H. Whitman, *Homer and the Homeric Tradition* [Cambridge, Mass., 1958], p. 258; J. Culler, *Structuralist Poetics* [Ithaca, 1975], pp. 67–68). The analogy seems plausible enough, but we should not fall into an unconscious assumption that the audiences of classical Greek poetry were profoundly naive ἰδιῶται.

In his article "Reader Response and Stylistics" (*Style* 11 [1977]: 1–18), E. R. Kintgen argues that critics may overestimate the role of formal linguistic analysis in readers' perceptions of style and underestimate factors that vary (perhaps widely) with readers' "cognitive styles"; he proposes empirical testing of readers' responses as a substitute for "idiosyncratic and anecdotal" criticism. Obviously, we cannot test fifth- and fourth-century audiences; even if we could, readers may not report genre-conditioned elements of style as frequently, or in the same manner, as other features, especially if they think such reports otiose because they merely identify aspects of the subcodes of literature. If the reports are so filtered, an absence of responses to genre features that critics have described in formal terms would not necessarily prove that those features are stylistically irrelevant or of only marginal importance.

41. The Greeks were certainly aware when prose incongruously lapsed into too regular a rhythm (see Arist. *Rhet.* 1408b22–27). Aristotle is speaking of people in general, not verbal sophisticates.

tomed to the mixture of metrical, but essentially colloquial, language with
the high style. To some degree this mixture occurs in lyrics, but particularly
important are the trimeter dialogues. There the phonology and meter
make the excursions into paratragedy especially prominent.[42] The frequent
use of paratragedy (and some parody of other genres) certainly points to
the comic poets' confidence that their public would appreciate the juxtaposition of styles. And the reverse effect is probable: the experience of
paratragedy trained the audience to a greater consciousness of the generic
characteristics when they heard them "straight." I must, however, at once
concede that the specific differentiae examined in this study make few
appearances in Old Comedy.

Third, several passages in Aristotle's discussions of rhetorical and poetical styles (mostly on the lexical level) give some hint of how people (some
not as serious as the Stagirite himself) tended to assimilate deviations from
standard speech. At *Rhet.* 3. 1404b5–14 he speaks of the pleasurable
surprise that comes from unconventional words and phrases in prose and,
more often, in poetry:

τῶν δ᾽ ὀνομάτων καὶ ῥημάτων σαφῆ μὲν ποιεῖ τὰ κύρια, μὴ ταπεινὴν
δὲ ἀλλὰ κεκοσμημένην τἆλλα ὀνόματα ὅσα εἴρηται ἐν τοῖς περὶ
ποιητικῆς· τὸ γὰρ ἐξαλλάξαι ποιεῖ φαίνεσθαι σεμνοτέραν· ὥσπερ
γὰρ πρὸς τοὺς ξένους οἱ ἄνθρωποι καὶ πρὸς τοὺς πολίτας, τὸ αὐτὸ
πάσχουσιν καὶ πρὸς τὴν λέξιν· διὸ δεῖ ποιεῖν ξένην τὴν διάλεκτον·
θαυμασταὶ γὰρ τῶν ἀπόντων εἰσίν, ἡδὺ δὲ τὸ θαυμαστόν ἐστιν. ἐπὶ
μὲν οὖν τῶν μέτρων πολλά τε ποιεῖται οὕτω καὶ ἁρμόττει ἐκεῖ (πλέον
γὰρ ἐξέστηκεν περὶ ἃ καὶ περὶ οὓς ὁ λόγος), ἐν δὲ τοῖς ψιλοῖς λόγοις
πολλῷ ἐλάττω.

This is clearly incompatible with the notion that the poet's audience had
become so inured to deviant expressions that it ceased to register them as
θαυμαστά. Aristotle can speak of rhetoric and poetry together precisely
because the foreign component is not uniformly absent in the former or
present in the latter (cf. *Poet.* 1458a23–25). Now it is true that Aristotle is
not saying in so many words that people hear the strange expression
ringing against the conventional, the παρόντα against the ἀπόντα, so to
speak; but it is difficult to understand his presentation except as involving
at least the unconscious opposition of the two.

Even more apropos is Aristotle's discussion in chapter 22 of the *Poetics.*
There the pedestrian gloss is quite explicitly employed as a critical instrument by Aristotle and the men whose opinion he cites. The glosses are

---

42. At least if it is true that iambic trimeter did, as Aristotle claims (*Poet.* 1449a24–28),
most closely approximate normal speech rhythm. I agree with M. Silk (*Interact.*, p. 220) that
Aristotle verges on the "quasi-prescriptive" in this passage.

drawn from that sort of language Aristotle denominates as the *lexis ἡ ἐκ
τῶν κυρίων ὀνομάτων* (1458a19), τὸ ἰδιωτικόν (21), τὸ κύριον (23), ἡ
διάλεκτος (1458b32–33), and perhaps ἡ αὐτὴ λέξις (1458b9).[43] The gloss
itself is provided by students of poetry or poets themselves *qua* replacement or substitution: Aristotle's verb for the process is μετατίθημι
(1458b18 μετατιθεὶς ἄν τις τὰ κύρια ὀνόματα, 20–21 ἐν δὲ μόνον ὄνομα
μεταθέντος, ἀντὶ κυρίου εἰωθότος γλῶτταν; cf. 24 and 26). Aristotle first
describes a poet's strategy: Euripides begins, so to speak, with the pedestrian gloss ἐσθίει, which he heard in Aeschylus' line, and substitutes the
γλῶττα in Aristotle's terminology, i.e., the *non*pedestrian word θοινᾶται.
Next Aristotle takes Homeric lines and makes them insipid, though
metrical. He gives no sign here that he thought of the glosses as automatic,
subaudible accompaniments of unconventional words or that the same
gloss would occur to everybody. But, at the very least, he endorses the
critical procedure of taking individual constituents of a poetic line and
substituting everyday expressions as a reliable guide in stylistic analysis.

Ariphrades' mockery of tragic poets (1458b31–59a4) is widely regarded
as foolish or a joke, perhaps made in a comedy:[44]

. . . Ἀριφράδης τοὺς τραγῳδοὺς ἐκωμῴδει ὅτι ἃ οὐδεὶς ἂν εἴπειεν ἐν
τῇ διαλέκτῳ τούτοις χρῶνται, οἷον τὸ δωμάτων ἄπο ἀλλὰ μὴ ἀπὸ
δωμάτων, καὶ τὸ σέθεν καὶ τὸ ἐγὼ δέ νιν καὶ τὸ Ἀχιλλέως πέρι ἀλλὰ
μὴ περὶ Ἀχιλλέως, καὶ ὅσα ἄλλα τοιαῦτα.

If Ariphrades meant to raise a laugh with his examples, we may infer that
he expected instant recognition of the deviant expressions. Aristotle
defends the deviations by claiming that they are meant as such: διὰ γὰρ τὸ
μὴ εἶναι ἐν τοῖς κυρίοις ποιεῖ τὸ μὴ ἰδιωτικὸν ἐν τῇ λέξει ἅπαντα τὰ
τοιαῦτα (1459a2–4). Thus he too implies that the deviations do not go
unnoticed in the stream of poetry. Both men testify to the audience's
consciousness of specific features as strange against the background of
conventional language.

If I am right about the Greek audience's perception of poetry, a poetic
utterance that could give rise to the pedestrian gloss was never sensed as
strictly *sui generis*. The Greek ear and mind would attribute the distinct
character of the poetry, in respect to the differentia at least, to a specific
alteration of everyday language. Everyday syntax impinges on poetry,
therefore, in a way that both heightens and systematizes the art. The

---

43. So J. Vahlen, who translates "in purer Prosa" (*Beiträge zu Aristoteles' Poetik* [Leipzig,
1914], p. 146), but Lucas is almost certainly right in saying that this translation leaves αὐτῇ
without point.
44. See Vahlen, *Beiträge,* p. 146, n. 43, pp. 148, 303–04, replying to Spengel.

differentiae operate as a precise signal that language is not routine in the text that includes them. Such a signal may appear redundant: after all, since meter is itself a pervasive device for signaling that the language is of a special sort,[45] why repeat the point? The answer, almost a platitude, is that poetry (together with much else in language) *is* highly redundant. It points to its difference from nonpoetic language repeatedly and with a great variety of means.[46]

In *Enallage and Greek Style* I examined a syntactical phenomenon that, on my interpretation, is based on the nearly explicit confrontation of poetic and everyday language. Indeed, the definition I follow rests on the concept of the pedestrian gloss, though I did not use the term: "enallage is the transfer to the governing substantive of an adjective which by logic, or at least convention, belongs with an expressed dependent genitive (*Enallage,* p. 1). I believe that enallage encapsulates the aesthetic principle at work in the differentiae examined in this book, but from the viewpoint of practical criticism an important difference should be noted. Each instance of enallage contains one pedestrian gloss specific to itself, namely, the adjective taken with the dependent genitive as if the two words were in grammatical agreement. Though there are some patterns to be observed in the body of collected enallages, if we take the phenomenon as a category we are limited to a generalization: the pedestrian gloss reflects the general habits of routine language subverted by the trope. Realizations of the trope are as different as the different words that are its material.

The differentiae studied here have, within each category, pedestrian glosses exactly or nearly like each other, for example, *ἄν* added to the differential expression, or one of a small number of prepositions added to a terminal accusative. Enallage is more ramified on the semantic level because the relationships expressible by the genitive function differ widely.[47] Thus, changing the adjective to the genitive case may produce

45. Rhyme (hardly a factor in Greek, of course) is *less* pervasive, since it affects only the verse ending.

46. In the terminology of Russian formalism, the devices by which literary language, especially poetry, breaks the automatic response elicited by the routine use of language constitute *ostranenie,* "defamiliarization" (see V. Erlich, *Russian Formalism*[3] [The Hague and Paris, 1969], pp. 190, 234–35; E. Stankiewicz, "Structural Poetics and Linguistics," *Current Trends in Linguistics* 12 [1974]: 635, cf. 640). The term "foregrounding," an unfortunate translation of J. Mukařovský's Czech word *aktualisace,* is best avoided. The topography suggested by the English word implies that one element of poetic contrivance stands before and blocks the view of other elements. As applied to the differentiae of this study, "foregrounding" might suggest that the audience was more aware of the nonstandard syntax than of, say, the semantic content or acoustic properties of an utterance. We cannot possibly establish any such hierarchy.

47. A. Hoekstra is quite justified in pointing out that the semantic range of noun + dependent genitive combinations varies more widely than many scholars (myself included) have acknowledged ("Enallage and the Transferred Epithet: Some Remarks on Condensed Effects

different results in different instances of the figure. Also it should be remembered that the identification of enallages is, on the whole, more difficult than the identification of instances of the differentiae that are my present concern. Despite the problematic nature of enallage, I am still convinced that in the minds of Greek poets it had a distinct stylistic shape uniting its manifold realizations.[48]

The notion of routine language as poetry's silent partner, a continual (if

---

in Aeschylus," in *Miscellanea Tragica in Honorem J. C. Kamerbeek*, ed. J. M. Bremer, S. L. Radt, C. J. Ruijgh [Amsterdam, 1976], pp. 167–68).

48. The issues of the pedestrian gloss and the perceived danger of atomistic analysis stand between me and A. Hoekstra, *Festschrift* (see n. 47). By insisting on a formal distinction between enallage and transferred epithet I certainly did not mean that the latter is poetically contemptible. On the contrary, I suggested that there could be a distinct poetic advantage in ignoring the semantic link made in ordinary language between the word in the genitive and the attributive adjective: "If a reader or listener takes an enallage literally, i. e. if he follows the grammatical concord and fails to note the transfer, he is forced to make metaphorical sense of the expression, find an *ad hoc* logical relation between the adjective and noun in agreement, or remain baffled. On the other hand, if he detects the enallage he can perceive the prosaic sense at once, *and so is in danger of leaving his poetic faculty unexercised*" (*Enallage*, p. 3, emphasis added; the point was not hopelessly obscure—cf. H. L. Hudson-Williams, *CR* 17 [1977]: 64–65). My formulation does not advance the claim, *pace* Hoekstra, that it is *only* "the presence of a dependent genitive that renders an expression striking" (Hoekstra, pp. 166–67). To be sure, among the effects to be perceived by the "poetic faculty" in the combination of attribute and governing noun we often find the condensation powerfully demonstrated by Hoekstra. But I do not agree that Hoekstra's experimental addition of a genitive renders the original phrase "less condensed" (his examples are Aesch. *Pers.* 240 φεράσπιδες σαγαί + ἀνδρῶν and *Sept.* 124–25 δορυσσοῖς σαγαῖς + ἀγανόρων). Acute members of Aeschylus' public could, I think, be alerted by the hypothetical enallage to greater appreciation of the effect of the two words in grammatical agreement. I had written (*Enallage*, p. 3), "Enallage bridges the figurative and the prosaic." I now offer an improved version: Enallage and other instances of the pedestrian gloss are bridges that invite two-way traffic.

A few other points raised by Hoekstra: He charges (pp. 157–58) that I have failed to notice the "intensity" and "pregnancy" of the passage containing the enallage at Soph. *OT* 1400–01 ("hardly, if ever, equalled in the rest of surviving Greek tragedy"). Of course there is magnificent pathos in that passage, but is it impious to compare an enallage there with other semantically related examples? I invite meditation on the *Eros* ode in the *Antigone*, which holds an enallage (at 793–94) that Hoekstra finds less impressive.

Hoekstra misapprehends my remark (*Enallage*, pp. 8–9) on Aesch. *Sept.* 64 κῦμα χερσαῖον στρατοῦ: "enallage [rather than an epexegetic genitive] is likely because Greek habitually attaches an adjective, typically πεζός or ναυτικός to στρατός in order to distinguish 'fleet' from 'army' or uses the adjective alone, with στρατός understood." Hoekstra (pp. 160–61) writes: "that is obvious enough, but quite irrelevant at [sic] issue, for here transference is out of the question: the alternative 'fleet' would hardly have suggested itself to inhabitants of the inland city of Thebes." My point was not that the adjective is needed here to exclude "fleet," but that there may have been a mechanical inclination to make a semantic connection between the adjective indicating "land" and the genitive. I am rather less confident now that this was the case.

I take this opportunity to correct a grievous blunder on p. 13 of *Enallage*: Antiphanes, not Antiphon, wrote διὰ πόντιον οἶδμα. My argument based on an alleged "contemporary prose usage" is, therefore, sheer nonsense.

not continuous) negative image of poetry, so to speak, may seem to contaminate poetry's aesthetic integrity. The pedestrian gloss will, I am sure, seem to some readers an offense against Art. In defense I invoke some remarks of Paul Valéry. Valéry can serve as a sort of *argumentum a fortiori,* since he usually insisted more strongly than modern theoreticians on an absolute distinction between poetry and prose.[49] "Commentaries on 'Charmes'" is typical:

> It is an error contrary to the nature of poetry, and one which may even be fatal to it, to claim that for each poem there is a corresponding true meaning, unique and conformable to, or identical with, some thought of the author's. A result of this error is the invention of that absurd school exercise which consists in having verses put into prose. This inculcates an idea most fatal to poetry, for it teaches that it is possible to divide its essence into parts which can exist separately. It implies the belief that poetry is an *accident* of the *substance* prose. But poetry exists only for those in whose eyes this operation is impossible and who recognize poetry by this impossibility. As for the others, by understanding poetry they mean substituting for it another language, whose condition is not to be poetic.[50]

Unlike the composer of music, whose raw material, sound, Valéry regards as pure and orderly, the poet faces the great challenge of creating "an artificial and ideal order by means of a material of vulgar origin," the "common language," the "fruit of the disorder of life in common":[51]

> if the poet could manage to construct works in which nothing of prose ever appeared, poems in which the musical continuity was never broken, in which the relations between meanings were themselves perpetually similar to harmonic relations, *in which the transmutation of thoughts into each other appeared more important than any thought,* in which the play of figures contained the reality of the subject—then

---

49. E.g., R. Jakobson, who identifies a "poetic function" that can be more or less present in texts of all sorts (his most recent statement is "A Postscript to the Discussion on Grammar of Poetry," *Diacritics* 10 [1980]: 22–35), and E. Stankiewicz: "There is no sharp demarcation-line between poetic and non-poetic language. The analogue of a line should be replaced by the analogue of two poles; i.e. a 'marked,' more explicit pole of poetic language, and an 'unmarked,' less explicit pole of non-poetic language, which admits a lesser or higher degree of poetic saturation" ("Poetic and Non-poetic Language in Their Interrelations," in *Poetics. Poetyka. Poètika* [International Conference of Work-in-progress Devoted to Problems of Poetics], Warsaw, 1961, p. 13). Valéry is aware that the extent to which poetic language is distinct varies with language and period (see "Variations on the 'Eclogues,'" in *The Art of Poetry,* trans. D. Folliot [Princeton, 1958], p. 306).
50. "Commentaries on 'Charmes,'" in *The Art of Poetry,* pp. 155–56.
51. "Pure Poetry," in *The Art of Poetry,* pp. 191–92.

one could speak of *pure poetry* as of something that existed. It is not so: the practical or pragmatic part of language, *the habits and logical forms* [my italics], and . . . the disorder and irrationality that are found in its vocabulary . . . make the existence of these creations of absolute poetry impossible.[52]

Here Valéry speaks of the inescapable impurity of language in its routine aspect as a regrettable defect. But elsewhere, in the midst of an attack on the "heresy of paraphrase," he expresses a notion of poetic technique that could serve as a license for this study:

The poet's use of words is quite different from that of custom or need. The words are without doubt the same, but their values are not at all the same. It is indeed nonusage—the *not saying* "it is raining" [i.e., the pragmatic statement demanded by those who equate excellence in prose with excellence in poetry]—which is his business; and everything which shows that he is not speaking prose serves his turn. Rhymes, inversion, elaborate figures, symmetries, and images, all these, whether inventions or conventions, are so many means of setting himself in opposition to the prosaic leanings of the reader (just as the famous "rules" of the art of poetry have the effect of constantly reminding the poet of the *complex universe* of that art).[53]

52. Ibid., p. 192.
53. "Problems of Poetry," in *The Art of Poetry*, p. 98.

1. Number

In its use of grammatical number Greek often surprises the English speaker. For example, he finds a strong predilection for the plural of the neuter demonstrative: μετὰ δὲ ταῦτα occurs far more often than μετὰ δὲ τοῦτο. Comparative adverbs are, in form, singular neuter adjectives, superlative adverbs are plural, e.g., ἥδιον, but ἥδιστα. Every beginner must be startled to learn that neuter plural subjects are used with verbs in the singular. Abstract words, idiomatic in English only as singulars in most contexts, appear as plurals in Greek: ἀμέλειαι and σιγαί (Plato), ἀλήθειαι (Isocrates). Conversely, some abstract nouns in the singular are used to denote a group of people: ἡ πρεσβεία = "seniority" but also "a delegation of ambassadors."

Our business, however, is not what surprises English speakers but what we have reason to believe a Greek understood as a variation between one branch of his language and another. Thus I am not here concerned with the rise of grammatical number in the early phases of the language. To choose correctly among singular, dual, and plural a Greek of the classical period did not need to know, for example, that neuter plurals took verbs in the singular because they derived from singular a-stem feminine collective nouns.[1] And he would have been astonished to learn that ὕδωρ was a sort of plural.[2] He simply knew, for instance, which nouns could be used as collective singulars (ἡ ἵππος was acceptable for οἱ ἵπποι, a poet could use ἡ ναῦς for αἱ νῆες [Aesch. Pers. 380], but one never said τὸ πλοῖον for τὰ πλοῖα). He said ἅλες for "table salt" (without, I am sure, perceiving the substance differently than we do). He was aware that in epic poetry τόξα means not "bows" but "bow and arrows." In short, he knew perfectly well the conventions of grammatical number obtaining in everyday Greek and

---

1. Schwyzer, *Gramm.* 1.581–82.
2. Johannes Schmidt, *Die Pluralbildungen der indogermanischen Neutra* (Weimar, 1889), p. 195.

many of the aberrant uses of literary Greek, whether earlier than his own time or contemporary.

Our stylistic investigations of any word must begin with ascertaining as well as we can just what was conventional.[3] But this preliminary task is not always elementary. In most circumstances, X and X-with-plural-marker (henceforth X-plural) signify merely "one X" and "more than one X." Also, X and X-plural may denote different but related things, e.g., English "water" and "waters" in the syntagma "take the waters." γάμοι, discussed at length on pp. 28–34 below, is this sort of plural. These differences in denotation hold no stylistic interest as long as the choice of X or X-plural is understood as dictated entirely by the singularity or plurality of that which the speaker is signifying. Style is a characteristic of language only when a choice of *signifiants* is possible. We must often go to considerable lengths to be sure whether this requirement is met in a particular Greek text.

Given that it is proper to regard the occurrence of X for X-plural or vice versa as stylistically motivated, the difference between the two forms can involve one or more contrasts in respect of denotation, connotation, or provenience. For the reader's convenience in following an unavoidably complex presentation, I set out below the various distinctions perceived by scholars:

1. X-plural = X + Y, the "elliptical" plural, as in τόξα = "bow and arrows."
2. X = Y_1, Y_2, Y_3, as in ὁ ἵππος = ἱππεύς$_1$ on his ἵππος, ἱππεύς$_2$ on his ἵππος, ἱππεύς$_3$ on his ἵππος.
3. X-plural of a proper noun = anyone or anything like X in some important aspect, as in 'Cassandras' = "unerring prophets believed by none."
4. X of a concrete noun = X-plural, as in ὁ Μῆδος = οἱ Μῆδοι, or πλίνθος = "bricks."
5. X of an abstract noun = persons characterized by X, as in ἡ πρεσβεία = "men, usually πρεσβῦται, i.e., old men, forming a diplomatic delegation."
6. X-plural = one particular X, with a glance at other Xs, as in τοὺς εὐεργέτας (Eur. *HF* 1309) = "Heracles, a representative of the class of εὐεργέται."
7. A special case of (6): X-plural of a word denoting a person as a relative = one particular X, with a glance at any and all persons in

---

3. See Wackernagel, *Vorl.* 1.98, criticizing Witte for neglecting this task in his *Singular and Plural*. Pedantry can make itself look foolish when it attempts to define proper usage: The teacher asks a pupil, "Is 'trousers' singular or plural?" The boy answers, "Singular on the top, plural on the bottom" (from Uriel Weinreich, *College Yiddish*).

that relationship to a given person. For example, τέκνα = "this τέκνον of mine, but what I say of him holds true for any child I have now, have ever had, or may have in the future."

8. X-plural of an abstract noun = the abstraction realized in more than one particular circumstance, as in οἱ καιροί = "the emergencies faced in the years 480, 403, and 346 B.C."

9. X-plural of an abstract noun = X in only one instance, as in φόνοι of a single murder.

10. X-plural = X of everyday Greek in some special type of Greek, as in μάχαιραι for "knife" in poetry, for μάχαιρα in everyday conversation.

11. X-plural = X the speaker wishes for some reason to conceal in a multiplicity, as at Soph. *OT* 336, τοῖς φιλτάτοις = Jocasta (the scholiast writes: εὐσχημόνως ἀπήγγειλε τὸ περὶ τῆς μητρός), and 1176, κτενεῖν νιν τοὺς τεκόντας ἦν λόγος, where τοὺς τεκόντας = Laius. These plurals are usually called "allusive."

12. X-plural = X!, the "affective" plural, claimed to exist by some scholars, as in φόνοι = "a terrible, violent φόνος," or νύκτες = "night, a time of extreme danger."

It will be seen from this list that the interchange of abstract and concrete is the constituent of many of the distinctions.

Pride of place should go to two ancient notices of the plural-for-singular. They are interesting in themselves and will serve to introduce problems in the stylistic interpretation of grammatical number.

Aristotle: Poetic or Rhetorical Plural?

The poetic plural comes to us with most imposing credentials: it is the subject of one of Aristotle's rare remarks on syntax. Among the devices that add ὄγκος to style, he lists τὸ ἓν πολλὰ ποιεῖν, ὅπερ οἱ ποιηταὶ ποιοῦσιν· ἑνὸς ὄντος λιμένος ὅμως λέγουσι

> λιμένας εἰς Ἀχαϊκούς (fr. adespot. 83 Nauck),
> καὶ
> δέλτου μὲν αἵδε πολύθυροι διαπτυχαί. (Eur. *IT* 727)
> *Rhet.* 3.1407b32–35

It is symptomatic of the philological quarreling that has erupted over the "poetic plural" that this remark has been widely criticized.

We take the second of Aristotle's examples first. In their commentary, Cope and Sandys charge Aristotle with an elementary blunder. Euripides, they say, is using a periphrasis that requires a plural expression, since the folds of the writing tablet are truly multiple: if he "had written δέλτοι he would have used the licence ascribed to him by Aristotle." They note that he does just that at 787: τάδ᾽ ἐστὶ τὰν δέλτοισιν ἐγγεγραμμένα. I prefer Maas's explanation ("Poet. Pl.," p. 492)—that what Aristotle is recommending is the "periphrasis of a singular notion (δέλτος) by means of a plural expression (δέλτου διαπτυχαί) as a rhetorical expedient." This seems plausible, since τὸ ἓν πολλὰ ποιεῖν does not need to refer exclusively to the direct pluralizing of a singular word, i.e., δέλτος to δέλτοι. (However, Maas is wrong in claiming that the simplex πτύχαι is unattested in the singular: Euripides himself wrote it at *Supp.* 979.)

Maas argues that Aristotle's first example is not a properly poetic plural but rather a "general" plural, types 6 and 11 in our list, not 10 ("Poet. Pl.," pp. 481, 492–93, 498–99). This is a surprising argument, considering Aristotle's introductory words: ὅπερ οἱ ποιηταὶ ποιοῦσιν (admittedly, it is possible that Aristotle means nothing more than "the sort of thing that occurs in prose and poetry but is rather more common in poetry"). Maas tries to draw a rigorous distinction between what he sees as proper "poetic" plurals like σκῆπτρα and μάχαιραι and the "general," or "rhetorical," plural. "Poetic," for Maas, is simply a "plural used where prose, uninfluenced by poetry, would use the singular" (p. 481).[4] He defines the general plural as plural-for-singular of "names and words for relationships and types [*Verwandtschafts- und Gattungsbezeichnungen*]"; the "general" plural has a specifically rhetorical tone, e.g., "mysterious obscurity," contempt, indignation, or irony ("Poet. Pl.," pp. 498–99). The "poetic" plural, by contrast, has no such force: "Every interpretation which attributes to the poetic plural the force to create a nuance of meaning (of whatever sort) is necessarily false" (p. 486). A more sensible description of the "general" plural is given by Löfstedt (*Synt.* 1.38):

> The essence of the general and rhetorical plural consists of generalizing the single thing or individual, either simply to indicate the general character of a phenomenon or to evoke a rhetorical intensification, in that one presents an individuality in a pathetic, ironic, or other way, as repeated and typical. . . . The general and rhetorical plural have often been combined with the poetic, although it usually shows an entirely distinct character; of course there are also instances where the boundary can hardly be fixed.[5]

---

4. Obviously, scholars will not always be unanimous in identifying poetic influence.

5. The terms "allusive" and "generalizing" are both used by scholars to refer to the device of naming with the word Xs a single X by reference to the class to which it belongs. It is best, I think, to confine the former term to cases where the word Xs has a singular referent unmistakable to the audience, but the speaker means to conceal, or at least avoid clearly indicating, that one X to an interlocutor. Where we suspect no desire to so conceal the one X,

Maas is quite wrong to rely on the adjective Ἀχαϊκούς as a mark of the "general" plural. Since the accidents of transmission have denied us the context of the tragic line, we have no way of telling what general rhetorical thrust was at play here; Aristotle says that the referent is a single harbor, which tells us nothing about the tone of the passage. Indeed, it is hard to see how any nuance of the sort Maas attributes to the general plural promotes ὄγκος, for Aristotle's other prescriptions in this section involve merely condensed or rotund expressions.[6] But the noun is geographical, a category of word long recognized as having a strong affinity for the plural.[7] This makes it probably that λιμένας is a plural assignable only to type 10. If this classification is correct, we need look only at the distribution of the word (not its connotation) as a singular-for-plural to determine its genre affiliation. In the classical period the use seems to be entirely poetic.[8]

If the phrase quoted by Aristotle is a general plural, it is more likely a general plural à la Löfstedt. The speaker might have meant to convey something like, "May Trojan ships never sail *into this* (*or any other*—this nuance is suggested by the plural) *Achaean* harbor."

It will be convenient to consider here type 7, a semantically narrower species of 6. Plural forms like τέκνα and τοκεῖς applied to single persons are explained by Wackernagel (*Vorl.* 1.95) as *pluralia tantum*; their grammatical number is determined "not by the number of persons in mind, but

---

but the speaker means only "one of the class of Xs," "generalizing" is the better term. At Eur. *Hel.* 595 and *Hipp.* 49 and 797–98 the poet has his characters partially bury their precise meaning; thus I would replace the rubric "generalizing" with "allusive" in Kannicht's and Barrett's comments on those lines. But K. H. Lee rightly explains λέκτροις at Eur. *Tr.* 203 lyr.: "the plural does not mean that she thought she would have to share the bed of several Greeks; it is simply a vague generalization." Jebb calls τυράννων at Soph. *Ant.* 60 an "allusive plural," which mistakes the nuance. B. Knox explains the plural accurately: "The word . . . emphasizes the absolute power of Creon, conferred on him by the *polis* in the emergency, and at the same time by its plural form generalizes the expression and thus lessens the suggestion that he is a 'tyrant'" (*The Heroic Temper* [Berkeley and Los Angeles, 1964], p. 63). Since there is no obvious singular referent corresponding to the plural ξυνωμότας (perhaps falsely transmitted: see A. H. Sommerstein, *CQ* 27 [1977]: 264) at Aristoph. *V.* 483, I would not join MacDowell in calling it a "generalizing plural."

6. Aristotle's general recommendation is to avoid ambiguity except for special purposes: see his remark on grammatical number at *Rhet.* 1407b9–10.

7. See Löfstedt, *Synt.* 1.29, or even Maas himself ("Poet. Pl.," p. 493), who regards μάχαιραι, σκῆπτρα, etc., as legitimate poetic plurals, but not λιμένες, yet one page later places λιμένες and μάχαιραι in the same list of poetic plurals taken over from Greek literature by Latin authors. Wackernagel (*Vorl.* 1.97) remarks that though Polybius uses λιμένες of a single harbor, for Aristotle's *Gefühl* "the plural was unusual, a poetic deviation."

8. Lysias 13.34 may look like an exception, λιμένες = "the Piraeus," but he may mean the several harbors of the Athenian port: cf. Xen. *HG* 2.4.31 τὸν κωφὸν λιμένα, and U. Judeich, *Topographie von Athen* (*Handbuch der Altertumswissenschaft* III 2.2 [Munich, 1931]), pp. 437, 443–44. I have checked all instances of the plural in Aristophanes (three and thirteen respectively) and have found no references to a single harbor.

by their relation to the speaker."[9] This usage is common in the language of tragedy, both trimeters and lyrics, but does not appear in comedy (even paratragedy), choral lyric, or epic.[10] It is curious that the distribution is so limited, since the corresponding use in Latin is attested in colloquial and literary language (see Löfstedt, *Synt.* 1.38–39). The restriction in Greek cannot be an epiphenomenon of a lexical restriction; most of the nouns in question are poetic, but not all.[11]

Not to be confused with type 7 are instances of the plural where reference to the singular is only an inference, not something intended by the speaker. H. L. Jones (*Poet. Pl.*, p.6) is not justified in seeing plural-for-singular at Lysias 1.4:

ἡγοῦμαι δέ . . . τοῦτό με δεῖν ἐπιδεῖξαι, ὡς ἐμοίχευεν Ἐρατοσθένης τὴν γυναῖκα τὴν ἐμὴν καὶ ἐκείνην τε διέφθειρε καὶ τοὺς παῖδας τοὺς ἐμοὺς ᾔσχυνε . . .

Though it is true that the speaker has only one child at the time of the trial, the jury hears about him in §6, after the alleged plural-for-singular. More important, the speaker's extravagant complaint is not that his infant son in particular has been shamed by Eratosthenes but that all his descendants have been shamed, present and future, from his unfaithful wife and any succeeding wives. Jones's explanation, that "such plurals of singular meaning took their origin, no doubt, in legal phraseology," is otiose.[12]

To my knowledge, τοὺς παῖδας in this passage is the only plural form in oratory that has been suspected of standing for the singular. Since the "generalizing" plural has rhetorical possibilities sometimes exploited by tragedians, it is striking that Greek orators abstained from it. Forensic speeches above all provided abundant opportunity to use a device that could suggest that the case at hand was paradigmatic, that the wrong verdict would embolden malefactors of the sort the opponent typifies to do their worst to victims much like the speaker himself. We may, I think, conclude that the plural of types 6 and 7 appeared appropriate to tragedy and no other genre.

9. It is not clear whether Wackernagel regards the general plural as necessarily distinct from the poetic plural. In any case, his remarks at *Vorl.* 1.97 show no sign that he follows Maas's interpretation of the first Aristotelian example.

10. Nouns and pronouns used this way are listed by Menge, *Poet. Scaen.*, pp. 26–27, and Jones, *Poet. Pl.*, pp. 150–58. Not every instance they cite has an unambiguously single referent, e.g., at Aesch. *Eum.* 152 lyr. τοκεῦσιν can be understood as a true plural, even if the Furies intend only "mother."

11. E.g., τοκεύς (Herodotus, Thucydides, Lysias [though only in the *Epitaphios*]), γονεύς (Herodotus, Isaeus, Plato), and with some frequency τέκνον. ἡ τεκοῦσα appears at Hdt. 1.116.4 and Isaeus 3.15, 8.7; together with ὁ φύσας it appears at Lysias 10.8, a passage of special interest since the issue there is the archaic language of Solon's law.

12. In fact, Athenian laws used both singular and plural to refer to malefactors and victims.

γάμοι: Semantics and Provenience

A second ancient notice of the poetic plural, Longinus 23.2–3, can serve to introduce a well-known—and quite problematic—example:

ἀλλ᾽ ἐκεῖνα μᾶλλον παρατηρήσεως ἄξια ὅτι ἔσθ᾽ ὅπου προσπίπτει τὰ πληθυντικὰ μεγαλορρημονέστερα, καὶ αὐτῷ δόξοκομποῦντα τῷ ὄχλῳ τοῦ ἀριθμοῦ· ταῦτα παρὰ τῷ Σοφοκλεῖ τὰ ἐπὶ τοῦ Οἰδίπου·

ὦ γάμοι, γάμοι,
ἐφύσαθ᾽ ἡμᾶς καὶ φυτεύσαντες πάλιν
ἀνεῖτε ταὐτὸ σπέρμα, κἀπεδείξατε
πατέρας, ἀδελφοὺς παῖδας, αἷμ᾽ ἐμφύλιον,
νύμφας γυναῖκας μητέρας τε, χὠπόσα
αἴσχιστ᾽ ἐν ἀνθρώποισιν ἔργα γίγνεται.   (OT 1403–08)

πάντα γὰρ ταῦτα ἓν ὄνομά ἐστιν, Οἰδίπους, ἐπὶ δὲ θατέρου Ἰοκάστη, ἀλλ᾽ ὅμως χυθεὶς εἰς τὰ πληθυντικὰ ὁ ἀριθμὸς συνεπλήθυσε καὶ ἀτυχίας.

Though the plurals that Longinus is using as an illustration are πατέρας, ἀδελφούς, παῖδας, νύμφας, γυναῖκας, and μητέρας,[13] γάμοι is also of considerable interest. Here we have a word whose plural form denotes one or more nuptial ceremonies, one or more states of matrimony, or one or more instances of sexual intercourse. The plural with a singular sense has been variously explained. Witte (Sing. u. Pl., p. 29) calls it an analogical construction: εὐνή in Homer means not only bed but also intercourse; the word gradually takes on a plural form; "and now it is but a small step for γάμος, a word of related meaning, to become plural." Volp's genial approach has often been quoted: "Pluralem ita explico, ut in notione matrimonii quasi rerum iucundarum varietas respiciatur" (Num. Pl., p. 69). Löfstedt (Synt. 1.36, n. 1) calls γάμοι a "secondary, poetic example" of the tendency of words for periods of time, festivals, and banquets to stand in the plural. The first explanation is farfetched, the second downright silly. Löfstedt's is the most probable, but it speaks of only one of the three meanings, wedding.[14] Whatever the origin of the plural, it is worth observing in detail how it was used from Homer on. Witte's treatment of the word (Sing. u. Pl., p. 29) requires correction.[15]

13. Pace Jones, Poet. Pl., p. 4. These are plurals of type 7.
14. There may also be some significance to the neuter plurals of festival names, but I see no way to disentangle the semantic analogy that presumably brings various celebrations into the plural from the interchange of neuter plural pronouns with singular forms, which can have the same effect (see Schwyzer, Gramm. 1.43–44). Thomas Magister remarked, γάμους ποιεῖν Ἀττικοί, οὐχὶ γάμον (quoted from F. W. Sturz, Lexicon Xenophonteum s.v.).
15. A partial job was done by Jones, Poet. Pl., p. 97.

He is not quite right in saying that Homer knows only the singular, for at *Il.* 18.491 we find γάμοι, probably meaning "marriage scene." (So Leaf, who adds that νύμφας and θαλάμων "perhaps need not imply more than one bride and chamber"; πολὺς δ᾽ ὑμέναιος ὀρώρει at 493 is not decisive in favor of the singular, since a single wedding song could be formed by the mingling voices of many celebrations.)[16] Witte cites Archilochus 326 West as the first plural, which would be significant indeed, since γάμοι there should mean matrimony; but its Archilochean authorship is not now accepted. West 197 Ζεῦ πάτερ, γάμον μὲν οὐκ ἐδαισάμην is a negative example because it shows the singular used of a wedding feast (the expression γάμον δαίνυμι, "I give a banquet," is well attested in Homer). Similarly, there is no doubt that the celebration is meant at Theognis 15–16 West and Pindar *N.* 1.71 (variously dated between 481 and 471). The meaning "coitus," primary at Pind. *Thren.* 3.7 = 128cS-M, is obscured by a euphemism in Slater, *A Lexicon to Pindar* s.v.: "i.e. on his wedding night."

The first unambiguous attestation of the plural for a single state of wedlock is probably Aesch. *Sept.* 780 (lyr.). The first such use in Aeschylean dialogue is almost certainly later.[17] Sophocles and Euripides show a strong preference for the plural.[18]

Herodotus and Aristophanes provide good controls for fifth-century usage. The former contains no instance of the plural with an unquestionably singular reference: at 1.196.1 ὡς ἂν αἱ παρθένοι γινοίατο γάμων ὡραῖαι (but cf. 6.122.2 [bracketed by Hude] ἐπειδὴ γὰρ ἐγίνοντο γάμου ὡραῖαι), and at 4.117 τὰ περὶ γάμων, the plural is distributive. Even in the expression ἡ κατάκλισις τοῦ γάμου (6.129.1), which means reclining at the wedding banquet, Herodotus uses the singular. No elevation of style is evident in these passages, so we are probably safe in saying that normal Ionic used the singular for a single wedding or state of matrimony.

The use of γάμος in Aristophanes is more illuminating. In every instance the singular plainly has the meaning "wedlock," or else "wedding celebration" is possibly, but not certainly, the meaning.[19]

16. Sensibly enough, Chantraine (*Hom.* 2, pp. 32–33) hedges. Witte strangely ignores the three meanings of γάμοι, though he speaks of ὑμέναια = *Hochzeit* on the same page.

17. At *PV* 739. Though 479 is the firm *terminus post quem* for the play, production after the *Persae* (472) is one thing virtually all Aeschyleans agree on: see C. J. Herington, *The Author of the "Prometheus Bound"* (Austin and London, 1970), chap. iv and appendix B, and M. Griffith, *The Authenticity of the Prometheus Bound* (Cambridge, 1977), p. 5.

18. Witte, *Sing. u. Pl.,* p. 195; Jones, *Poet. Pl.,* pp. 98–99. Witte, arguing as always for metrical convenience, claims (p. 50) that the accusative singular is used only before vowels or in line-final position, and that virtually all instances of the singular genitive and dative, which inconvenience his theory because they are as iambic as the corresponding plurals, are textually unreliable (pp. 196–98). The special pleading is patent.

19. Cf. Menge, *Poet. Scaen.,* p. 34: "In the comic poets this plural-for-singular is seen

Nub. 438 anap. τὸν γάμον ὅς μ᾽ ἐπέτριψεν

Av. 717–18 ἐλθόντες γὰρ πρῶτον ἐπ᾽ ὄρνις οὕτω πρὸς ἅπαντα
τρέπεσθε,
πρός τ᾽ ἐμπορίαν, καὶ πρὸς βιότου κτῆσιν, καὶ πρὸς
γάμον ἀνδρός.
(The chorus means selection of a spouse rather than of a wedding
day, I think, since the other applications of bird divination are
general or persistent activities, not nonce decisions.)[20]

Av. 1725 lyr. ὦ μακαριστὸν σὺ γάμον τῇδε πόλει γήμας.
(All instances of γαμέω γάμον in LSJ refer to marriage itself, not
marriage rites.)

Lys. 786 lyr. φεύγων γάμον ἀφίκετ᾽ ἐς ἐρημίαν

Th. 975–76 lyr. [Ἥραν] ἣ πᾶσι τοῖς χοροῖσι συμπαίζει τε καὶ / κλῇδας
γάμου φυλάττει
(Despite χοροῖσι and the similarity to *Pax* 976 [see below],
wedlock, not the celebration, is almost certainly meant. There is
no example in Greek of "keys to a festival, celebration, or rite" in
RE s.v. Kleiduchos.)

Conversely, the plural is regularly used for a wedding or weddings:

Ach. 1049–50 ἔπεμψέ τίς σοι νυμφίος ταυτὶ κρέα / ἐκ τῶν γάμων.

Pax 774–79 lyr. Μοῦσα σὺ μὲν πολέμους ἀπωσαμένη μετ᾽ ἐμοῦ
τοῦ φίλου χόρευσον,
κλείουσα θεῶν τε γάμους ἀνδρῶν τε δαῖτας
καὶ θαλίας μακάρων.[21]

976 δέσποινα χορῶν, δέσποινα γάμων

1192 ὅσον τὸ χρῆμ᾽ ἐπὶ δεῖπνον ἦλθ᾽ εἰς τοὺς γάμους.

---

rarely, and indeed it is used in such a way that the force of the plural number recedes from the
singular and a new noun, as it were, emerges. Thus . . . γάμοι are the *dies festi nuptiarum*" at
Aristoph. *Pax* 1192 and other passages. This is true, except that the noun is, of course, not a
creation of comedy.
20. Also, the timing of an Athenian wedding was largely conventional: days near the new
moon of Γαμηλιών were favored (*RE* VIII² col. 2129 s.v. Hochzeit). But cf. T. F. Higham,
CQ 26 (1932): 106, who proposes γόνον = "birth."
21. Cf. Stesich. 210 P. Marks of the high style—"Du" predication in a prayer (see
E. Norden, *Agnostos Theos*⁴ [Stuttgart, 1956], pp. 143ff.), τε . . . τε joining single words
(Denniston, *Particles*, pp. 503–04—would make it very likely that γάμοι = "wedding feast"
is a very old usage, even if we did not have the scholiast to tell us that the lines are
"Stesichorean."

1206 τὰ δῶρα ταυτί σοι φέρομεν εἰς τοὺς γάμους.

Αv. 132 μέλλω γὰρ ἑστιᾶν γάμους˙
(The verb guarantees the meaning of γάμους.)

1688–89 εἰς καιρὸν ἄρα κατεκόπησαν οὑτοιὶ
εἰς τοὺς γάμους.

1737–40 Ἔρως . . . Ζηνὸς πάροχος γάμων.
(An explicit description of the nuptial procession.)

1755 lyr. ἕπεσθε νῦν γάμοισιν
(Meineke conjectures γαμοῦσιν. Cf. Αv. 1725, quoted above, where the birds have the lasting blessedness of the marriage in mind.)

The three remaining Aristophanic examples of the plural of γάμος need to be discussed separately. At Lys. 942–43 γάμων is used of intercourse:

οὐχ ἡδὺ τὸ μύρον μὰ τὸν Ἀπόλλω τουτογί,
εἰ μὴ διατριπτικόν γε κοὐκ ὄζον γάμων.[22]

At Ra. 850 Aeschylus is made to speak of the many unlawful liaisons in Euripidean tragedy. But most interesting is Th. 890–91, a passage from the parody of Euripides' Helen: βιάζομαι / γάμοισι Πρωτέως παιδὶ συμμεῖξαι λέχος. Here alone in Aristophanes the plural appears to mean "mating" and "wedlock," not "wedding." Though in the Helen Theoclymenus, Proteus' unsympathetic son, looks forward to celebrating his wedding (1431–35), βιάζομαι and the expression συμμεῖξαι λέχος surround γάμοισι and virtually guarantee that γάμοισι is erotic, not celebrational. (συμμεῖξαι λέχος is redolent of tragic style: see Rau, Paratrag., p. 60.)

I conclude that γάμοι for wedlock, not wedding, and not a true plural, is an innovation of tragedy. Its appeal for tragedians is to be understood as lying in its combination of two ideas related but distinct in ordinary Attic (and even earlier poetry), namely, wedlock and the celebration that inaugurates it. The identification (not mere symbolizing) of a concrete event with an event that has not yet occurred or with a chain of future events is an example of poetic condensation. Further, γάμοι aids tragic decorum because it contains, but does not make blatant, a sexual connotation far less apparent in the more abstract singular. To translate γάμοι in Oedipus' speech as "marriage rites" (so Jebb) holds the advantage of being ambiguous as to which marriage rites are meant—Jocasta and Laius' or

22. See J. Henderson, The Maculate Muse (New Haven, 1975), p. 135.

Jocasta and Oedipus'? But at the same time it bowdlerizes the sexual connotation required by ἐφύσατε ταὐτὸν σπέρμα and αἷμ' ἐμφύλιον. (I would follow Jebb's explanation of αἷμ' ἐμφύλιον as "blood-kinship" and take those words in apposition with both πατέρας . . . παῖδας and νύμφας . . . μητέρας τε.²³)

Perhaps the passage was influenced by Cassandra's ἰὼ γάμοι γάμοι Πάριδος, / ὀλέθριοι φίλων (Aesch. Ag. 1156–57 lyr.). There too γάμοι is ambiguous, suggesting both Paris' quasi-wedlock with Helen and the wedding celebration that soon turned into a funeral (681–716 lyr.).²⁴

γάμοι, then, is a plural with a semantic value that plays on the distinction rigorously observed in ordinary fifth-century Attic between singular and plural.²⁵ Not that this semantic possibility is exploited each time a tragedian used γάμοι with a suggestion of the meaning "wedlock": inspection of context is necessary before declaring an instance of γάμοι merely a type 10 plural or a mixture of that type and the "waters" type.

Fourth-century prose writers show some erosion in the distinctions observed by Aristophanes, but the "poetic plural" of γάμος is not yet dead. Plato uses γάμος/γάμοι almost exclusively in the context of legislation. His word for wedding was almost certainly γάμοι. Two examples:

R. 383a οὐδὲ [sc. τοῦτο ἐπαινεσόμεθα] Αἰσχύλου, ὅταν φῇ ἡ Θέτις τὸν Ἀπόλλω ἐν τοῖς αὐτῆς γάμοις ᾄδοντα ἐνδατεῖσθαι τὰς εὐπαιδίας . . .²⁶

Lg. 841d εἴ τις συγγίγνοιτό τινι πλὴν ταῖς μετὰ θεῶν καὶ ἱερῶν γάμων ἐλθούσαις εἰς τὴν οἰκίαν.

There are no instances in Plato of γάμοι with an unequivocally singular present. It is true that in writing of marriage legislation he often uses the plural together with the singular of other words (in coordination or subordination),²⁷ but at other times he stays with the plural.²⁸ Unless he is

---

23. I cannot understand why Kamerbeek thinks "the idea of 'womb' is foremost to be felt in the expression."

24. Aeschylus probably used the singular for wedlock at 745 lyr. γάμου πικρὰς τελευτάς, if the manuscripts are correct. (For the association of τέλος and its cognates with marriage ceremonies see A. Lebeck, The Oresteia [Cambridge, Mass., 1971], pp. 70–73.) I suspect, however, that Eur. Med. 1388 preserves the number that Aeschylus had used: πικρὰς τελευτὰς τῶν ἐμῶν γάμων.

25. Regrettably, Antiphon and Thucydides do not use the word at all. The latter has γαμικά, which tells us nothing.

26. There is an outside chance that Plato's quotation begins before ἐνδατεῖσθαι, which Burnet indicates as the first word in the quotation from Aeschylus.

27. R. 459a τοῖς τούτων γάμοις τε καὶ παιδοποιίᾳ, Ti. 18d εἰς τὴν τῶν γάμων σύνερξιν, Lg. 771e πρὸς . . . τὴν τῶν γάμων κοινωνίαν καὶ σύμμειξιν, 773c τῇ τῶν γάμων κοινωνίᾳ, 773d τῆς τῶν γάμων ἰσότητος, 925a τὴν . . . τούτων γάμων χρόνου συμμετρίαν (if the second hand of O is correct as against the first hand's and A's γάμων).

28. R. 459d τοῖς γάμοις . . . καὶ παιδοποιίας (a few lines after the first example in n. 27), Smp. 192b πρὸς γάμους καὶ παιδοποιίας, Lg. 721a ἡ τῶν γάμων σύμμειξις καὶ κοινωνία.

merely striving for some *variatio*, we may suspect a poeticizing tendency in two respects, the assimilation of number and the pluralization of an abstract (see p. 35, below). But he does not use γάμοι itself as a "poetic plural" in the tragic manner.

Isocrates uses the singular of wedlock (10.42, 49; 16.31) and the plural either of the nuptial ceremonies (9.16 ἐν τοῖς γάμοις ὑμέναιον ᾀσθῆναι) or as a true plural (10.39 ὑπεριδόντες τοὺς οἴκοι γάμους ἦλθον μνηστεύσοντες). Since Isocrates was exceptionally free in using the plural of abstract nouns,[29] his failure to use γάμοι as a "poetic plural" even in epideictic (9 and 10) is of interest. It shows that he was not willing to buy a bit of elevation and a means to secure a consonantal ending for the genitive and dative of a word at the cost of introducing semantic confusion.

A wide range of possibilities appears in Demosthenes. He uses γάμος for wedlock:

19.194 ἡλικίαν γάμου
(in a quotation referring to several girls)

39.26 γάμῳ γεγαμηκὼς τὴν μητέρα.

And the plural for the wedding:

30.21 . . . οὐδὲ πρὸς ἄλλον οὐδ᾽ ἂν εἷς οὐδένα τοιοῦτον συνάλλαγμα ποιούμενος ἀμαρτύρως ἂν ἔπραξεν· ἀλλὰ τῶν τοιούτων ἕνεκα καὶ γάμους ποιοῦμεν καὶ τοὺς ἀναγκαιοτάτους παρακαλοῦμεν . . .
(The point is the public character of the ceremony.)

He also uses the plural for disgraceful intercourse:

45.39 χρημάτων τοσούτων κλοπή, γυναικὸς διαφθορά, γάμοι δεσποίνης, πράγματ᾽ αἰσχύνην καὶ ὕβριν τοσαύτην ἔχοντα.

18.129 ἡ μήτηρ τοῖς μεθημερινοῖς γάμοις ἐν τῷ κλεισίῳ τῷ πρὸς τῷ καλαμίτῃ ἥρῳ χρωμένη τὸν καλὸν ἀνδριάντα καὶ τριταγωνιστὴν ἄκρον ἐξέθρεψέ σε.[30]

The author of the epideictic *Epitaphios* included in the Demosthenic corpus, on the other hand, selected γάμοι as a decent expression for the mating of a god with the mother of an Athenian tribe's eponymous founder:

60.31 ἐμέμνηνθ᾽ Ἱπποθωντίδαι τῶν Ἀλόπης γάμων, ἐξ ὧν Ἱπποθῶν

---

29. Gildersleeve, *Synt.* 1.21: "In Isocrates the plural is so marked a mannerism, and is so often suggested by the avoidance of hiatus, that it is not necessary to insist on sharp distinctions in that author."

30. Some, e.g, Mathieu in the Budé, who translates "marriages en plein jour," have seen an ironic nod to the meaning "nuptials."

ἔφυ, καὶ τὸν ἀρχηγὸν ᾔδεσαν· ὧν, τὸ πρέπον φυλάττων ἐγὼ
τῷδε τῷ καιρῷ, τὸ σαφὲς εἰπεῖν ὑπερβαίνω.

As Xenophon did not write the purest Attic (see above, p. 13), one
should not overestimate the importance of his using the plural at *Cyn.* 1.7
τῶν τότε μεγίστων γάμων μόνος ἔτυχεν Ἀταλάντης, where we should
probably translate γάμοι as "marriage" or "match," not "wedding." The
plural at *Lac. Pol.* 1.6 is somewhat difficult to interpret because Xenophon perhaps meant us to understand that Lycurgus was thinking of the
ceremony that initiates marriage and referred to it in his decree:
ἀποπαύσας τοῦ ὁπότε βούλοιντο ἕκαστοι γυναῖκα ἄγεσθαι, ἔταξεν ἐν
ἀκμαῖς τῶν σωμάτων τοὺς γάμους ποιεῖσθαι.

Abstract and Concrete, Singular and Plural

Aristotle initiated and Longinus continued the stylistic interpretation of
plural-for-singular as somehow grander than the "expected" singular. Both
ancient critics speak in synchronic terms and assume that the singular in
their examples is grammatically normal. They have left it to modern
scholars to explain the apparent substitution of singular for plural and the
principles by which we can discriminate "normal" and stylistically motivated pluralization.

In my discussion of γάμοι large differences of denotation were prominent. Although "wedlock," "wedding," and "coitus" have much to do with
one another, they are still different things. But far more often the semantic
differences seem absent altogether, in which case a plural can be assigned
to type 10 or can be said to involve a connotative difference of a particular
sort, namely, the shift of an expression from the concrete to the abstract.

Before proceeding to consider this shift in detail, I wish to emphasize
what I regard as the essential aesthetic point to be derived from Aristotle
and Longinus. Both are giving voice to their perception of unexpected
plurals as inevitably different in tone from the normal form. Now, it is not
as important to characterize the altered tone (and perhaps no characterization of nuance can be fully adequate) as it is to be clear that X and X-plural
can never be perfect synonyms. This is seen most readily when in a brief
span a single speaker uses both numbers to refer to the same event. As, in
music, the character of what precedes and what follows makes quite
different things of the same note, so in language the change of immediate
context can alter the associations and emotional coloring of a word used
twice with the same referent.[31] When the word is altered in form, the

31. A specific example: a given note will sound like a return if it follows one sequence of
notes, but will announce a departure after a different sequence. A word uttered by one

probability of a difference in nuance is greater, especially when the word is uttered by a speaker whose mental state is in flux. An illustration from Soph. *OT* 960–62, where Oedipus questions the messenger who brings word of Polybus' death:

> Οἰ. πότερα δόλοισιν, ἢ νόσου ξυναλλαγῇ;
> Ἀγ. σμικρὰ παλαιὰ σώματ᾽ εὐνάζει ῥοπή.
> Οἰ. νόσοις ὁ τλήμων, ὡς ἔοικεν, ἔφθιτο.

νόσου and νόσοις are no different in denotation.[32] Though I could never prove it, I see the change from singular to plural as an appropriate means to follow the contour of Oedipus' emotions as they move from guarded question to relieved restatement of the messenger's obliquely worded report. The actor, I fancy, pronounced νόσοις with stronger voice than νόσου.

Oedipus contrasts δόλοι and νόσος—he has no interest in which disease in particular was to blame.[33] He speaks of "disease," or perhaps "some disease," with equal generality in both lines. But according to grammarians' theories, singular and plural differ in the extent to which they present abstractions as αὐταὶ καθ᾽ αὑτάς or as incorporated, so to speak, in specific persons and events. These differences are said to be genre conditioned. I will argue that current accounts err in the specifics of genre distribution and, more important, in their underestimating of the tension *within the language* between abstract and concrete modes of expression.

Kühner-Gerth (1.15–19) begin by assuming that the abstract is properly a singular, and proceed to explain divergences into the plural as appropriate to multiple instances of the abstraction. The frequent plurals of abstract notions in the *Iliad* and, even more, the *Odyssey* reflect the "sensual and objective" character of Homeric language. Lyric and tragic poets have a predilection for abstract terms of "perceptions, feelings, passions, and resolutions." Prose, Kühner-Gerth maintain, "distinguishes strictly the use of the singular from that of the plural by denoting with the singular always the actual abstract concept, and with the plural individual types, cases, and so forth of the abstract activity." Gildersleeve (*Synt.* 1.22) says much the same in simpler language: "Pluralizing abstract nouns makes them concrete."[34] The general principle enunciated by Kühner-

---

character sounds straightforward, but it seems ironic when repeated by another in verse-initial position.

32. Cf. Jones, *Poet. Pl.*, p. 10: "There is apparently no call for a sharp distinction nor indeed is there any such distinction."

33. Until 969–70, when he speculates that πόθος for him might have killed Polybus.

34. His next remark is unquestionably true: "Pluralizing proper nouns makes them common."

Gerth and Gildersleeve is substantially correct, in my judgment, but requires some refinements. I offer a short discussion, *exempli gratia,* of a singular/plural opposition cited in both grammars.

μανία/μανίαι

Gildersleeve translated μανίαι "attacks of madness." This implies, I take it, that the plural corresponds to a perceived multiplicity of discrete phenomena occurring in a particular person, a type 8 plural. In this camp of interpretation is Jones (*Poet. Pl.,* pp. 100–01), who after examining each occurrence of μανίαι in the tragedians saw only one passage (Eur. IT 283–84) where he would not translate the word as "fits" or "successive attacks" of madness. But the three passages he chooses to quote are not compelling:

Aesch. *PV* 878–79 anap.   ὑπό μ' αὖ σφάκελος καὶ φρενοπληγεῖς
                          μανίαι θάλπουσ(ι)

          1057 anap.   τί χαλᾷ μανιῶν;

Soph. *Ant.* 959–65 lyr.   οὕτω τᾶς μανίας δεινὸν ἀποστάζει
                          ἀνθηρόν τε μένος. κεῖνος ἐπέγνω μανίαις
                          ψαύων τὸν θεὸν ἐν κερτομίοις γλώσσαις.
                          παύεσκε μὲν γὰρ ἐνθέους γυναῖκας εὔιόν
                          τε πῦρ,
                          φιλαύλους τ' ἠρέθιζε Μούσας.

To follow Jones we must deny what seems certain in the first passage, namely, that Io is describing the sudden reappearance of the various aspects of her affliction *tout ensemble,* not describing a span of time long enough to contain discrete paroxysms; and to understand μανιῶν in the second passage as anything other than madness conceived as a condition would require us to suppose that Hermes was dissecting madness into separate, probably distinct, parts.[35] In the Sophoclean lines, "fits of madness" is right if we can believe that μανίαις is as much an instrumental as γλώσσαις. Most would prefer to translate with something like "in lunatic fashion."[36]

35. Jones says that the singular at 959 "seems to be in contrast as meaning *state of madness*," but he neglects to mention the iterative παύεσκε, a point that buttresses his argument to a small degree.

36. Though the plural need not imply a succession of events in time or a number of different symptoms each time the word is used, such a notion may underlie the origin of the plural. Eur. *HF* 835–36 can be read as an analysis of one case of madness: μανίας τ'... καὶ παιδοκτόνους φρενῶν ταραγμοὺς καὶ ποδῶν σκιρτήματα. Perhaps it was felt that all lunacy (catatonia excepted?) manifested itself in a plurality of component actions.

Also doubtful is the genre distribution claimed by Kühner-Gerth for words like μανίαι, namely, lyric and tragic poetry. How elevated a usage is μανίαι? True, we have already seen several instances in tragedy. Bacchylides' one use of the word in either number is a distributive plural:

> πιθοῦσα δ᾽ Ἥραν
> παῦσεν καλυκοστεφάνους
> κούρας μανιᾶν ἀθέων·
> 11.107–09

Pindar makes μανίαισιν almost parallel to σοφία, a word he uses in the plural in the same poem (at 107):

> ἐπεὶ τό γε λοιδορῆσαι θεούς
> ἐχθρὰ σοφία, καὶ τὸ καυχᾶσθαι παρὰ καιρόν
> μανίαισιν ὑποκρέκει.
> O. 9.37–39

(Gildersleeve's translation might make too much of the plural: "Keeps in unison with the discordant notes of madness.") And the plural occurs in a prayer sung by the women at Aristoph. Lys. 341–42:

> ἅς, ὦ θεά, μή ποτ᾽ ἐγὼ πιμπραμένας ἴδοιμι,
> ἀλλὰ πολέμου καὶ μανιῶν ῥυσαμένας Ἑλλάδα καὶ πολίτας.

Beside the meter, elevation is marked by the absence of the article with πολίτας and perhaps by the use of ῥύομαι with the meaning "rescue."[37] But there is no sign of stylistic adornment at Aristoph. Nub. 832–33:

> σὺ δ᾽ εἰς τοσοῦτο τῶν μανιῶν ἐλήλυθας
> ὥστ᾽ ἀνδράσιν πείθει χολῶσιν;[38]

In expressions of the sort ἔρχεσθαι ἐς τοσοῦτον + genitive, the singular is almost invariable. A law on will making, perhaps of great antiquity, quoted at Dem. 46.14 shows the plural in parallel with several singulars:

> . . . ἂν μὴ παῖδες ὦσι γνήσιοι ἄρρενες, ἂν μὴ μανιῶν ἢ γήρως
> ἢ φαρμάκων ἢ νόσου ἕνεκα, ἢ γυναικὶ πειθόμενος . . .

37. The only Attic prose occurrence of ῥύομαι in the meaning "deliver" attested for our period is Thuc. 5.63.3, a passage thought to reproduce Spartan diction (see Gomme-Andrewes-Dover). The next appearance of the verb in Attic prose (in any sense) comes in Hypereides (see Veitch).

38. Strepsiades' answer, εὐστόμει, may be high style, perhaps an Aeschylean reminiscence: see Rau, Paratrag., p. 190. The scholiast says μανίαι is an Attic peculiarity (this is noted by Menge, Poet. Scaen., p. 34).

And at Aristoph. *Pax* 65 μανίαι is used precisely where a general expression for "madness" is required:

τὸ γὰρ παράδειγμα τῶν μανιῶν ἀκούετε.

It appears, then, that everyday Attic of the fifth century (and much earlier, if the wording of the law can be trusted) and poetry both used μανίαι. Literary prose never, to my knowledge, attests the form, either distributively or for the affliction of a single person. I would interpret this as fastidiousness, reflecting a sense that the plural was logically superfluous or indecorous.

Whether singular or plural is the "proper" grammatical number for words like μανία cannot be ascertained by considering the "objective correlate." Appealing, but impossible to verify, is the theory of the affective plural, type 12. Havers states an extreme version: plurals like *gli odi, le ire,* and *le gelosie* are symptomatic of dangerous tendencies in Italian temperament ("Bedeut. Pl.," pp. 42–43, following P. D. Fischer). Löfstedt (*Synt.* 1.34, 52–54) is less alarming. He holds that the plural was once intensifying, but in classical Latin, at least, has settled down to a cliché used by poetry as a means of distinguishing itself from everyday language. But no generalization can be drawn from the use of μανίαι.[39] θυμοί, for instance, another noun pertaining to emotional life, and abstract in the sense "fits of anger, passions," is not attested before Plato (LSJ s.v. II.4). And plurals like *gaudia,* attested both in Plautine and late vulgar Latin, derive independently from the same "mysterious impulses."[40] Though there might have been some connection in language between repetition, as indicated by a plural marker, and intensity of feeling, this putative phenomenon does not contribute to our analysis. μανίαι in the law quoted above shows that the supposed expressive vigor of the plural had faded enough for a sober context. And if a new intensifying plural-for-singular occurred spontaneously in the colloquial Greek of our period, how could we identify it? If we cannot distinguish the affective plural from others, we cannot tell what notion of genre appropriateness underlies its scarcity in oratory, much of which is highly excited (see p. 54).

39. The other abstract nouns of perceptions, etc., listed by Kühner-Gerth 1.16 together with μανίαι as exemplifying lyric and tragic poets' use of the plural are all exclusive to poetic texts; thus they do not allow the genre comparison possible in the case of μανίαι.

40. As a stick against those who would explain poetic plurals as nothing but sheer metrical expediency, Wackernagel adduces French *la joie,* which comes from *gaudia,* not *gaudium* (*Vorl.* 1.98).

Prose: General Trends

When the situation requires a way to speak of multiple occurrences of an abstraction, English, tending to the Platonic, by and large stays with the singular. Greek prefers to use the type 8 plural. An expression like κυπαρίττων . . . ὕψη καὶ κάλλη θαυμάσια (Pl. *Lg.* 625b, answering ἀνάπαυλαι . . . ἐν τοῖς ὑψηλοῖς δένδρεσίν εἰσι σκιαραί) is not, for Greek, a stylistic monstrosity. Still, there are signs of what we might call the English sensibility in Greek. In prose we can almost always be certain that the plural is justified by a plurality of instantiations. Dem. 18.246 contains a chain of plural abstracts:

τὰς ἑκασταχοῦ βραδυτῆτας ὄκνους ἀγνοίας φιλονικίας.

Wackernagel (*Vorl.* 1.96) points out that the plural is made intelligible by ἑκασταχοῦ.

Although the number of examples is far too small to permit certainty, it does appear that the distributive abstract singular is more restricted in prose than in poetry. All but two prose examples of plural adjective + abstract accusative of respect or "genitive of cause" listed by Gildersleeve (*Synt.* 1.22), Kühner-Gerth (1.14–15, 307), and Schwyzer (*Gramm.* 2.85–86) include the article. Some examples:

Thuc. 8.96.5 διάφοροι τὸν τρόπον
Xen. *An.* 2.3.15 θαυμάσιαι τοῦ κάλλους καὶ μεγέθους
Pl. *R.* 452b μὴ ἡδεῖς τὴν ὄψιν
Aeschin. 3.47 κακοὶ τὴν ψυχήν
Arist. *HA* 505b13 παραπλήσιαι τὸ εἶδος

With these compare Aesch. *Pers.* 441–42:

. . . ἀκμαῖοι φύσιν,
ψυχήν τ᾽ ἄριστοι κεὐγένειαν ἐκπρεπεῖς.

The exceptions in prose are Thuc. 5.34.2 ἀτίμους ἐποίησαν, ἀτιμίαν δὲ τοιάνδε, where the deictic force of τοιάνδε functions like the article, and Pl. *R.* 490d τοὺς πολλοὺς κακοὺς πᾶσαν κακίαν, where inclusion of the article might have turned the intended meaning, "every kind of evil," into "all evil."[41] Now, it is generally true that the article is less frequent in poetry and that adjectives in the singular also favor the article. But it may be that we see here a fastidiousness in prose in connection with number. If a singular abstract noun applies to many persons, the article alleviates the

41. Gildersleeve, *Synt.* 2.308–09, 312.

strangeness by showing that the abstraction is not floating but fixed, something well known and present at every place and time. This is especially true when the article seems to function as a possessive, as in *κακοὶ τὴν ψυχήν*. By contrast, poetic usage makes the abstraction less substantial.

Isocrates

Isocrates is notorious for lavish use of abstract nouns in the plural. He does *not* balk at employing the number without obvious semantic justification. In successive clauses at 6.97 he moves from the plural (otherwise unattested) of one word to the singular of a synonym:

πρότερον μὲν μηδὲ τὰς τῶν ἐλευθέρων ἰσηγορίας ἀνέχεσθαι, νῦν δὲ
καὶ τὴν τῶν δούλων παρρησίαν ὑπομένοντας φαίνεσθαι.

The dependent genitive with each abstract noun is plural; *a priori* *παρρησίας* would be possible, but Isocrates never uses the plural, and the word following, *ὑπομένοντας*, does not create the sequence of double -αν that could have prompted the exceptional pluralization of *ἰσηγορία*.

At 5.116 the same word appears twice, first as a singular, then as a plural:

καὶ μὴ θαυμάσῃς, εἰ διὰ παντός σε τοῦ λόγου πειρῶμαι προτρέπειν
ἐπί τε τὰς εὐεργεσίας τὰς τῶν Ἑλλήνων καὶ πραότητα καὶ φιλανθρω-
πίαν· ὁρῶ γὰρ τὰς μὲν χαλεπότητας λυπηρὰς οὔσας καὶ τοῖς ἔχουσι
καὶ τοῖς ἐντυγχάνουσι, τὰς δὲ πραότητας οὐ μόνον ἐπὶ τῶν ἀνθρώπων καὶ τῶν ἄλλων ζῴων εὐδοκιμούσας . . .

It is not impossible that Isocrates means to contrast mildness as a quality with manifestations of that quality *in concreto,* but I am inclined to think that his ear was attending to the consonant following the word at its first appearance in the passage, and to the vowel after the second.

θάνατοι in Poetry and Prose

Prose confines the plural of *θάνατος* very carefully indeed. The distributive plural is found at Antiphon 1.28, *οἱ ἐπιβουλεύοντες τοὺς θανάτους τοῖς πέλας* (where the plurality of the perpetrators and victims is beyond question), but as far as I am aware no orators or other prose writers use the same construction. There are numerous instances of the plural for the multiple deaths a speaker wishes on an enemy or miscreant; but in each case a cardinal or other word implying multiplicity aids the sense, e.g., at Dem. 19.131, where the "normal" singular is followed by the plural of the impossible multiple death:

ᾤχετο μὲν παρὰ τὸν νόμον, ὃς θάνατον κελεύει τούτων τὴν ζημίαν
εἶναι· ἐλθὼν δ' ἐκεῖσε ἑτέρων θανάτων ἄξια ποιῶν πέφανται.⁴²

The other common prose use is as part of a litany of dread events, usually
political, and thus applying to many, e.g., Pl. *Ep.* 7.327d:

μεγάλας ἐλπίδας εἶχεν ἄνευ σφαγῶν καὶ θανάτων καὶ τῶν νῦν
γεγονότων κακῶν βίον ἂν εὐδαίμονα καὶ ἀληθινὸν ἐν πάσῃ τῇ χώρᾳ
κατασκευάσαι.⁴³

In tragedy, on the other hand, θάνατοι is used for one person's death, as
at Aesch. *Ch.* 53 lyr. δεσποτᾶν θανάτοισι (of Agamemnon) and, according to Jebb (but cf. Kamerbeek), at Soph. *Tr.* 1275–78 anap.:

λείπου μηδὲ σύ, παρθέν', ἐπ' οἴκων,
μεγάλους μὲν ἰδοῦσα νέους θανάτους,
πολλὰ δὲ πήματα ⟨καὶ⟩ καινοπαγῆ.

Just how the tragedians came to this use of θάνατοι is far from clear. Witte
(*Sing. u. Pl.*, pp. 36–37) and Volp (*Num. Pl.*, p. 72) believe it is some sort
of analogical construction, the former diffidently proposing κῆρ, the latter
δύσμαι as the model. Jones (*Poet. Pl.*, p. 91) more reasonably claims that
it is "an extension . . . of the plural use where more than one person is
referred to." In this particular passage assimilation is another possibility,
θάνατοι coming under the influence of οἴκων and πήματα. The contention
that θάνατοι suggests violent death (Havers, "Bedeut. Pl.," p. 44) can
hardly be tested, since the victims of tragedy so rarely come to a peaceful
end (cf. Jones, *Poet. Pl.*, p. 91). Decisive refutation would require the
plural used of an individual's unquestionably serene demise, say, as
bestowed by Apollo or Artemis.

The ἀπορία created in poetry when θάνατοι is used for a single death
varies precisely in proportion to the perceived concreteness of the word,
i.e., the extent to which it designates the physical actualization of an

42. Also Dem. 21.21 and Pl. *Lg.* 908d (the dual); in comedy at Aristoph. *Pl.* 483, where I
see no high-style features.
43. I believe this formulation holds even for Pl. *R.* 492d ἢ οὐκ οἶσθα ὅτι τὸν μὴ πειθόμενον ἀτιμίαις τε καὶ χρήμασι καὶ θανάτοις κολάζουσι; τὸν μὴ πειθόμενον is singular but
generic, and therefore one thinks of a class of men. Other examples, all unambiguously
plural: [Dem.] 17.15 (cf. Menge, *Poet. Scaen.*, p. 34 on φυγαί), Pl. *Ep.* 7.351c, Isoc. 20.8.
This sort of list easily finds a place in patriotic rhetoric, e.g., Isoc. 6.89 ἐγὼ μὲν γὰρ ὑπὲρ
τούτων οὐ μόνον πόλεμον ἀλλὰ καὶ φυγὰς καὶ θανάτους οἶμαι προσήκειν ἡμῖν ὑπομένειν.
Is Plato (*R.* 399a–b) not quoting from such a declaration in his description of the song of a
single man facing death? κατέλειπε ἐκείνην τὴν ἁρμονίαν, ἢ ἔν τε πολεμικῇ πράξει ὄντος
ἀνδρείου καὶ ἐν πάσῃ βιαίῳ ἐργασίᾳ πρεπόντως ἂν μιμήσαιτο φθόγγους τε καὶ προσῳδίας,
καὶ ἀποτυχόντος ἢ εἰς τραύματα ἢ εἰς θανάτους ἰόντος ἢ εἴς τινα ἄλλην συμφορὰν
πεσόντος, ἐν πᾶσι τούτοις παρατεταγμένως καὶ καρτερούντως ἀμυνομένου τὴν τύχην.

abstract idea. One might well say that to the malicious plural of an enemy's imagination there should be a corresponding painful plural in the imagination of the potentially bereaved or killed, but every preserved instance of the phenomenon in tragedy looks back to an actual death. A few instances include details of the murder scene. Also, if the tragic examples were intended to suggest the same notion of literally impossible multiple deaths that we see in Aristophanes and prose authors, the poets could have so indicated by adding a word of multiplicity.[44] (The possibility of some faint resonance of multiple deaths cannot, however, be utterly rejected.)

The safest way out of the ἀπορία—safest because it asserts the least—is to regard the alteration of number as pure *licentia*: the poets use many plurals-for-singular, θάνατοι is one of them, and it is intelligible simply as a *differentia*. We can go farther by regarding θάνατοι as an inversion of the usual arrangement of grammatical number and the contrast between general notion and multiple instantiations *in concreto*. The normal idiom, found in prose and (less certainly) colloquial Greek, employs the singular to designate the general idea and its instantiation in a single case, the plural only for multiple instantiations. The poetic variation presents the plural-for-singular to designate a single concrete instance. As the change in number in the normal idiom accommodates abstract to concrete, the change in the opposite direction perhaps accommodates concrete to abstract. The plural θάνατοι would, if this is correct, suggest as an undertone, roughly " 'death,' the word for the general idea."

Concrete Plural-for-Singular

This speculation is not entirely arbitrary. The manipulation of abstractness in expression is a prominent feature of Greek style. Moreover, poets manipulate the grammatical number of concrete words in a way that appears to achieve the converse effect.

We have already discussed an especially rich source of plurals for the singular in tragedy, *pluralia tantum* denoting a set of persons in a particular relationship to the speaker (pp. 26–27, above). Tragedy alone exploits the ambiguity latent in these expressions, i.e., it uses some plurals of type 7 as type 11. Bruhn's list (*Anhang*, pp. 3–5) of plurals "of persons, sometimes with intentional ambiguity, often only as a linguistic ornament, especially

---

44. We can exclude altogether any influence of one meaning the plural can bear, "ways of death." The strongest motive for imagining an iterated death seems to be intense hatred (as in the prose examples) and, on the part of the bereaved, not knowing how the death occurred. Cf. Vladimir Nabokov, *Pnin* (Avon paperback ed., New York, n.d.), p. 13: "And since the exact form of her death had not been recorded, Mira kept dying a great number of deaths in one's mind, and undergoing a great number of resurrections, only to die again and again . . ."

in designations of relationship" contains fifteen examples of the primary sort (e.g., τέκνον); eight constructed with words for blood relations (e.g., τοὺς πρὸς αἵματος); seven with words of intimacy, friendship, or enmity; and five, perhaps extensions of the first group, that speak conspiratorially of the living, the dead, and the murderers. Seven expressions with words for political authority probably belong to the primary group as well: a τύραννος is a τύραννος over someone. Nearly all entries in the list occur in trimeter passages.

The frequency of plurals in this semantic region is not surprising. Most characters in tragedy suffer precisely because they are related to one another by ties of family or kinship. Reference to one child as "children" calls attention to the categorical, as well as specific, relationship of the speaker to the child. "Relationship" is itself abstract; and being conscious of the categorical relationship takes one beyond the persons specifically designated. (τὰ παιδικά, the only plural used in prose for a single person, is discussed by K. J. Dover, *Greek Homosexuality* [Cambridge, Mass., 1978], pp. 16–17.)

Both poetry and prose use plural expressions, like ἅλες, which "proceed from different conceptions" (Gildersleeve, *Synt.* 1.23–24).[45] Though the singular ἅλς does exist (e.g., Hdt. 4.181.2 ἁλὸς τρύφεα), the plural could even be used for the transferred meaning "friendship": Aeschin. 3.224 τοὺς τῆς πόλεως ἅλας περὶ πλείονος ποιήσασθαι τῆς ξενικῆς τραπέζης. Similarly, a splendid royal enclosure is composed of many discrete buildings, thus δώματα for δῶμα. Though there must have been at least some structures grand enough for a plural of this sort, δώματα never occurs in Attic prose or comedy (LSJ s.v.). But the word in either number is poetic, so we cannot say that prose abstains from the plural. οἶκος, by contrast, is a prosaic word; thus abstention from οἶκοι for a single dwelling is a discrete phenomenon. But it too behaves like a lexical item, i.e., even if a single dwelling consisted of several buildings, one could not call it οἶκοι in everyday Greek, merely because that would be using a part of the paradigm of that noun reserved for poets as a type 10 plural.[46]

Witte notices that Pindar, Aristophanes, and the three tragedians shy away from δόμοι though making free use of the oblique cases of the plural,

---

45. κρέα = "prepared meat" is usually mentioned together with ἅλες. Assuming the morphology has been correctly understood, this usage appears (at line 12) in an inscription recently published by L. H. Jeffery and Anna Morpurgo-Davies, "An Archaic Greek Inscription from Crete," *The British Museum Quarterly* 36 (1971): 24–29; cf. *Kadmos* 9 (1970): 147.

46. By "everyday Greek" I mean, in this instance, language that disregards a distinction of Attic law between "estate" and "dwelling place" (see LSJ s.v. οἰκία). Whereas a tragic character may use οἶκοι to mean either, a competent speaker in an inheritance action would not use the singular of the same word except to indicate "estate."

the number that for them is *a priori* the one to use (*Sing. u. Pl.*, pp. 51, 184ff., 208). He argues that the oblique cases are "colorless," whereas the nominative plural if used as a subject with a plural verb brings "the plural character of the form in its full meaning to consciousness," and precisely this plural verb frightens the poets into using the singular. (There is no such problem, of course, with the neuter δώματα.) This seems to show that the plural is an ornament, something to be deployed so as to forestall semantic embarrassment. It is true that almost all of the few instances of nominative δόμοι are simply in apposition with a noun or stand as subject to a form of εἰμί (e.g., Eur. *Med.* 139). There is a counterexample at Eur. *El.* 870 (cf. 359), but more interesting is Cassandra's line (*Ag.* 1309). Evidently Aeschylus thought he could put δόμοι + noncopulative verb only into the mouth of a delirious mantic. The reason for this preference is perhaps positive rather than, as Witte maintains, negative. Personification of the house using words found in prose, δόμος and οἶκος (especially the latter), may have carried a hint of popular speech: see Fraenkel on *Ag.* 37–38 οἶκος δ᾽ αὐτός, εἰ φθογγὴν λάβοι, / σαφέστ᾽ ἂν λέξειεν, and on the more clearly popular expression one line before. If so, poets will have regarded the yoking of the personification with the plural of the high style as incongruous.[47]

The poets of our period took over numerous words from their predecessors that appeared to them as plural-for-singular, and created many more by analogy. This process has been amply (though not always accurately) documented by Witte in his *Singular und Plural.* Wackernagel (*Vorl.* 1.98) chides Witte for neglecting the essential preliminary task of determining ordinary usage in each case, but it must be remembered that writers in the fifth and fourth centuries could not—if they conceived such a desire—determine how Homer's or Sappho's literary language differed from their common speech. Unless some body of writing has eluded us altogether, they could compare earlier poetry only with some quite useless prose inscriptions, mostly in the special language of governmental or religious records, the relatively late Ionian prose writers, and their own casual speech. Nothing requires us to assume that they interpreted their predecessors' language on sound historical principles (so much should be clear from any page of Plato's *Cratylus*). It follows that plurals for fifth-century Theban or Athenian singulars could be taken over with no rationale other than their status as traditional poetic diction. This alone seems enough to create what Aristotle calls ὄγκος.

σκῆπτρον is a clear example of a word that combines a concrete and

---

47. The chart at *Sing. u. Pl.* p. 202 shows but one use of οἶκοι in Aristophanes and the tragedians. I find Witte's metrical argument unpersuasive.

abstract meaning, stick and royal authority. Jones (*Poet. Pl.*, p. 38, n. 3) understood the origin of σκῆπτρα for σκῆπτρον as somehow reflecting the plurality of abstract "official powers and prerogatives" enjoyed by a king and his lieutenants and symbolized by the scepter. In my view, the abstract side of the word did not originally motivate the plural, though the plural, once created, may have emphasized the abstract sense.

Regrettably there is no clear relationship between the Homeric usage of σκῆπτρον/σκῆπτρα—perfectly explicable singulars (except for a strange plural at *Il.* 18.505)—and the many plurals for both the concrete and abstract senses of fifth-century usage.[48] The plural does not appear to be merely a poetic innovation: Herodotus uses it in a speech Xerxes makes to Artabanus (7.52.2), and its appearances in Aristophanes are not notably elevated (*Av.* 510, 636 lyr., *pace* Menge [*Poet. Scaen.*, p. 34]). But the word makes no appearance in prose outside Herodotus, even in its meaning "walking stick," presumably because in the classical period the object was known only as a thing possessed by divinities and kings of the heroic age and by oriental potentates.[49] The literary and archaeological evidence shows that the scepter as described by Herodotus (1.195), imagined by vase painters, and implied by Aristophanes is composite, an ornament of some sort mounted on a wand.[50] The passage in Aristophanes relies on the audience's knowing that a bird was commonly used as a finial:[51]

> ἦρχον δ᾽ οὕτω σφόδρα τὴν ἀρχήν, ὥστ᾽ εἴ τις καὶ βασιλεύοι
> ἐν ταῖς πόλεσιν τῶν Ἑλλήνων Ἀγαμέμνων ἢ Μενέλαος,
> ἐπὶ τῶν σκήπτρων ἐκάθητ᾽ ὄρνις μετέχων ὅ τι δωροδοκοίη.
>
> *Av.* 508–10[52]

48. I am inclined to think that Leaf ad loc. was wrong to assume that the scepter(s) held by the elders on Achilles' shield had the purpose of establishing which speaker had the floor. Perhaps we have here the conflation of two notions: (1) the γέροντες (Hesiod would call them βασιλῆες) are all σκηπτοῦχοι, at least in the Dark Age, and (2) the assembly procedure often described in both epics dictates a single scepter.

49. Jones (*Poet. Pl.*, p. 38, n. 3) remarks on the eunuchs called σκηπτοῦχοι at Xen. *Cyr.* 7.3.16. The wand used in the Athenian courts was called βακτηρία.

50. See *RE, Zweite Reihe* 3, s.v. Sceptrum (cols. 368–70), and the upper portions of the royal scepters belonging to Phineus, Creon, Cepheus, et al. in A. D. Trendall and T. B. L. Webster, *Illustrations of Greek Drama* (London, 1971), pp. 52, 61, 65 (an elongated knob), 78, 110.

51. The scholiast remarks, εἰώθασιν ἐν τοῖς σκήπτροις ἐπὶ τοῦ ἄκρου ἐκτυποῦν ὄρνιθας εἰς κόσμον. This could be just a reasonable deduction from the sense.

52. If the figure of a bird did in fact perch on the heroic scepter, there can be little doubt that it was an eagle, in imitation of the royal scepter par excellence: see Pind. *P.* 1.5–10. To extend this speculation, σκήπτω, the verb from which the noun derives, may have been a *vox propria* for the hurling of Zeus' thunderbolts: see Aesch. *Pers.* 514 (θεός = Ζεύς; cf. 532–34), 740, *Sept.* 429, *Ag.* 366, and (ironically of Zeus' victim) *PV* 749. More general uses of aerial or subterranean attacks by divine being: Aesch. *Eum.* 801, Soph. *OT* 28, or of an apparently benign sign (Hephaestus' fire) Aesch. *Ag.* 302ff.

All this makes it appear that σκῆπτρα was an elliptical plural, type 1, for wand + crowning member. The abstract sense latent in the word is never entirely absent in tragedy, but a concrete sense is apparent in virtually all Jones's examples. In some, a character points to or brandishes the scepter:

> ἀλλ' ὧδέ μ' αἰεὶ ζῶσαν ἀβλαβεῖ βίῳ
> δόμους 'Ατρειδῶν σκῆπτρά τ' ἀμφέπειν τάδε
> Soph. El. 650–51

A nearly pure abstract meaning is exceptional; perhaps the clearest such is Soph. OC 448–49:

> τὼ δ' ἀντὶ τοῦ φύσαντος εἰλέσθην θρόνους
> καὶ σκῆπτρα κραίνειν καὶ τυραννεύειν χθονός.

Here the verb with σκῆπτρα precludes a concrete sense, and we may speak of a distributive abstract.

But elliptical plurals were not created in the fifth century; therefore σκῆπτρα, as I have tried to explain it, must be an archaism. (Some archaic attestation would, admittedly, strengthen my argument.) Whether this theory is correct or not, those uses of the word requiring a concrete sense must have appeared strange to the fifth-century audience. Even erudite connoisseurs among them who recognized the putative archaism of the word (though not its origin as an elliptical plural) would, I imagine, try to align the plural with the usual habits of their language. Less sophisticated members of the audience would probably try even harder. The solution to their perplexity was close at hand: it is the Jones solution, to remember that "in a sense the king possesses *scepters* just as he possesses *powers* (κράτη)" (*Poet. Pl.*, p. 38, n. 3). In any case, the plural of the concrete noun more strongly suggests something intangible than the singular does because it can no longer be understood literally.

Concrete Singular-for-Plural[53]

The type 4 plural, ὁ Πέρσης for the Persians, ὁ Χαλκιδεύς for the Chalcidians, and the like, is frequently used by historians. That the "national appellative" (Gildersleeve) was common in ordinary speech is clear from the way it is presented in two pieces of verse:

> πὰρ πυρὶ χρὴ τοιαῦτα λέγειν χειμῶνος ἐν ὥρῃ
> ἐν κλίνῃ μαλακῇ κατακείμενον, ἔμπλεον ὄντα,

53. Discussed by Gildersleeve (*Synt.* 1.28–29), Kühner-Gerth (1.13–15), Wackernagel (*Vorl.* 1.93–94), Löfstedt (*Synt.* 1, chap. 2), Schwyzer (*Gramm.* 2.41–42).

πίνοντα γλυκὺν οἶνον, ὑποτρώγοντ᾽ ἐρεβίνθους·
"τίς πόθεν εἰς ἀνδρῶν; πόσα τοι ἔτε᾽ ἐστί, φέριστε;
πηλίκος ἦσθ᾽, ὅθ᾽ ὁ Μῆδος ἀφίκετο; . . ."

Xenoph. 13 Gentili-Prato

κεἰ μὲν οἱ Λακωνικοὶ
ὑπερβάλοιντο μικρόν, ἔλεγον ἂν ταδί·
"ναὶ τὼ σιὼ νῦν ὠττικίων δωσεῖ δίκαν."

Aristoph. *Pax* 212–14

Wackernagel sees this sort of expression as especially appropriate to oriental despotisms, whose kings could be regarded as complete embodiments of their nations, and perhaps derived from oriental languages themselves; its application to Greek states was secondary. Löfstedt, on the other hand, argues that it is *"volkstümlich,"* native to Latin (and, by implication, to Greek). I believe Löfstedt is right. The collective singular in place of the plural is a natural expedient for speaking with some immediacy and concreteness of people one does not know.

But it is not the only expedient. Wackernagel (*Vorl.* 1.93) summarizes the choices and the practice as follows:

if the utterance has to do not so much with a plurality as with a type as such, and therefore with an abstract plurality, the singular or plural can be used. Then the singular has a much more abstract meaning. I have in mind such expressions as *es irrt der Mensch, solang er strebt.* Precisely so could the Greek and the Latin speak from the very beginning, although in the older language the plural predominates. Homer would have said ἄνδρες in that sentence.

I think that the early predominance of the plural in the "older language" may reflect an accident of transmission, that our chief source of early Greek, the Homeric poems, favors the plural (as enjoying a higher tone?). The singular, characteristic of the gnomic style, though underrepresented in our corpus, is likely to be of considerable antiquity. Consider Hesiod's

καὶ κεραμεὺς κεραμεῖ κοτέει καὶ τέκτονι τέκτων,
καὶ πτωχὸς πτωχῷ φθονέει καὶ ἀοιδὸς ἀοιδῷ.

Op. 25–26

It has been observed, e.g., by Volp (*Num. Pl.,* pp. 76–77), that the national appellative is excluded from tragedy. Epideictic oratory, so far as I know, contains no examples despite numerous opportunities, as when the topos of "our ancestors' glorious resistance to the Mede" is trotted out. Nor do there seem to be any instances in Pindar. The high style has, if anything, a persistent interest in abstract expression: why, then, this particular exclusion? In part, perhaps, because these singulars had a banausic tone. But also, I suggest, because they are insufficiently abstract. ὁ Πέρσης is abstract in that it presents the Persians as a mass, not as many distinct individuals: "If you've seen one Persian, you've seen them all." Yet its ethnic specificity makes it less general than ὁ ἄνθρωπος or ὁ πέλας (Eur. *Med.* 86). To this "pseudo-abstraction" poets and orators of the high style preferred οἱ Πέρσαι.

Both poetry and prose use the type 2 collective singular of various military terms, e.g., ἡ ἵππος, ἡ ἀσπίς (poetry and prose), ὁ ὁπλίτης (prose only, since the hoplite is post-heroic). No surprise here: generals and poets both tend to consider military forces and their weapons *en bloc*, the former out of necessity, the latter out of indifference to detail in this area coupled with a general willingness to appropriate technical language.[54]

A poetic specialty is the distributive use of σῶμα referring to more than one body (human or animal) and of the singular for parts of the body that come in pairs (see lists at Kühner-Gerth 1.15). A most obvious variation within poetry is Euripides' ταχύπορος πόδα of Achilles (*El.* 451 lyr., part of an elaborate circumlocution for Achilles' name). The motive, I believe, is to propel these supposedly concrete words gently away from the visual and toward the abstract. This maneuver is clearest in those periphrases that replace a verbal form by a concrete noun + genitive, e.g., (from Kühner-Gerth 1.280) Eur. *Or.* 1216–17 σὺ μὲν νῦν . . . παρθένου δέχου πόδα = παρθένον ἀνελθοῦσαν. (Greek can achieve the same effect more directly, sometimes without poetic intention, by using words like βάσις = "foot.")[55]

We can distinguish two uses of singular-for-a-pair. In one type the singular is used to lead the mind's eye to imagine (in a strict sense) a detail, as at Pind. *P.* 1.6–7:

εὕδει δ'ἀνὰ σκά-
πτῳ Διὸς αἰετός, ὠκεῖ-
αν πτέρυγ' ἀμφοτέρωθεν χαλάξαις.

Here ἀμφοτέρωθεν leads the imagination from one wing to another. The combination of adverb and singular suggests the alternate drooping of the eagle's wings far better than the plural could. This is why Dornseiff

---

54. Thus Dornseiff (*Pindars Stil*, p. 24) should not have included *O.* 7.19 'Αργείᾳ σὺν αἰχμᾷ in his list of unexpected singulars.

55. Cf. Long, *Lang. Soph.*, p. 13 and passim. It would be arrogant to chide Aristophanes for missing a trick when he wrote πόδες instead of πόδα in the paratragic lines at *Th.* 47–48 θηρῶν τ'ἀγρίων πόδες ὑλοδρόμων / μὴ λυέσθων (which Kühner-Gerth [1.280] translate *bestiae circumcursantes*).

(*Pindars Stil,* p. 25) regards some singulars as promoting a visual effect.[56]

Dornseiff (p. 24) identifies another consequence of writing singular for plural: "There too [as in plural-for-singular] there is something abstracting, an expressive gathering together of individual things to stand for the slightly symbolic idea of the thing itself." I believe this is correct, though not all his examples seem apropos.[57] It is not that one arm or leg is less tangible than two; but to mention only one part when, logically, both are involved and, far more important, everyday language mentions both, is to speak less literally. To use the singular in this way is to assume that the listener understands that both arms or wings are meant. This not very difficult mental step, whereby we understand the pair when one member is mentioned, is a sort of abstraction.

Plural for First-Person Singular

Scholarly opinion is nearly unanimous on the fundamental meaning of the first-person plural verb and pronoun when uttered by a single person.[58] At the highest level of generality, Benveniste (*Prob.,* p. 203 [235]) writes: "The verbal person in the plural expresses a diffused and amplified person. 'We' annexes an indistinct mass of persons to 'I'." In Greek, at any rate, the plural indicates a positive feeling for the "annexed mass." To say "we" for "I" is to assert some sort of solidarity with persons for whom or to whom one is speaking. "We" can embrace inferiors, as when Achilles says (*Il.* 22.393) ἠράμεθα μέγα κῦδος· ἐπέφνομεν Ἕκτορα δῖον. He means, in Wackernagel's paraphrase (*Vorl.* 1.98), "Through the glory I have won, the Achaeans in general are made richer in glory." The plural can also suggest a community of persons sharing a journey, dangers, gender, historical era, or simply humanity (see Slotty, "soz. affekt. Pl.," pp. 349–51). Slaves use the plural of themselves, but never to unite themselves with their masters (cf. Menge, *Poet. Scaen.,* p. 30; Slotty, p. 350, no. 7, p. 351, no. 8). The best term for these plurals is "sociative," for it ex-

---

56. The passage is cited by Dornseiff, but without comment of any kind, in a list that mixes singulars of the "visual" type and those with a flavor of abstraction (see next paragraph). I am confident, however, that I can at least tell which type of singular Dornseiff thought was exemplified by each of his citations.

57. *O.* 7.19 should not be cited as an example (see above, n. 54). Pind. *Dith.* 2.11 (*Pap. Oxy.* xiii 1604. ii.10–11) is questionable because the context permits, but does not demand, that the listener imagine a multiplicity of torches when he hears αἰθομένα . . . δαῒς ὑπὸ ξανθαῖσι πεύκαις.

58. Discussions at Gildersleeve, *Synt.* 1.27–28; Kühner-Gerth 1.83; Wackernagel, *Vorl.* 1.99–100; F. Slotty, "Die Stellung des Griechischen und anderer idg. Sprachen zu dem soziativen und affektischen Gebrauch des Plurals der ersten Person," *IF* 45 (1927): 348–63; Löfstedt, *Synt.* 1.40; Schwyzer, *Gramm.* 1.243.

presses the unity of meaning that is obscured by the two terms it replaces, namely, *pluralis maiestatis* and *pluralis modestiae*.[59]

Especially remarkable is the frequent (but not inevitable: see Eur. *Hipp.* 671 lyr.) masculine plural for feminine singular that appears in tragedy and, perhaps, comedy as well. Gildersleeve puts it well: "The particular is sunk in the generic, the individual in the class, the woman in her male kindred." In modern jargon we could say that the women of tragedy revert to the unmarked gender.[60] According to Slotty ("soz. affekt. Pl.," p. 361), only this switch in the gender accompanying the plural distinguishes the Greek sociative plural from that of Latin and German.

Regardless of the origin of the sociative plural, are there instances where the speaker intends no annexation of others though he uses a plural form? And is the sociative plural largely confined to poetry, as Kühner-Gerth, Wackernagel, and Schwyzer claim? Slotty ("soz. affekt. Pl.," pp. 348–49) argues that it made more than sporadic appearances in prose and colloquial Greek. His trump card (or so he regards it) is the story related by Plutarch at *Mor.* 816d–e. As a young man Plutarch was sent with another man on an embassy to the Roman proconsul; but when, for some reason, his colleague remained behind, Plutarch executed the mission on his own. Plutarch's father advised him how to couch his report to the citizens:

μὴ λέγειν 'ᾠχόμην' ἀλλ' 'ᾠχόμεθα,' μηδὲ 'εἶπον' ἀλλ' 'εἴπομεν,' καὶ τἆλλα συνεφαπτόμενον οὕτω καὶ κοινούμενον ἀπαγγέλλειν. οὐ γὰρ μόνον ἐπιεικὲς τὸ τοιοῦτο καὶ φιλάνθρωπόν ἐστιν, ἀλλὰ καὶ τὸ λυποῦν, τὸν φθόνον ἀφαιρεῖ τῆς δόξης.

This tale does not support Slotty's argument: the event took place long after our period, the need for self-effacement (possibly even excuse) via the sociative plural arises from a special circumstance, and it was not a form that the young Plutarch would have employed on his own initiative. Slotty claims that the abundance of examples from poetry actually proves the usage was *"volkstümlich,"* for poetry and popular speech share a "more animated vividness and a stronger dependence on the emotions [*eine lebendigere Anschaulichkeit und eine stärkere Abhängigkeit vom Gefühlsleben*]," i.e., than literary prose. Arguing for a kinship of poetry and popular speech is reasonable: indeed, this is what I claim in my

---

59. According to Havers ("Bedeut. Pl.," p. 60), the term *pluralis sociativus* or *inclusivus* was devised by Vico. Havers subsumes the first-person plural under his general notion of affective plurals (see below, appendix 1a).

60. Menge (*Poet. Scaen.,* pp. 27–28) resists the idea that the masculine plural is favored as being (in Kühner-Gerth's phrase) more general. K. J. Dover points to a clear use of the masculine with reference to both sexes, οἱ καλοί at Xen. *Cyr.* 5.1.14 (*Greek Homosexuality* [Cambridge, Mass., 1978], p. 66).

discussion of μανίαι, certain uses of the optative, and the jussive infinitive with nominative subject. But this kinship must be demonstrated in *praxis*, not assumed as a working principle.

Slotty has added considerably to the number of examples of the sociative plural previously known in prose dialogue. That the usage is colloquial, however, is still unclear. Aristophanes does not exhibit any convincing examples. Slotty can, in fact, show only two instances:

> ὥρα βαδίζειν, ὡς ὁ κῆρυξ ἀρτίως
> ἡμῶν προσιόντων δεύτερον κεκόκκυκεν.
>
> προσιουσῶν Le Febvre
>
> *Ecl.* 30–31
>
> ξύναυλον ὕμνων βοὰν
> φθεγξώμεθ', εὔγηρυν ἐμὰν
> ἀοιδάν, κοαξ κοαξ
>
> *Ra.* 212–14 lyr.

The masculine plural is easily excused in both: the first because the line is probably addressed to a number of women dressed as men (so Ussher), the second because the chorus (Slotty says "coryphaeus," but I cannot see why) has both an individual and a collective aspect.[61] Further, Slotty argues throughout his article against the common interpretation of various instances of the plural as unjustified. For example, Nestor's οὔ τι καθ' ἡμέτερόν γε νόον (*Il.* 9.108) is for Wackernagel a clear example of an "our" that can only mean "my," whereas Slotty (pp. 350–51) speaks of the "sociative plural of peers [*Standesgenossen*]."[62] Elsewhere he tries to show that the plural is contextually or psychologically motivated, or part of a linguistic tendency of various special or fortuitous groupings. He is reduced to explaining some passages by the rather woolly concept of the *pluralis affectus* (see below, appendix 1). He argues (pp. 359–61), for instance, that this rubric applies to the plural at *Od.* 16.441, where Eurymachus tells Penelope

> αἶψα οἱ αἷμα κελαινὸν ἐρωήσει περὶ δουρὶ ἡμετέρῳ.

61. The masculine participle may be simultaneously paratragic and appropriate to women masquerading as men: see Ussher ad loc. M. Kaimio, in his discussion of all instances of hortatory subjunctives in the first-person plural in choral parts in tragedy and comedy, conjectures that the usage reflects "the prokerygma announcing the hymn in actual cult ceremonies" (*The Chorus of Greek Drama within the Light of the Person and Number Used* [*Commentationes Humanarum Litterarum* 46, Helsinki, 1970], p. 143; for his convenient summary of earlier work see pp. 12–17).

62. A compelling argument for the Wackernagelian position is the confusion of the plural possessive adjective ἁμός with the singular ἐμός (Wackernagel, *Vorl.* 1.99; Schwyzer, *Gramm.* 2.203).

(The lines that follow make clear that Eurymachus is speaking of his own sword: he has special reason to defend Odysseus' household.)

Slotty's line of argument tends to reduce the genre distinctiveness of the sociative plural. To agree with Slotty means to assimilate very different sorts of "we" for "I." Consider these two examples, both from well-known passages:

Μάλα τοι, φάναι τὸν Περικλέα, ὦ 'Αλκιβιάδη, καὶ ἡμεῖς τηλικοῦτοι ὄντες δεινοὶ τὰ τοιαῦτα ἦμεν· τοιαῦτα γὰρ καὶ ἐμελετῶμεν καὶ ἐσοφιζόμεθα οἷάπερ καὶ σὺ νῦν ἐμοὶ δοκεῖς μελετᾶν. τὸν δὲ 'Αλκιβιάδην φάναι· Εἴθε σοι, ὦ Περίκλεις, τότε συνεγενόμην ὅτε δεινότατος ἑαυτοῦ ἦσθα. [Xen. *Mem.* 1.2.46]

παθόντες ἂν ξυγγνοῖμεν ἡμαρτηκότες
Soph. *Ant.* 926

In the first I hear the "we" of condescension, in the second a literary usage, proper to the genre and far removed from everyday language. (Slotty's analysis of the latter is impossibly strained: "not . . . an individual utterance of Antigone's but a periphrasis, not very appropriate in her connection, of the well-known proverb *πάθος μάθος*.")

APPENDIX 1a.
SOME MODERN CONTRIBUTIONS

Theories of the poetic plural range from austere preoccupation with meter (Witte) to enthusiastic but uncritical notions of the primitive mind (Havers). Scholars of the middle ground admit to uncertainty (Wackernagel) and sometimes look wistfully at one or both poles of the argument (Schwyzer, Löfstedt).

In his *Singular und Plural* Witte tries to show that the immediate motive for changing the number of a word expected in the singular to the plural, or vice versa, is metrical necessity. He opens his book with an acknowledgment that poets cannot alter the expected number of a word without justification, viz., the analogy of another word of similar or related meaning that would be expected in the metrically desirable number. But his method is to hurry through the semantics and then conduct a leisurely investigation of the metrical properties of the singular and plural of the word in question. Nothing in his book contradicts Maas's manifesto ("Poet. Pl.," p. 486): "Every interpretation which attributes to the poetic plural the force to create a nuance of meaning, of whatever sort, is necessarily false." This is not a position I accept (see above, esp. pp. 34–

35). Decisive against the argument from metrical expediency is the evidence of Old Comedy: Aristophanes wrote in verse and must have sometimes felt the pressure of *Verszwang,* yet he abstained from poetic plurals except in parody (see below, appendix 1c). I cannot believe that the alteration of number was not sought for its own sake much of the time. (For other criticisms see Maas, "rev. Sing.," Wackernagel, *Vorl.* 1.98.)

Havers's fundamental thesis in "Zur Bedeutung des Plurals" is that the plural, both nominal and verbal, conveys emotional intensity, especially feelings of horror and awe for things or people endowed with mysterious powers. He declines a pursuit of the specifically poetic plural (p. 40) but does remark (p. 59): "Naturally poetry will make greater use of this intensive plural than prose, since in the former, emotional processes take a bigger place. But one must also consider that this plural will be preferred in poetry as being archaic."

Löfstedt devotes much of the third chapter of *Syntactica* 1 to scandalized criticism of Havers, conceding only that his hypothesis contains "here and there a small kernel of truth." Löfstedt brings against Havers an acute argument, pertinent to Greek, that can serve as an example of his critique. Havers (p. 56) explains δώματα and *aedes* as manifestations of a primitive belief that power hides in place designations, especially in those for human habitations. Löfstedt (p. 32, n. 2) sensibly objects that if the plural were indeed magical or mystic one could expect what one does not find, a tendency to use the plural especially for temples. Havers's work is, moreover, of little help to a comparative study of genre. His remark (p. 42) that abstracts like ἀνίαι, δείματα, ἐλπίδες, ἡδοναί, λύπαι, and so forth appear in Greek prose as well as in poetry tells us virtually nothing. Finally, his theory, even if true, leaves only two ways in which poetry and prose might differ: the relative importance of intense emotion and poetry's partiality for archaic language (pp. 57–60). There seems little or no place in his scheme for developments internal to the language, e.g., analogically constructed plurals (cf. Löfstedt, *Synt.* 1.31, n. 1). According to Havers's interpretation, poets of the classical period, wanting to infuse their verses with great emotion, made abundant use of the affective plural. Since certain semantic fields account for a disproportionate share of unexpected plurals, this theory would be credible only if we could show that Greeks of the fifth and fourth centuries expressed their superstitions in designating the same classes of things as their ancestors in the common Indo-European period had done, or that analogy from pre-existing affective plurals led them to those semantic fields where Indo-European *Weltanschauung* had located hidden forces. Havers, however, does not try to demonstrate the former, and he underestimates the importance of the latter. And if emotion per se, apart from the tradition of genre-appropriate diction, could generate new plurals in the poetry of our period, Havers would need to explain the absence of numerous examples in excited rhetoric or the colloquial speech of Old Comedy. (There are only, to my knowledge, a few type 9 plurals in oratory, e.g., Antiphon 2.γ.1. κινδύνους, Lysias 3.48 ἀγῶνας [but ἀγῶνα at §§20, 38]: these are adduced by M. H. Jameson, *Historia* 20 [1971]: 554, n. 38 apropos ἀγῶνας, the reading of some manuscripts at Thuc. 8.68.2. Of course, litigation can be perceived, with no strain, as a series of hazards. For the plural in Old Comedy see below, appendix 1b.)

In his *Indogermanische Grammatik* (vol. 6, *Syntax* I, pp. 25–26) Hirt complains that previous investigations (by Witte, Maas, Bednara, and Landgraf) have come to no satisfying result. He notes the predominance of "unjustifiable" plurals of abstract concepts in Greek, Latin, and several other Indo-European languages. His argument then runs as follows: the *Rig-Veda* contains many words, especially abstracts, that are *pluralia tantum* instrumentals in *-bhis,* an ending related to Greek *-φι.* In Homer, words ending in *-φι* are sometimes singular, sometimes plural, but gradually the ending comes to be interpreted only as a plural. Under the influence of this practice, other plurals begin to be used where a singular is expected. Thus, argues Hirt, the poetic plural is born. Though my own interpretation makes the manipulation of abstractness one motive for the use of the poetic plural, and the poetic singular as well, I simply see no evidence for Hirt's assertion that the plural of abstracts is the basic type from which all others sprang.

Hainsworth also focuses on *-φι* in his article "The Plural of Abstract Nouns in the Greek Epic" (*BICS* 4 [1957]: 1–7). He proposes that abstract plurals derive ultimately from ἶφι, "formally the instrumental plural of a word meaning 'sinews'." ἶφι serves as a model for the Ionic βιῆφι, which is "analysable as a case form of a noun, the instrumental plural of an abstract." For the most part, *-σι* functions in the place of *-φι* in Ionic, giving the *-ησι* of ā-stem dative plural abstracts. (A problem in this reconstruction is that it would be very difficult, perhaps impossible, to determine how long Greek speakers continued to understand the case ending of the model word ἶφι as plural.) Hainsworth (p. 2, commenting on Cauer) explicitly accepts as possible the analogical spread from "legitimate" plural uses of abstract words.

APPENDIX 1b.
THE POETIC PLURAL IN PROSE

Witte's account of occurrences in prose authors of plurals associated with poetry (*Sing. u. Pl.,* pp. 248–56) is sketchy and inadequately argued.[63] His general conclusion (p. 255) seems to me quite unsubstantiated: Herodotus and Plato, he writes, "not infrequently" use the secondary forms of epic and tragic *Dichtersprache*, both singulars and plurals, whereas Thucydides and the Attic orators use them "only where their language rises above the average." In fact, Witte gives no examples of poetic plurals from Thucydides and the orators and exaggerates the number that he has found in Herodotus and Plato. I offer here some specific remarks on some of the plurals that Witte treats.[64]

ἅρματα (*Sing. u. Pl.*, p. 253)

Witte gives one instance in prose of ἅρματα with a singular meaning, Pl. *Lg.* 899a:

αὐτοῦ δὴ ἄμεινον ταύτην τὴν ψυχήν, εἴτε ἐν ἅρμασιν ἔχουσα ἡμῖν
ἥλιον ἄγει φῶς τοῖς ἅπασιν, εἴτε ἔξωθεν, εἴθ᾽ ὅπως εἴθ᾽ ὅπῃ, θεὸν
ἡγεῖσθαι χρεὼν πάντα ἄνδρα.

Poeticizing features may be present in this passage: the omission of the article with ἥλιον and the ellipsis of ἐστί with χρεών (less common in prose than in poetry [LSJ s.v. χρεών]).

πελάγεσσι (*Sing. u. Pl.*, p. 254)

Witte (pp. 244–45) shows that poets employ the plural (but in the dative case only) of πέλαγος to denote waves. The one prose attestation known to Witte is Pl. *Plt.* 298b:

οἵ τ᾽ αὖ κυβερνῆται μυρία ἕτερα τοιαῦτα ἐργάζονται, καταλείποντές
τε ἔκ τινος ἐπιβουλῆς ἐν ταῖς ἀναγωγαῖς ἐρήμους, καὶ σφάλματα
ποιοῦντες ἐν τοῖς πελάγεσιν ἐκβάλλουσιν εἰς τὴν θάλατταν, καὶ
ἕτερα κακουργοῦσιν.

A playful poeticism here looks perfectly appropriate, just as we might say "into the brine" vel sim. in the middle of an otherwise unpoetic piece of writing.

αἵματα (*Sing. u. Pl.*, p. 252)

According to Witte, the plural at Pl. *Lg.* 872d is to be associated with the poetic plural pioneered by Aeschylus (*Sing. u. Pl.*, pp. 229–30):

ὁ γὰρ δὴ μῦθος ἢ λόγος, ἢ ὅτι χρὴ προσαγορεύειν αὐτόν, ἐκ παλαιῶν

---

63. Maas ("rev. Sing.," col. 1409) called this section "entirely unsatisfactory," a fair judgment considering the scope implied by Witte's title.
64. Plato's use of θάνατοι (discussed by Witte on pp. 254–57) has been treated above, on p. 41.

ἱερέων εἴρηται σαφῶς, ὡς ἡ τῶν συγγενῶν αἱμάτων τιμωρὸς δίκη
ἐπίσκοπος νόμῳ χρῆται τῷ νυνδὴ λεχθέντι καὶ ἔταξεν ἄρα δράσαντί
τι τοιοῦτον παθεῖν ταὐτὰ ἀναγκαίως ἄπερ ἔδρασεν.

We should be on guard, as Plato emphasizes that the law, and almost
certainly its formulation, is archaic. Further, the plural is distributive: it
looks to the shedding of the blood of any number of relations. I doubt,
therefore, that αἵματα was meant to sound poetic, even if its form is first
found in tragedy.

πόθοι (Sing. u. Pl., pp. 206–07, 251–52)

Witte regards the plural as an innovation introduced by Sophocles or
Euripides. It occurs three times in Plato. At *Phil.* 48a the plural follows
shortly after a quotation from the *Iliad,* and it shares a preposition with
θρήνοις: καὶ τὰς ἐν τοῖς θρήνοις καὶ πόθοις ἡδονὰς ἐν λύπαις οὔσας
ἀναμεμειγμένας. It is unclear to me whether πόθοι evoked associations
with the Sophoclean and Euripidean uses or has been semantically con-
verted by Plato into the plural of πόθος in a new meaning, "song of
yearning." At *Lg.* 633d the plural is distributive, and so not a clear
example of plural-for-singular. At *Lg.* 870a Plato wrote ψυχῆς ἐξηγριω-
μένης ὑπὸ πόθων. Here again the plural appears to refer to more than one
instance of πόθος, since the soul would, I imagine, survive a single attack
of the emotion. In that case only the form would have seemed poetic. We
cannot, however, be certain that the plural was not meant as a poetic plural
of an abstraction, or even a single concrete instance.

στήθη (Sing. u. Pl., pp. 252–53)

Witte cites six instances of στήθη in Attic authors. He is surely right to
call the plural in Thucydides' description of plague symptoms (2.49.3) a
borrowing of the plural used in Ionic medical writings. Four of Plato's five
uses of στήθη are plainly technical: *Prot.* 352a (an amateur medical examination), *Ti.* 69d, 79c, *Smp.* 191a (where διαρθρόω is a suitable verb for
the tooling of the chest into two distinct μαστοί). *Ti.* 91e is not technical.
Of course στήθη is a well-established poetic usage, and Maas ("rev. Sing.,"
col. 1410) has this in mind when he writes: "We must reckon with the
possibility that colloquial language moves from one number to another
without poetic influence," as in Gothic *brusts* as against modern German
Brust. We can also add that if the prose authors were borrowing the plural
from poetry, they might have sounded more Homeric than the tragedians
and lyric poets of the fifth century, who attest στήθη only five times (see
LSJ s.v.). The case for a colloquial plural would have to rest on the slender
evidence of a single occurrence in Middle Comedy, Eubulus 138K, where

the anapestic meter makes the reflection of routine speech all the less likely:

οἶνον γάρ με ψίθιον γεύσας
ἡδὺν ἄκρατον, διψῶντα λαβὼν
ὄξει παίει πρὸς τὰ στήθη.

But in Aristophanes the singular appears twice, the plural never.

τόξα (*Sing. u. Pl.*, pp. 248, 255)

Witte cites, without comment, two Herodotean examples of the plural designating the weapon of a single man: 2.106.3 and 3.78.2. For Witte τόξα is a plural constructed on the analogy of ὅπλα, ἔναρα, and τεύχεα (*Sing. u. Pl.*, p. 31; he does not mention the theory that τόξα is an elliptical plural). In evaluating the first example, a description of a statue of Sesostris, we can refer to a stone sculpture found at Ninfi, perhaps the very one seen by Herodotus.[65] Sesostris holds a bow, but no arrows, in his *right* hand, though Herodotus says τῇ . . . ἀριστερῇ τόξα. In any case, he does not have more than one bow. The second plural, which appears in Herodotus' account of the slaughter of the Magi, is explained by Stein as "bow and quiver," but I see no justification for this. It seems improbable to me that Herodotus would have used τόξα in these two passages as an epicism. Both are narrative, and both are free of conspicuous stylistic heightening. Further, he twice uses the singular in speeches, where a poeticism is on the whole more likely (see above, p. 10). On the other hand, an Ionicism is possible, though it would have to count as a stray dialect feature, as there are twenty-nine instances of the singular in narrative (see Powell, *Ind. Herod.*). Worse, there is no evidence beside the two Herodotean attestations of Ionic τόξα for τόξον, whereas the thirty-one singulars in Herodotus are certified as good Ionic by a Samian inscription and a passage of Heraclitus (see Favre, *Thes. Verb.* s.v.).

APPENDIX 1c.
SOME POETIC PLURALS IN ARISTOPHANES

In a previous section (pp. 36–38) I argued that μανίαι for "madness," the abstraction, is a colloquial usage; the evidence came from Aristophanes. As that discussion might suggest that other "poetic" plurals were also part

---

65. Drawing and discussion in G. Rawlinson, *The History of Herodotus* (New York, 1880), 2.149.

of everyday Greek, I thought it prudent to examine each instance in Aristophanes of a few "poetic" plurals par excellence, δόμοι, δώματα, οἶκοι, μάχαιραι, and θάνατοι. As the list below shows, Aristophanes uses these plurals (always in oblique cases: cf. above, pp. 43–44) outside verbatim quotations from tragedy or paratragedy only to designate "true" plurals, i.e., in instances where the singular would be anomalous. Witte has made a similar but more comprehensive survey; he concludes that "forms which were first used by the tragedians preserve throughout a specifically tragic color" and could not have been used by Aristophanes except in parody (*Sing. u. Pl.*, pp. 233–34). (In no instance does the classification "paratragic" rest solely on the plural. For most examples, readers who wish to confirm the marks of paratragedy for themselves will find the index of Rau's *Paratragodia* sufficient.)

δόμων: Paratragic or tragic quotation
   Ach. 450, 456: parody of Eur. *Telephus*.
   Av. 1241: allusion to Eur. *Likymnios*.
   Lys. 707: a high-style line (ἄνασσα at 707, δόμων without the article).
   Ra. 1360 lyr.: parody of Euripidean pathos.
   Ecl. 11: "paratragic prayer-hymn" (Rau).

δόμοις: Paratragic or tragic quotation
   Ach. 460: parody of Eur. *Telephus*.
   Nub. 1162: "tragic pot-pourri" (Dover).
   Av. 1708: "messenger speech in exquisite poetic style" (Rau).

δόμοισιν: True plural
   Ach. 543

δόμους: Paratragic or tragic quotation
   Av. 1247 = Aesch. *Niobe* fr. 276 Mette

δωμάτων: Paratragic or tragic quotation
   Ach. 479 = Eur. fr. 1003 N
   Th. 871 = Eur. *Hel.* 68

δώμασι(ν): Paratragic or tragic quotation
   Nub. 1159: from a mélange of tragic lines.
   Pax 115: parody of Eur. *Bellerophon*.

δώματα: Paratragic or tragic quotation
   Ach. 1072: in style of tragedy (cf. Eur. *Ba.* 60, *Or.* 1312).
   fr. 268K: Eur. *Or.* 1361 has identical beginning, but closes with the singular, δῶμα.

οἴκων: Paratragic or tragic quotation
   Nub. 1165: parody of Eur. *Hec.* 173.
   True plural
   Th. 826 anap.: ὁ κανών occurs at 825, but the plural ἀνδράσι at 824 makes it clear that the speaker means a multiplicity of households. Unlike most of the paratragic plurals, this one appears with the article.

οἴκους: Paratragic or tragic quotation
Pax 88: parody of Eur. *Bellerophon*.

The following are true plurals that never appear as "poetic" plurals in Aristophanes:

μαχαίρας: *Eq.* 489
fr.684 N
θανάτους: *Pl.* 483, of reiterated death (cf. above, pp. 40–42).

APPENDIX 1d.
χεροῖν AND ποδοῖν IN TRAGEDY

Preservation of the dual number is a conspicuous archaism of the Attic dialect. The dual of the noun, with or without δύο, is always used on Attic inscriptions until 409; the verbal dual is not much less persistent (see Meisterhans, *Inschrift.*, pp. 199–200).[66] Aristophanes has some 380 duals as against 290 plurals where dual is possible, a ratio of about 1.3:1. By comparison, the figures for the three tragedians—627 and 1,030 respectively, a ratio of about 1:1.6—show a relative disinclination to use the number.[67] Certain categories show a more or less systematic exclusion, e.g., tragedy abstains from the duals in -ματε/-μάτοιν found in comedy.[68] The conventional view of the matter, which I see no good reason to discard, holds that we see here an Ionic influence. The Ionic iambic and trochaic verse, which served as the chief linguistic model for tragic dialogue, contained no duals whatever, and the dual was felt to be a feature of Attic incompatible with the dignity of the genre (see Meillet, *Aperçu*, p. 218).[69]

66. Cuny (*Nombre Duel*, pp. 78–83) goes further, claiming that there is no plural before 404 in Attic inscriptions where the dual is possible.
67. Radko, "Synt. Trag.," p. 99. Cf. Cuny, *Nombre Duel*, p. 245.
68. Cuny, *Nombre Duel*, pp. 95–96. According to Cuny (pp. 85ff.) the dual is at first excluded altogether, and with time becomes more frequent, though we cannot chart the growth of the number with great precision because the evidence includes plays unusually short or lacking characters who appear as couples. This process actually runs counter to the trend of the spoken language (p. 363). It must be remembered that for Cuny (writing in 1905) the *Supplices* of Aeschylus is the oldest extant tragedy: the redating of that play upsets his account.
69. Schwyzer ("Synt. Arch.," p. 5) writes: "The avoidance of the dual, which was banal for the Attic ear [*Sprachgefühl*], is due to the Ionic influence on Attic poetic language." This Björck (*Alpha Imp.*, p. 314) finds an "unfortunate sharpening of Meillet's assertion." If I understand Björck correctly, his complaint is twofold: (1) that Schwyzer replaces Meillet's "partial" avoidance with "complete" avoidance, a reasonable objection if Schwyzer did in fact intend to make a categorical statement, and (2) that the dual was felt not as too common, but as archaic, something that up-to-date, "highbrow" (Björck's word) language would shun. But if this were so, later tragedy should show relatively fewer duals (cf. n. 68, above). We are

E. Hasse discovered, but did not explain, a curious rule observed by the tragedians: aside from χεροῖν and ποδοῖν they avoided the dual of words for parts of the body and for footwear, though Aristophanes shows no such restriction.[70] To my knowledge, the only exceptions are ὄσσε at Aesch. *Pers.* 1065 lyr. and Eur. *Tr.* 1315 (Homeric reminiscences according to Hasse, but only the second closely reproduces the sense of *Il.* 4.461 and 5.310); χεῖρε, attested at Eur. *Andr.* 115 (but in elegiac couplets, a metrical form found nowhere else in tragedy and, furthermore, within a phrase apparently modeled on Hom. *Od.* 11.211, so almost "the exception that proves the rule") and conjectured at Aesch. *Ag.* 1559 by Porson and at Eur. *Ba.* 615 by Nauck; and, in satyr drama, σκελοῖν at Eur. *Cyc.* 183. ποδοῖν is far less frequent than χεροῖν; there are but seven examples, even less than the overall proportion of πούς:χείρ in tragedy would yield if the percentage of duals were uniform for the two words.[71]

As I see it, what needs to be explained is not so much the negative part of Hasse's rule as its relaxation for χεροῖν and ποδοῖν. For not only is the dual rather scarce in tragedy, but the specific category of paired parts of the body is, in dialects other than Attic, that semantic field from which the dual most quickly retreated (Cuny, *Nombre Duel,* p. 192).[72] Now if tragedy is to yield to normal Attic at all, it is hardly surprising that it will make its concession for the most frequently named body parts, hands and feet, both in literal and figurative uses. The hands are, of course, specially favored, being the instruments of human action (see Fraenkel ad Aesch. *Ag.* 1357 and Müller, "Der Dual bei Euripides" [n. 70], p. 18). The feet serve, *inter alia,* as an index of a man's enthusiasm: see LSJ s.v. πούς 1.6–7. On the whole, the tragedians seem to use the dual of these words for literal signification of hands and feet. Thus Soph. *Ph.* 1150–51 lyr.

---

on safer ground in regarding the dual as something specifically Attic, for this was clearly the view of later antiquity: see Wackernagel, *Vorl.* 1.80. Radko's criticism ("Synt. Trag.," p. 98) rests on his opinion that there was no statistically significant avoidance of the dual by tragedy, a position I would not accept in light of Cuny's discussion. Radko's remark (pp. 100–01) that "tragedy is less a reflection of the language of the people" seems an almost self-contradictory concession.

70. *Ueber den Dual bei den attischen Dramatikern* (Bartenstein, 1891), p. 11. Footwear is perhaps not a major interest of the tragic poets. Hasse's rule is an extension of Hermann Joseph Müller's observation that the tragedians intentionally avoided χεῖρε ("Der Dual bei Euripides," *Prog. Königl. Kath. Gymnasium* [Sigmaringen, 1889], p. 12).

71. The attestations of ποδοῖν are Aesch. *Ch.* 207, 982, Soph. *El.* 567, Eur. *Andr.* 1139, *Ion* 495 lyr., IA 206 lyr., 212 lyr. (This list combines instances cited by Müller, Hasse, Cuny, and Radko.)

72. Cuny understands this phenomenon as a consequence of the dialects' tendency not to use the dual except with δύο and δυοῖν, words hardly ever used with objects naturally found in pairs.

οὐ γὰρ ἔχω χεροῖν
τὰν . . . ἀλκάν

is more typical than *El.* 1349–50, where χείρ means "authority":

οὗ τὸ Φωκέων πέδον
ὑπεξεπέμφθην σῇ προμηθίᾳ χεροῖν.[73]

What accounts for the discrimination against the nominative/accusative duals of χείρ and πούς? Cuny (*Nombre Duel,* p. 128) remarks that the frequent χεροῖν at iambic verse end was "doubtless a convenient formula from the point of view of meter."[74] Radko ("Synt. Trag.," p. 128) goes further: "Almost all instances of χεροῖν in the dual appear to be metrically conditioned. The genitive-dative dual χεροῖν occurs at those points in a line which require an iamb. The one metrically unconditioned form is Soph. *OC* 483." These arguments are insufficient. An iambic word can be used in any of the six positions in the line that begin a foot, is obligatory in verse-final position after fifth-foot diaeresis, is favored in the fifth foot by Porson's law, and throughout the line by various strictures.[75] Given so many opportunities for an iambic word and the failure of tragedians to offer similar hospitality to words of the same shape (say, σκελοῖν), any claim of metrical conditioning must be considered improbable.[76] Although he does not apply his findings to the words in question, it appears from Cuny's extensive canvass of the dual that those in -ε were subject to more rapid erosion than those in -ω and, more significantly, that the genitive/dative dual persisted longer than nominative/accusative duals (see his remarks on the dual in Thucydides, *Nombre Duel,* p. 403). What seems to shelter χεροῖν and ποδοῖν is the combination of a favored semantic status, the morphologically selective decay of the dual number, and in the case of χεροῖν a vocalization distinct from the normal Attic form, χειροῖν.

---

73. The enallage of the possessive adjective with προμηθίᾳ may help lead the listener away from the literal meaning.

74. Müller ("Der Dual bei Euripides," p. 18) had already called χεροῖν a welcome ending for the trimeter line.

75. For instance, anapests are allowed outside the first foot only to adjust for proper names and the tragedians are disinclined (later Euripides excepted) to resolve long syllables.

76. Radko's suggestion ("Synt. Trag.," p. 89) that the six examples of χεροῖν in choral passages "again appear to be metrically conditioned" is made without specific argumentation, and so cannot be assessed. He does not anywhere mention the tragedians' abstention from χεῖρε and πόδε.

2. The Terminal Accusative

Among the syntactical differentiae examined in this study, the terminal accusative, or "accusative without preposition" (I reserve the term "allative" for certain datives), is at once the most genre specific and the most frequently encountered. My canvass, which is not exhaustive, shows more than two hundred examples in fifth-century lyric and tragic poets but only one (and that one far from secure) in Attic prose; only a handful occur in fifth- and fourth-century comedy.

This construction is, without question, one of great antiquity. Old Indic and Old Iranian use the terminal accusative even more freely than Homeric Greek does (Schwyzer, *Gramm.* 2.67). Already in Homer the adverbial notion present in the accusative case may be augmented by a preposition; and the construction with bare accusative, though common, is not obligatory with any verb of motion or with any noun denoting the terminus of motion (Chantraine, *Hom.*, pp. 45–46).[1] Lexical and semantic specialization are already evident: ἱκνέομαι and ἵκω favor the construction more than ἔρχομαι, νέομαι, ἄγω, ἡγέομαι, and other verbs, and dwelling places more than other nouns or pronouns (Chantraine, pp. 45–46). The abundance of terminal accusatives in "serious" poetry of our period, even in tragic dialogue (see below, pp. 84–85), is all the more surprising when considered against other developments in the realm of prepositions and the cases they govern. As compared with Homer, Greek of the fifth and fourth centuries, Attic in particular, shows a sharp reduction in the permissible combinations. (For instance, μετά with the dative, common in epic, is extremely rare in tragedy and never appears in comic dialogue or prose [Wackernagel, *Vorl.* 2.206–09]. This trend resulted finally in the restriction of all prepositional phrases, save a few *expressions glacées,* to the accusative case in Modern Greek.) Common terminal accusatives like οἶκον and

---

1. Whereas the adverbial "home" of English is obligatory: one cannot say, "I am going to home." This is more like Greek οἴκαδε, which cannot be replaced by *εἰς οἴκαδε (though εἰς ἅλαδε is attested at Hom. *Od.* 10.351).

Ἀθήνας are especially striking archaisms, since ordinary Attic already had corresponding expressions, οἴκαδε and Ἀθήναζε, that also indicate place whither without recourse to prepositions.

An accusative that is neither governed by a preposition nor functions as a terminal accusative can stand in one of several other relations to a verb signifying motion:

1. as an external, direct object, in some sense conceived as affected by the verb, e.g., φεύγω τὸν λέοντα, "I flee the lion."

2. as an accusative of the extent of space, i.e., a word naming an object that exists apart from the verbal action and designates a "place or way over which the movement occurs" (Page ad Eur. *Med.* 1067),[2] e.g., Hdt. 4.12.2 τὴν [sc. ὁδὸν] παρὰ θάλασσαν ἔφευγον.

3. as an "internal accusative" designating motion in substantival form, but not precisely the same motion connoted by the verb, e.g., Eur. *Ion* 1238–39 lyr. τίνα φυγὰν . . . πορευθῶ; (One can also say πορεύεται τις of movements unconnected with exile or flight.)

4. as an "internal accusative" that is simply the noun corresponding to the verb, e.g., Eur. *Hel.* 1041 τίνα φυγὴν φευξούμεθα; This construction is also known as the *figura etymologica.*

Types 3 and 4 are easily distinguished from terminal accusatives, but instances bearing a similarity to 1 or 2 can be problematic.

Terminal Accusative or Direct Object?

The temptation to deny the existence of a terminal accusative is strong when the verb can be translated by an English verb requiring the (atrophied) objective case in English. Gildersleeve, for instance, rejects a terminal interpretation of accusatives with ἵκω, ἱκνέομαι, and compounds thereof on the ground that "these verbs are felt as transitives, 'reach'" (*Pind.,* p. 286).[3] One of his examples of terminus as object of the verb is Pind. *N.* 3.3:

ἵκεο Δωρίδα νᾶσον Αἴγιναν

We may, however, invoke Gildersleeve against himself. In his remarks on the categories "transitive" and "intransitive" he says that the distinction is "from a higher point of view . . . futile"; what matters is "habits"

---

2. Page used the term "cognate accusative," which risks confusion with type 4. Pind. *P.* 8.69 ὅσα νέομαι probably belongs to this category: Slater, *Lexicon to Pindar* s.v. νέομαι, translates "at every step of my path." E. Clapp strangely supposes that the accusative is a direct object ("Pindar's Accusative Constructions," *TAPA* 32 [1901]: 22).

3. Gildersleeve here nearly transgresses his own warning against regarding particular uses as canonical for English ("Probs.," p. 126).

("Probs.," p. 125). Greek habits with the verb at *N.* 3.3, then, are the issue. If a passage of poetry places an accusative answering the question "whither" and dispenses with a preposition, though it is obligatory in prose, I am prepared to call it a "terminal accusative." And I would so classify the syntax with greatest confidence when the verb in question frequently appears with the preposition in the same sense as it bears in the passage under examination. Since ἵκω and its by-forms ἱκάνω and ἱκνέομαι are attested far more often *with* the preposition,[4] Pindar's usage here must have been felt as unusual; because the terminal accusative is common in poetry, that syntactical interpretation is more likely to have suggested itself to Pindar's audience than Gildersleeve's direct object.

Rather different are those passages in which there is reason to regard the accusative as an unmistakable direct object, i.e., something clearly altered as a consequence of the verbal action. In those Homeric expressions, for example, in which the onset of an emotional state is often represented as the movement of the emotion toward or into the person, the accusative is more than a destination: we understand *Il.* 1.240 Ἀχιλλῆος ποθὴ ἵξεται υἷας Ἀχαιῶν as predicting that the sons of the Achaeans will be afflicted. Significantly, in no expression of this type does Homer include a preposition. At the very least, the adverbial, purely local sense is submerged. The same may be true in passages from the classical period where the verb of motion can be glossed with a transitive verb implying that the subject strongly affects the person designated by the accusative noun, e.g., Soph. *OT* 711–13, where Jocasta says

> χρησμὸς γὰρ ἦλθε Λαΐῳ ποτ᾽,
>
> . . . .
>
> ὡς αὐτὸν ἥξοι μοῖρα πρὸς παιδὸς θανεῖν
>
> ἕξοι (ἕξει Canter) K. Halm: ἥξοι Lᵃᶜ rec: ἥξει LᶜA rec.

Jebb argues that ἥξοι = καταλήψοιτο and therefore requires the accusative object αὐτόν. This interpretation, which implies that the case forces the audience to take the verb in a sense unusual in the fifth century, is possible but not inevitable. Jocasta wants to deny that Oedipus is Laius' son and to suggest that the oracle may not have been

---

4. Prose examples of these verbs are rare, but when they appear the preposition is at hand, e.g., Pl. *Phdr.* 276d εἰς τὸ λήθης γῆρας ἐὰν ἵκηται (a quotation from poetry) and Hdt. 1.216.3 and 2.29.4, which have ἐς. English does in fact have a frankly transitive use of "reach," as in "Reach me the sugar," but the grammar is called "informal" by the *American Heritage Dictionary* s.v. The syntax is venerable enough: the *OED* cites examples as far back as 1000.

authentic (711). Her presentation of the oracular response is concise (710: σύντομα) and devoid of vivid detail. The flat expression, "fate would come to him," is better suited to the tone of her speech.

The sense of motion is more plausibly conveyed by transitive glosses in two other passages from Sophocles:

> OC 942–43 οὐδείς ποτ᾽ αὐτοὺς τῶν ἐμῶν ἂν ἐμπέσοι
> ζῆλος ξυναίμων . . .
>
> αὐτοῖς Lb: αὐτοὺς cet.

Jebb: "ἐμπέσοι has here the constr[uction] of ἕλοι: cp. Eur. *IA* 808 δεινὸς ἐμπέπτωκ᾽ ἔρως τῆσδε στρατείας Ἑλλάδ᾽, οὐκ ἄνευ θεῶν. This is decisive against here reading αὐτοῖς, the commoner constr[uction]."

> *El.* 137–78   ἥ σε πολλὰ δὴ
> ἀφ᾽ ὧν ἔχοιμι λιπαρεῖ προύστην χερί.

Kamerbeek: "In the context the verb takes the meaning of ἱκετεύω and its construction."

In the passages with ἐμπίπτω a clear transitive sense is probable because the verb frequently, as in these lines, connotes a violent attack: the approach of ζῆλος or ἔρως drastically alters those it visits. In the last passage the approach to the god, though not truly concrete since he is not physically present to receive the sacrifices, is recognizable as an act of supplication. Nevertheless, the syntax of these constructions would, I think, have provoked some sense of anomaly. Possibly the audience noticed, subconsciously, that in these passages the poet exploited the semantic ability of a verb to straddle two sorts of syntax. The construction is archaic and elevated if the verb is understood literally, but banal if the verb is understood in an extended sense.

Two examples from Herodotus are of particular interest because they would constitute exceptions to the strong genre-specificity of the terminal accusative:

> 2.36.1 τοῖσι ἄλλοισι ἀνθρώποισι νόμος ἅμα κήδεϊ κεκάρθαι τὰς κεφαλὰς τοὺς μάλιστα ἱκνέεται (Stein: "ἱκνέεται = προσήκει, attinet sc. τὸ κῆδος.")
>
> 9.26.1 φαμὲν ἡμέας ἱκνέεσθαι ἡγεμονεύειν
>
> ἐς add. Koen post φαμὲν (Stein translates the verb as "falls to our share.")

By the criterion applied above to the syntagma ποθὴ ἵξεται υἷας, an expression that never appears in Homer with a preposition, these instances of ἱκνέομαι + accusative might be called terminal accusatives, for in another use of the verb in the same sense, "concern, have to do with, befit," the manuscripts show a preposition:

6.57.4 ἐς τὸν ἱκνέεται ἔχειν⁵

My intuition, however, is that the abstract sense given to both the verb and the subjects (impersonal or Stein's understood τὸ κῆδος in the first passage; ἡγεμονεύιν, impersonal, or just possibly the infinitive, in the third) drains away any residual local sense from the verb. Diachronically considered, the accusative might be adverbial, but this is not an issue for our present purposes. If in fact the accusatives were intended as terminals, and were felt by Herodotus as poeticisms, it would make more sense for the ἐς to appear in the first and third passages, both ethnographic narrative, than in the second, which is a speech.⁶ It goes without saying that the paucity of evidence forbids any certainty.

At Soph. *Ph.* 921 the accusative πεδία is, strictly, terminal (so Escher, *Acc.*, p. 63), but it seems to me pedantic not to read it as a direct object of πορθῆσαι as well:

ξὺν σοὶ τὰ Τροίας πεδία πορθῆσαι μολών.

Pace Escher (*Acc.*, pp. 61–64), who declares himself agnostic on the point, I would regard all instances of δύω as intransitives, and accusatives associated with them as terminal, except for the few times (all in Homer) when a person is said to put clothes or armor around or on a part of the body (see LSJ s.v. δύω II.2). At Aesch. *Ag.* 218 lyr. δύω is used of Agamemnon's assumption of "necessity's yoke": ἀνάγκας ἔδυ λέπαδνον (cf. Aesch. fr. 261N = 461 Mette ἔδυ . . . ἐς ἄντρον). At first sight, the translation "put on" seems natural, and that would make the accusative a direct object. But three of the passages cited by Fraenkel suggest that Italie (*Index Aeschyleus* s.v. δύω II.2) is probably right to render the verb "*subire.*" Euripides has his Agamemnon describe the yoking as a fall: ἐς οἷ' ἀνάγκης ζεύγματ' ἐμπεπτώκαμεν (*IA* 443). Motion toward the yoke figures as well at Eur. *Or.* 1330 ἀνάγκης δ' ἐς ζυγὸν καθέσταμεν and in a late Hellenistic poem in anapests (D. Page, *Greek Literary Papyri*, p. 414): ἦλθεν ὑπ' αὐτὴν ζεύγλαν ἀνάγκης. I conclude, therefore, that λέπαδνον can be construed as a terminal accusative. (Could ambiguity between the two possible constructions, transitive verb + direct object and intransitive verb + terminal accusative, reflect ambiguity surrounding Agamemnon's "choice"?)

The remaining examples with δύω cited by Escher are:

5. Cf. Hdt. 6.109.4.
6. Cf. p. 10 on the probable locus of poeticisms in Herodotus. With some hesitation, J. López Facal classifies as "directivo o lativo" bare accusatives with five verbs, ἐξικνέομαι, ἐφικνέομαι, ἐσέρχομαι, ἐσκαταβαίνω, and ἱκνέομαι (*Los Usos Adverbiales del Accusativo Dativo y Genitivo en la lengua de Heródoto* [Madrid, 1974], pp. 59–60). K. H. Lee ad Eur. *Tr.* 92 should not have referred *tout court* to the construction as one that "also occurs in Herodotus."

Soph. *Aj.* 1192–94 lyr. ὄφελε πρότερον αἰθέρα δῦναι μέγαν ἢ τὸν πολύκοινον ῞Αιδαν

Eur. *El.* 1271 πάγον παρ' αὐτὸν χάσμα δύσονται χθονός

Terminal Accusative with Compound Verbs

It is not altogether clear whether accusatives with compound verbs can be classified as terminal. One might argue that the case is felt as falling under the regimen of the prefix, especially when the prefix alone, i.e., the preposition, ordinarily governs the accusative. As in the last section, I would argue that the habits of the particular verb must be considered.

By the criteria established above (p. 64), we might suspect that the accusative after ἐπιβαίνω at Hdt. 7.50.4 (a speech) is terminal: ἐπιβέωμεν γῆν καὶ ἔθνος. The verb, in its meaning "enter," rather than "attack," is attested with the preverb repeated and with the preposition εἰς (LSJ s.v. A.III). There is, however, a chance that the speaker (Xerxes) thinks of any entrance into a γῆν or ἔθνος as an attack; in that case, the accusative is distinctly a direct object and the verb designates more than motion.

πρόσειμι is attested both with preposition + accusative and with the accusative alone in a variety of genres:

Tragedy: Eur. *El.* 1278
Satyr drama: Eur. *Cyc.* 95
Comedy: Aristomenes 4 K (unless the reading τοῖς is preferred to τοὺς)
Forensic oratory: Andoc. 1.122

It seems safer, therefore, to exclude instances with πρόσειμι from the category of terminal accusative.

I am rather more inclined to see a terminal accusative at Eur. *Ion* 700 lyr.: πολιὸν ἐσπεσοῦσα γῆρας (cited by Schwyzer, *Gramm.* 2.68; other examples at LSJ s.v. εἰσπίπτω 3, 4). Here, unlike the example with ἐπιβαίνω, the genre distribution gives us something of a clue: with εἰσπίπτω the goal of motion appears without a preposition only in poetry.[7] At some risk of circularity, we could suppose that prose authors did not regard the force of the prefix as extending to the noun; verse writers, then, would consider the accusative without preposition as adverbial, i.e., the same syntactically as accusative goal of motion with simplex verb. It would, however, be rash to reach any other conclusion than *non liquet.*

We need not, on the other hand, have any qualms about classifying an accusative as terminal when it complements a compound verb whose prefix

7. See Dodds ad Eur. *Ba.* 5.

cannot govern that case. There are numerous instances of bare accusative
with ἀφικνέομαι. Since ἀπό is not attested with the accusative until several
hundred years past our period, there is no need to relinquish these
examples as legitimate attestations of the construction.[8]

Terminal, Spatial, or Cognate Accusative?

Accusatives designating "extent of space" are found in all genres and
periods of Greek literature. Normally the context is sufficient to show
whether the accusative is the route traversed or the destination. It is the
former, for instance, at Bacchylides Dith. 19.12–13:

> πρέπει σε φερτάταν ἴμεν
> ὁδὸν παρὰ Καλλιόπας . . .

In principle, one should be able to arrive at a ὁδός, but for some reason
Greek never said *πρὸς ὁδόν. This confirms what is anyway probable from
context, that the correct reading at Soph. OC 1590 speaks of a "thresh-
old," not a "road":

> ἐπεὶ δ᾽ ἀφῖκτο τὸν καταρράκτην ὁδὸν

> καταφράκτην Suid. v. ὁδός: ὁδὸς LA

Given the reading ὁδόν, the accusative is terminal.[9]
    More difficult is Bacchylides 9.40–41:

> τοῦ κ[λέος π]ᾶσαν χθόνα
> ἦλθε[ν καὶ] ἐπ᾽ ἔσχατα Νείλου·

> καὶ Kenyon: τοι Weil

We might translate either "His kleos came across the whole earth, even to
the farthest parts of the Nile," or "to every land, even to the farthest parts
of the Nile." To me, the prepositional phrase "even to the farthest parts of
the Nile" suggests that χθόνα is more probably "country" than "earth." If
χθόνα is "country," it follows that the accusative more likely denotes goal
than spatial extent.[10]
    The analysis of Eur. IT 1112 lyr. is also difficult:

8. I see nothing significant in the comparative distribution of terminal accusatives with
ἀφικνέομαι and the uncompounded form of the verb.
    9. See A. von Blumenthal, Hermes 69 (1934): 457.
    10. It is true that the Ethiopians are, for Homer, the ἔσχατοι ἀνδρῶν, but I doubt that
Bacchylides meant ἔσχατα Νείλου as a way of saying "the southernmost ἔσχατα τῆς γῆς," an
expression which would imply that χθόνα means "the earth."

νόστον βάρβαρον ἦλθον

νᾶσον Bothe: νόμον Musgrave

Escher (*Acc.*, p. 138) classifies the accusative as terminal, but this requires us to understand νόστος as "place," rather than "journey"—an unparalleled usage that would divorce the phrase from the description of the forced march given by Euripides just before the line under consideration. (The adverb immediately following, ἔνθα, which can mean either "to that place where" or, simply, "where," is not decisive.) Read as an internal or cognate accusative, with νόστος treated like κέλευθος or ὁδός, the construction makes sense and requires no emendation. (For a clear example of the cognate construction see Pind. *P.* 11.39.)

We should admit into the category of terminal accusatives some complements of verbs of sitting, e.g., ζυγὸν at Soph. *Aj.* 249:

... θοὸν εἰρεσίας ζυγὸν ἑζόμενον.

That there can be an adverbial notion in the accusative is made clear by those instances where a preposition governs the case, e.g., Soph. *Ant.* 999–1000 ἐς παλαιὸν θᾶκον ἵζων (so Escher, *Acc.*, p. 64). On the other hand, the accusative as destination of the haunches is not inevitable: at Soph. *OT* 2 Oedipus' question is about the meaning of the suppliant posture assumed by the Chorus:

τίνας ποθ᾽ ἕδρας τάσδε μοι θοάζετε ... ;

Here the accusative is, of course, cognate. Aristoph. *Th.* 889 is similar:

τί δὴ σὺ θάσσεις τάσδε τυμβήρεις ἕδρας;

Bruhn (*Anhang*, §56) lists several alleged examples of the "accusative for the designation of the goal with verbs of motion" that I would not regard as properly "terminal," e.g., Soph. *OC* 332:

Οἰ. τί δ᾽ ἦλθες; Ἰσ. σῇ, πάτερ, προμηθίᾳ.

τί means "why?" and Ismene's answer and Oedipus' next question (333) contain datives, which make it all the clearer that Oedipus is not asking, "To what end have you come?" Also in Bruhn's list is Soph. *Tr.* 159:

πολλοὺς ἀγῶνας ἐξιών

Two passages in Thucydides, 1.15.2 and 1.112.3, with ἐξῇεσαν and ἐστράτευσαν respectively, show that the accusatives are cognate; the ἀγῶνες are not conceived as lying at a distance. (Soph. *Tr.* 505 lyr. ἔξηλθον ἄεθλ᾽ ἀγώνων, also cited by Bruhn, is different: at 517 the fight begins, hence the accusative here can well indicate a site.) Internal accusa-

tives, even if they can be translated so as to answer the question "to what end?" suggest goals in a sense so abstract that they have no spatial quality. Thus they cannot be interpreted as terminal.
(Internal accusatives are collected at Schwyzer, *Gramm.* 2.77.*θ* and Krüger, *Att.* 46.4 An. 2: this item of syntax is not genre specific.)

Miscellaneous

In two passages discussed by Escher (*Acc.*, p. 63) the syntactical flexibility of prepositions makes it impossible to tell for sure whether the accusative is terminal:

Soph. *El.* 1391–92 lyr.   παράγεται γὰρ ἐνέρων
                                            δολιόπους ἀρωγὸς εἴσω στέγας.

Escher argues that in Sophocles εἴσω is absolute or to be taken with the genitive; if the former is correct, στέγας is a terminal accusative. In view of the closeness of εἴσω to στέγας, it is more probable that εἴσω is preposi-tional, not adverbial, and, in accordance with Homeric usage, governs a subsequent accusative.

Soph. *OT* 174–77 lyr.   ἄλλον δ' ἂν ἄλ-
                                            λῳ προσίδοις ἅπερ εὔπτερον ὄρνιν
                                            κρεῖσσον ἀμαιμακέτου πυρὸς ὄρμενον
                                            ἀκτὰν πρὸς ἑσπέρου θεοῦ.

ἀκτάν might be a terminal accusative, since πρός is sometimes used with the genitive (here it would be the two words immediately following it) to designate direction (LSJ s.v. A.2). The prevailing opinion holds that πρός here follows its object and is followed by an attributive phrase depending on ἀκτάν (see LSJ s.v. πρός F.1 and Jebb ad loc.).
     The verb of motion and the terminal accusative normally stand quite close together, perhaps to avoid any uncertainty in meaning. Here are some instances of greater than normal separation, but where there cer-tainly exists a terminal accusative:

Aesch. *Supp.* 238–40   ὅπως δὲ χώραν οὔτε κηρύκων ὕπο
                                            ἀπρόξενοί τε νόσφιν ἡγητῶν μολεῖν
                                            ἔτλητ' ἀτρέστως

Eur. *Ph.* 1043–45 lyr.   χρόνῳ δ' ἔβα
                                            Πυθίαις ἀποστολαῖσιν
                                            Οἰδίπους ὁ τλάμων
                                            Θηβαίαν τάνδε γᾶν

At Aristoph. *Ra.* 1175–76 we might have the phantom, so to speak, of a terminal accusative designating persons:

τεθνηκόσιν γὰρ ἔλεγεν, ὦ μόχθηρε σύ,
οἷς οὐδὲ τρὶς λέγοντες ἐξικνούμεθα.

LSJ s.v. ἐξικνέομαι II.1 and Stanford explain οἷς as "relative by attraction for οὕς." Since the prefix ἐκ does not, as a preposition, govern the accusative case, the accusative lost through assimilation might be regarded as terminal. It is not clear, however, whether colloquial usage or *Kunstprosa* would demand the accusative, as the one prose instance listed by LSJ, Thuc. 1.70.2, cannot serve as a reliable touchstone. Krüger ad loc. translates the verb "accomplish" (*durchzuführen*), which effaces the sense of motion, and he remarks that he cannot vouch for either that meaning or the construction.

Text

As compared with other items of poetic syntax, say the omission of ἄν with the subjunctive in temporal clauses or enallage, the terminal accusative appears to have suffered little in scribal transmission. The restriction of the construction to poetry and its frequency made it familiar and respectable in the eyes of copyists. The addition of a preposition by a scribe, unless it is elided, would add at least one syllable, and this would, in most cases, upset the scansion. Nevertheless, a few manuscripts report both the terminal accusative and the normal construction with preposition, e.g., at Eur. *Alc.* 8:

ἐλθὼν δὲ γαῖαν τήνδ' ἐβουφόρβουν ξένῳ

δ' ἐς αἶαν citat Athenagoras suppl. pro Christ. p. 104

Here the principle *difficilior lectio potior* favors δὲ γαῖαν over ἐς αἶαν.

When the transmitted text includes the terminal accusative, no emendation should be accepted if either verb or noun is commonly found in the construction (see below, pp. 80–83); such is the case at Soph. *Tr.* 58:

ἐγγὺς δ' ὅδ' αὐτὸς ἀρτίπους θρῴσκει δόμους

ἄρτι που 'σθρῴσκει coni. Westcott

On the other hand, one does sometimes see the terminal accusative as a scholar's conjecture:

Aesch. *Pers. 862* εὖ πράσσοντας ἆγον οἴκους

οἴκους Porson: ἐς οἶκον Ha, ἐς οἴκους rell.

It certainly makes little sense to reject the terminal accusative at the cost of admitting something far more anomalous. At Pind. *I.* 3/4.70–72 the construction is eliminated if, following a *varia lectio* (reported by Slater, *Lexicon to Pindar* s.v. ἔρχομαι c), we accent πότ᾽, thus making it a preposition:

καί τοί ποτ᾽ ᾿Ανταίου δόμους

. . . .
. . . προσπαλαίσων ἦλθ᾽ ἀνήρ
τὰν πυρφόρον Λιβύαν

But there is only one secure instance of elided ποτί in Pindar (*O.* 7.90: see LSJ s.v.).

Provenience

The restriction of the terminal accusative in the classical period to lyric and tragic poetry is observed with surprising rigor. We have already considered the possible occurrences of the construction with ἱκνέομαι in Herodotus (pp. 65–66). The manuscripts also show one example with διαβαίνω, toward the end of a speech (4.118.4):

νῦν δὲ ἐπείτε τάχιστα διέβη τήνδε τὴν ἤπειρον

ἐς ante τήνδε add. Dietsch

The same verb is offered with a terminal accusative by all but one manuscript at Thuc. 8.38.2:

οἱ δ᾽ ἐκ τῆς Λέσβου ᾿Αθηναῖοι ἤδη διαβεβηκότες ἐς τὴν Χίον

ἐς B: om. cett.

The loss of preposition can be easily explained as haplography after the participle, and Krüger endorses the reading of B on the ground that the terminal accusative "would be poetic." A poeticism here would be peculiar indeed, though it would not be aesthetically repugnant in the Herodotean passage. I would, however, accept neither. διαβαίνω regularly governs the accusative of words designating bodies of land or water traversed, and this may explain copyists' errors. Also, the verb is not found with the terminal accusative in Homer (not decisive evidence, of course: see Schwyzer, "Synt. Arch.," p. 16). I am prepared to say that the construction was never admitted into Ionic or Attic prose.[11]

11. There is a scintilla of a possibility that Gorgias used a terminal accusative at *Hel.* (82B76D-K)12 ὕμνος ἦλθεν ῾Ελένην. It is altogether more likely that the collocation is corrupt.

There are several apparent occurrences in the philosophical poetry of Empedocles and Parmenides:

Emp. 20 Wright (36 D–K) ἔσχατον ἵστατο νεῖκος
47 Wright (35 D–K).3–4 νεῖκος . . . ἵκετο βένθος / δίνης
(cf. 53 Wright [62 D–K].6 πρὸς ὅμοιον ἱκέσθαι)
Parm. B1.25 D–K ἱκάνων ἡμέτερον δῶ

In comedy the terminal accusative is scarce, almost to the point of vanishing. I have seen only one instance where the construction is used without parodistic intention:

Aristoph. *Nub.* 300 lyr. ἔλθωμεν λιπαρὰν χθόνα Παλλάδος

This line falls within a choral song of exceptional beauty; the use of the construction here virtually proves that Aristophanes associated it with the high style.

All other examples known to me are paratragic:

Aristoph. *Nub.* 30 ἀτὰρ τί χρέος ἔβα με μετὰ τὸν Πασίαν;

Eubulus 53 K μετὰ ταῦτα Θήβας ἦλθον, οὗ τὴν νύχθ' ὅλην
τήν θ' ἡμέραν δειπνοῦσι καὶ κοπρῶν' ἔχει
ἐπὶ ταῖς θύραις ἕκαστος, οὗ πλήρει βροτῷ
οὐκ ἔστι μεῖζον ἀγαθόν· ὡς χεζητιῶν
μακρὰν βαδίζων, πολλὰ δ' ἰδίων ἀνήρ,
δάκνων τὰ χείλη, παγγέλοιός ἐστ' ἰδεῖν.

Θήβαζ' C et Eustath.

Eubulus 54.1 K Κόρινθον ἦλθον . . .

The Aristophanic passage is explained by the scholiast to E as borrowed from a Euripidean line (fr. 1011 N lyr. τί χρέος ἔβα δῶμα;). The scatological theme of the first passage from Eubulus might have been seen as guaranteeing the colloquial nature (at least in the fourth century) of the terminal accusative. This would be a regrettable complication, and it is fortunate that βροτός, surely poetic in fourth-century lexicon, confirms what we would have ample reason to suspect, that the poet is throwing the odd high-style element into the undignified material. The second passage from Eubulus is valuable in that it offers the terminal accusative without the worry of a variant reading.

I find it mysterious that a construction used so often in tragedy would not appear more often in comic parodies.[12]

___

12. I have independently checked the fifth-century comic fragments for terminal accusatives; for the fourth, I am relying on Krüger, *Poet.* §46.3, and Wackernagel, *Vorl.* 2.222.

(For the distribution of the construction in the various subsections of drama see below.)

Affect and Stylistic Nuance

Despite its exclusion from prose and comedy, the terminal accusative does not seem to have any particular aura to it within serious poetry. Just as it was deemed appropriate to metrically, and stylistically, different sections of tragedy (see below, pp. 83–85), it seemed suitable to the depiction of a variety of individual speech styles and emotional states. It is found in the mouths of very angry characters:

> Soph. *OT* 533–34   . . . τὰς ἐμὰς στέγας
> ἵκου . . . ,

in hurried commands:

> Soph. *Aj.* 804 καὶ σπεύσαθ᾽ οἱ μὲν Τεῦκρον ἐν τάχει μολεῖν,

and in expressions of great pain:

> Eur. *Hipp.* 1371 lyr. anap. αἰαῖ αἰαῖ
> καὶ νῦν ὀδύνα μ᾽ ὀδύνα βαίνει.

But it also has a place in calm declarations:

> Eur. *Andr.* 3 . . . ἑστίαν ἀφικόμην

Further, it does not shun the company of possible colloquialisms: an example at Soph. *OC* 1386–87 comes shortly after συλλαβών (1384), which Jebb calls "a colloquial phrase, bitter here":

> . . . μήτε νοστῆσαί ποτε
> τὸ κοῖλον Ἄργος . . .

Another passage combining the terminal accusative with a touch of the colloquial is Eur. *Alc.* 872 lyr.:

> πρόβα, πρόβα· βᾶθι κεῦθος οἴκων . . .

The distribution of -βα, the short form in the second-person singular imperatives of compounds of βαίνω, suggests that it is more colloquial than the ending -βᾶθι (Stevens, *Colloq. Eur.*, p. 63). The simple imperative βᾶθι, however, occurs only in tragic lyric (Veitch, *Grk. Verbs* s.v.). Conceivably, the movement from the repeated, colloquially formed πρόβα to βᾶθι is a deliberate elevation of tone within the line. In that case, the terminal accusative is insulated from the colloquialism.

The terminal accusative is also mixed with prosaic, rather than strictly colloquial, usage:

Eur. *Or.* 1289–90 lyr. τάχα τις Ἀργείων ἔντολος ὁρμήσας
ποδὶ βοηδρόμῳ μέλαθρα προσμείξει.

Di Benedetto points out that βοηδρόμος is a variant of the prosaic βοηθόος; the intransitive use of προσμείγνυμι is prosaic, but its prosaic quality is tempered by the use of the simple accusative in place of the normal dative or πρός + accusative.

Terminal Accusative Combined with Preposition + Accusative

Poets have no hesitation in placing a terminal accusative in the vicinity of an accusative governed by a preposition:

Soph. *Ant.* 1216–17 . . . ἁρμὸν χώματος λιθοσπαδῆ
δύντες πρὸς αὐτὸ στόμιον . . .

Soph. *OT* 637 οὐκ εἶ σύ τ' οἴκους, σύ τε, Κρέον, κατὰ στέγας

Eur. *El.* 1198–99 ἰὼ ἰώ μοι. ποῖ δ' ἐγώ, τίν' ἐς χορόν,
τίνα γάμον εἶμι; . . .

Eur. *Hipp.* 974–75 καὶ μήτ' Ἀθήνας τὰς θεοδμήτους μόλῃς
μήτ' εἰς ὄρους . . .

A likely motive for deploying the construction is a desire to avoid a long chain of prepositions and other words designating local relations:

Aesch. *Supp.* 14–15 anap. φεύγειν ἀνέδην διὰ κῦμ' ἅλιον,
κέλσαι δ' Ἄργους γαῖαν, ὅθεν . . .

Soph. *OT* 798 στείχων δ' ἱκνοῦμαι τούσδε τοὺς χώρους, ἐν οἷς

In these passages an added preposition with the accusatives would, I think, make the Greek fussier, but with no significant gain in clarity.[13]

Terminal Accusatives of Words Designating Persons

Grammarians have in various ways underestimated the freedom with which Greek poets of the classical period used words designating persons in the terminal accusative construction. Krüger (*Poet.* §46.3 An. 2) thinks that, in the dramatists, persons are hardly found at all as grammatical subjects where the goal of their motion is the bare accusative designating

13. Cf. below, pp. 79–80.

another person. K-G 1.212 attributes the personal terminal accusative only to Homer. Smyth §1599 claims that examples in tragedy are largely confined to lyric passages. Schwyzer (*Gramm.* 2.67–68) doubts that clear examples of this sort occur in the tragedians. In fact, the construction is not nearly as restricted as these scholars claim: persons are well attested as accusative *termini* in tragic lyrics and dialogue, particularly with proper nouns.[14]

Pronouns

Soph. *OT* 713 αὐτὸν ἥξοι μοῖρα   (see above, pp. 64–65)
   Ph. 601 τίς ὁ πόθος αὐτοὺς ἵκετ(ο)
   Ph. 141–42 lyr. σὲ . . . τόδ᾿ ἐλήλυθεν πᾶν κράτος (σοὶ T)
   El. 137–78 σε πολλά . . . προύστην (but see above, p. 65)
Eur. *Hipp.* 1371 anap. καὶ νῦν ὀδύνα μ᾿ ὀδύνα βαίνει
Aristoph. *Nub.* 30 = Eur. fr. 1011 τί χρέος ἔβα με

Common Nouns[15]

Eur. *Ba.* 847 ἥξει . . . βάκχας (βάκχαις Lenting) (Pentheus is the subject.)
Ba. 1354 βαρβάρους ἀφίξομαι (Personal subject.)

Proper Nouns

Aesch. *PV* 709 Σκύθας . . . ἀφίξῃ νομάδας (Io is the subject.)
Soph. *Aj.* 804–06 Τεῦκρον . . . μολεῖν (Subject is οἱ μέν.)
Eur. *Andr.* 287 lyr. ἔβαν . . . Πριαμίδαν (Subjects are goddesses.)
   El. 917 ἐλθὼν Φρύγας (Aegisthus is the subject. Denniston: "The simple accusative is made easier by the fact that Φρύγας is a geographical term, and virtually = Φρυγίαν.")
   El. 1281 ἦλθεν Φρύγας (Menelaus is the subject.)
   Hel. 595–96 οὐδ᾿ ἀφίξομαι / Ἕλληνας οὐδὲ πατρίδα.
   (Helen speaks. Kannicht: "Ἕλληνας instead of Ἑλλάδα, a variation from πατρίδα.")

To the extent that one thinks of Hades as a person rather than a place, one might add to this list:

Soph. *Aj.* 607 lyr. ἀνύσειν τὸν ἀπότροπον ἀΐδηλον Ἀΐδαν[16]
   (Subject is με.)

14. This list includes examples with ἀφικνέομαι.
15. Some of these may be regarded as derived from proper nouns.
16. Jebb's parallel passages show ἀνύω without prep. at Eur. *Supp.* 1142 and Soph. *OC* 1562. But at *Tr.* 657 Sophocles wrote πρὸς πόλιν ἀνύσειε.

Aj. 1192 lyr. αἰθέρα δῦναι μέγαν ἢ τὸν πολύκοινον Ἅιδαν
(Subject is ἀνήρ.)

The first seems to me to partake more of personification. In the second, the parallelism with αἰθέρα strongly suggests that Sophocles meant Hades the place.

If body parts are, as seems reasonable, considered stand-ins for persons seen under a particular description (e.g., "hands" = powerful person, "heart" = person susceptible to emotion), four Euripidean passages may be added:

Ba. 1286 ἐμὰς ἦλθεν χέρας (ἦλθ᾿ ἐς Musurus)
(Pentheus is the subject.)
IT 1421 μολοῦσα δεσποτῶν χέρας
(Iphigenia is the subject.)
Hipp. 840–41 dochm. τύχα . . . σὰν ἔβα . . . καρδίαν
Hipp. 1103 φρένας ἔλθῃ

There are, to my knowledge, three likely examples of personal terminal accusatives in Pindar,[17] two with simplex verbs of motion, one with a compound whose prefix cannot, in prepositional form, govern the accusative case:

N. 5.50–51 εἰ δὲ Θεμίστιον ἵκεις
ὥστ᾿ ἀείδειν . . .
(One might claim that ἵκεις is absolute, and Θεμίστιον the object of ἀείδειν, but the juxtaposition of Θεμίστιον and ἵκεις favors the terminal accusative construction.)

P. 5.86 οἰχνέοντές σφε δωροφόροι

σφι? Drachmann

P. 11.34b–35 γέροντα ξένον Στρόφιον ἐξίκετο

Because the preposition πρός can govern the accusative, I am reluctant to certify the accusatives in Timocreon 10 West = *Anth. Pal.* 13.31 troch. tetr. as terminals:

Κηΐα με προσῆλθε φλυαρία οὐκ ἐθέλοντα·
οὐ θέλοντά με προσῆλθε Κηΐα φλυαρία.

17. With Clapp ("Pindar's Accusative Constructions," p. 28, n. 2) I omit, e.g., *O.* 6.83 μ(ε) . . . προσέρπει.

Semantic Distribution

At *HF* 408–10 lyr. Euripides employs στρατός as a terminal accusative:[18]

> τὸν ἱππευτάν τ᾽ Ἀμαζό-
> νων στρατὸν Μαιῶτιν ἀμφὶ
> πολυπόταμον ἔβα.

Wilamowitz remarks: "a perfectly characteristic [*recht bezeichnendes*] example of the limitless boldness with which poetic language can join any goal in the accusative case to a verb of motion." Just why this passage struck Wilamowitz as a bold use of the construction I cannot say. And, at least for our period, his statement requires modification. The semantic repertory found in the construction is, on the whole, not broad. As can be expected from the subject matter of tragedy and lyric, the poets speak most frequently of motion toward the principal sites of heroic legend and toward the dwelling places of great families. Accordingly, it is not surprising that a large proportion of terminal accusatives are found with words designating these places. The list on pp. 80–83 holds about a third of all the examples I have collected; the fraction would be even larger if questionable candidates and examples with compound verbs were more freely admitted. An inspection of the verbs employed and complements of the noun in the accusative (adjectives and dependent genitives) will, I think, show that the construction tended to be cast from a small range of lexical materials.

Further, we might regard as close relations to these favored categories of terminal accusative instances where a noun meaning, say, "earth," is found as a genitive dependent on the accusative, e.g., at Eur. *El.* 1271: πάγον παρ᾽ αὐτὸν χάσμα δύσονται χθονός.[19]

Nevertheless, we should not think of the construction as inevitably dressed in one of only a few garments. Sometimes an abstraction appears as the goal:

With Simplex Verb of Motion

Pind. *N.* 7.19–20 θανάτου πέρας . . . νέονται

> *O.* 10.86–87 . . . ὥτε παῖς ἐξ ἀλόχου πατρὶ
> ποθεινὸς ἵκοντι νεότατος τὸ πάλιν ἤδη

τοὔμπαλιν Av, ἔμπ. cᵒo, δ᾽ ἔμπ. N: byz.

Bacchyl. fr. 25.3 Snell γῆρας ἱκνεῖσθαι

---

18. στρατόν is also a terminal accusative at Pind. *P.* 11.17 and Aesch. *PV* 723–24.
19. Cf. Soph. *OC* 668–69, Eur. *Hel.* 659.

Eur. *El.* 1198–99 lyr. ποῖ δ᾽ ἐγώ, τίν᾽ ἐς χορόν, / τίνα γάμον εἶμι
(but ἐς might be ἀπὸ κοινοῦ)
 Med. 920–21 ἥβης τέλος / μολόντας

With Compound Verb of Motion (cf. above, pp. 67–70)

Pind. *O.* 2.95 αἶνον ἐπέβα κόρος
Eur. *Ion.* 700 lyr. πολιὸν ἐσπεσοῦσα γῆρας (but cf. p. 67)

Also atypical is the appearance of an inanimate subject:

Eur. *Rh.* 223 φάος μολεῖν χθόνα
 fr. 1011 lyr. τί χρέος ἔβα δῶμα;

Insofar as the construction is characteristically used of literal movements
of persons toward concrete objects, I believe it reasonable to assume that
some of these atypical uses, especially in Pindar, are meant to place
concrete and abstract in a subtle juxtaposition.

Conclusion

P. T. Stevens (ad Eur. *Andr.* 3) offers an aesthetic appreciation of the
terminal accusative and similar constructions:

> The use of case endings alone where Attic prose requires a preposition
> belongs in general to an earlier stage of the language and is an instance
> of the archaizing tendency in the language of Tragedy. Apart from the
> touch of remoteness provided thereby, a reduction in the number of
> small 'empty' words adds something to the weight and dignity of a line
> of verse.

By "remoteness" Stevens means, I take it, distance from the one other
sort of language he mentions, Attic prose. With respect to the terminal
accusative, at least, we may add Ionic prose, comic verse, and colloquial
Attic as branches of Greek whose difference from serious poetry is
signaled by the "omission" of the preposition. I would not, however,
accept Stevens's premise that prepositions were regarded as "empty"
words, nor the idea that verse acquires added "weight and dignity" by their
relative scarcity. The language could, it is true, dispense with prepositions
and yet succeed in indicating the terminus of motion, though perhaps with
a loss of precision: εἰς, πρός, ἐπί, and κατά are not entirely interchange-
able. But in none of the examples of terminal accusative that I have
examined is there ambiguity: provided one knows the context one is not
left worrying whether a movement is, e.g., "toward," "into," "down

upon," or "against with hostile intent." Because a category of word is optional in certain genres does not mean that it is but a filler.

"Weight" and "dignity" are terms often meaningful in stylistic analysis, but it seems to me that they are not always usefully applied to individual constituents of style on a syntactic or lexical level. Obviously, the terminal accusative can derive an aura of "weight and dignity" merely from its exclusive association with serious poetry, but without any particular hue within the poetic palette. (I consider on pp. 190–92 the notion of poetic syntax as logically less elaborated than the syntax of *Kunstprosa*.)

Semantic Fields Commonly Found in Terminal Accusative Constructions

Excluded from this list are highly dubious examples and all those with compound verbs of motion, ἀφικνέομαι excepted.

"Earth" or "land"
γῆν/γᾶν: 11 examples
    Aesch.   *Pers.* 809 γῆν μολόντες Ἑλλάδ᾽
              PV 807–08 γῆν ἥξεις
    Soph.   *El.* 163 lyr. μολόντα τάνδε γᾶν
              Ph. 1174–75 lyr. τὰν . . . στυγερὰν Τρῳάδα γᾶν . . . ἄξειν
    Eur.   *Hipp.* 29 ἐλθεῖν τήνδε γῆν
              IA 1627 anap. γῆν ἱκοῦ Φρυγίαν
              Ph. 5–6 ἦλθε γῆν τήνδ(ε)
              Ph. 295 lyr. ἔβας . . . γᾶν πατρῴαν
              Ph. 638 lyr. ἔμολε τάνδε γᾶν
              Ph. 681 lyr. βᾶθι βᾶθι τάνδε γᾶν
              Ph. 1043–45 lyr. ἔβα . . . Θηβαίαν τάνδε γᾶν

γαῖαν/αἶαν: 6 examples
    Pind.   *P.* 4.117–18 ξείναν ἱκάνω γαῖαν
    Aesch.   *Supp.* 15 anap. κέλσαι . . . Ἄργους γαῖαν
    Eur.   *Alc.* 8 ἐλθὼν . . . γαῖαν τήνδ(ε)
              IT 402 lyr. ἔβασαν ἔβασαν ἄμεικτον αἶαν
              Med. 1384 γαῖαν εἶμι τὴν Ἐρεχθέως
              Tr. 1110 lyr. γαῖαν . . . ἔλθοι Λάκαιναν

χθόνα: 11 examples
    Bacchyl. 9.40–41 π]ᾶσαν χθόνα ἦλθε[ν
    Aesch.   *Supp.* 768 μολόντες ἀλίμενον χθόνα
    Soph.   *OT* 1178–79 ἄλλην χθόνα . . . ἀποίσειν

Eur.   *Alc.* 560 Ἄργους διψίαν ἔλθω χθόνα
        Hipp. 36 τήνδε . . . ναυστολεῖ χθόνα
        IT 480 τήνδ᾽ ἐπλεύσατε χθόνα
        Med. 12 ἀφίκετο χθόνα
        Ph. 112 ἦλθε Πολυνείκης χθόνα
        Rh. 223 φάος μολεῖν χθόνα
        fr. 819.2 ἦλθε Θηβαίαν χθόνα
Aristoph. *Nub.* 300 ἔλθωμεν λιπαρὰν χθόνα Παλλάδος

πατρίδα: 1 example
   Eur. *Hel.* 1092 πατρίδα . . . ἐλθεῖν

"City"
πόλιν/πόλεις: 14 examples
   Pind.   *P.* 5.52–53 ἦλθες . . . Λιβύας πεδίον . . . καὶ πατρωῖαν
          πόλιν
   Aesch. *Supp.* 955 στείχετ᾽ εὐερκῆ πόλιν
   Soph.   *OC* 1–2 τίνας χώρους ἀφίγμεθ᾽ ἢ τίνων ἀνδρῶν πόλιν;
        Tr. 259–60 ἔρχεται πόλιν τὴν Εὐρυτείαν
   Eur.   *El.* 1194 lyr. τίνα δ᾽ ἑτέραν μόλω πόλιν;
        Hel. 105 ἦλθες . . . κλεινὴν πόλιν;
        Heracl. 362 lyr. πόλιν ἐλθὼν ἑτέραν
        HF 652–53 lyr. θνατῶν δώματα καὶ πόλεις ἐλθεῖν
        IA 1520 Ἰλίου πόλιν μολεῖν
        Med. 757 πόλιν σὴν . . . ἀφίξομαι
        Or. 1209 Φωκέων . . . ἔλθοι πόλιν
        Or. 1648 ἐλθὼν τὴν Ἀθηναίων πόλιν
        Rh. 115 τήνδ᾽ οὐ μὴ μόλῃς πόλιν (LP: τήνδε μὴ
               [τήνδ᾽ ἐμὴ O] μόλῃς πόλιν [V]: οὔτι μὴ μόλῃς
               πάλιν Cobet)
        Supp. 621 lyr. πόλιν μόλω

ἄστυ: 3 examples
   Soph.   *OC* 757 ἄστυ . . . μολεῖν
        OT 35 ἄστυ Καδμεῖον μολών
   Eur.   *Med.* 771 μολόντες ἄστυ καὶ πόλισμα Παλλάδος

"House" or "hearth"
δόμον/δόμους: 15 examples
   Bacchyl. 17.97–100 φέρον δὲ δελφῖνες ἁλι- / ναίεται μέγαν θοῶς /
        Θησέα πατρὸς ἱππί- / ου δόμον· (δόμονδ᾽ Chr. Jur. aut verbis
        insequentibus transpositis numeros sanant: μέγαρόν τε θ.
        μόλεν Bl[ass] Housm[an] Wil[amowitz] alii)
   Pind.   *I.* 3/4.70–71b Ἀνταίου δόμους . . . ἦλθ᾽

          O. 14.20–21 *μελαντειχέα . . . δόμον Φερσεφόνας ἔλθ᾽*
          P. 5.29 *ἀφίκετο δόμους θεμισκρεόντων*
Aesch.   *Pers.* 159 troch. *ἱκάνω χρυσεοστόλμους δόμους*
Soph.   *El.* 63–64 *δόμους ἔλθωσιν*
          OC 757–58 *δόμους μολεῖν τοὺς σοὺς πατρῴους*
          OT 643 *δόμους στείχειν ἐμούς*
          Tr. 58 *θρῴσκει (ἄρτι που ᾽σθρῴσκει* coni. Westcott) *δόμους*
Eur.   *Hel.* 144 *ἦλθον . . . βασιλείους δόμους*
          Ion 71 *ἐλθὼν δόμους*
          Ion 702 lyr. *ἐλθὼν δόμους*
          Ion 1455 *δόμον ἔβα Λοξίου*
          Or. 1490 lyr. *ἔμολε . . . δόμους*
          Tr. 984 *ἐλθεῖν . . . Μενέλεω δόμους*

δῶμα/δώματα: 5 examples
Eur.   *Andr.* 1167 anap. *δῶμα πελάζει*
          HF 652–53 lyr. *θνατῶν δώματα καὶ πόλεις ἐλθεῖν*
          Ion 1021 *δῶμ(α) . . . τοὐμὸν μόλῃ*
          IT 521 *ἀφῖκται δῶμα Μενέλεω*
          fr. 1011 lyr. *ἔβα δῶμα*

οἶκον/οἴκους: 6 examples
Aesch.   *Pers.* 862 lyr. *ἆγον οἴκους* (cf. above, p. 71)
Soph.   *OT* 434 *οἴκους τοὺς ἐμοὺς ἐστειλάμην*
          OT 637 *εἶ . . . οἴκους*
Eur.   *Ion* 458 lyr. *μόλε Πύθιον οἶκον*
          IT 534 *νενόστηκ᾽ οἶκον*
          IT 1124 lyr. *οἶκον ἄξει*

μέγαρον: 2 examples
Bacchyl. 17.100–01 *ἔμολεν . . . θεῶν μέγαρον*
Pind.   *P.* 4.134 *ἦλθον Πελία μέγαρον*

μέλαθρον/μέλαθρα: 2 examples
Eur.   *IT* 1216 troch. *Ἰφ.* *ἄγνισον πυρσῷ μέλαθρον*
              Θο. *καθαρὸν ὡς μόλῃς πάλιν*
          Tr. 841 lyr. *μέλαθρα . . . ἦλθες*

στέγας: 3 examples
Soph.   *OT* 533–34 *τὰς ἐμὰς στέγας ἵκου*
          Tr. 329 *πορευέσθω στέγας*
Eur.   *Med.* 1143 *στέγας . . . ἑσπόμην*

ἑστίαν: 4 examples
Aesch.   *Ag.* 968 *σοῦ μολόντος δωματῖτιν ἑστίαν*
Eur.   *Alc.* 545 *ἄλλου . . . ἑστίαν μολεῖν*

Andr. 3 Πριάμου τύραννον ἑστίαν ἀφικόμην
Med. 681 πατρῴαν . . . ἑστίαν μόλω

Proper Nouns Designating Places: 29 examples
Pind.   *N.* 3.3 ἵκεο Δωρίδα νᾶσον Αἴγιναν
Soph.   *Aj.* 1341 Τροίαν ἀφικόμεσθα
           OC 378 τὸ κοῖλον Ἄργος βάς
           OC 1769–70 Θήβας . . . τὰς ὠγυγίους πέμψον
           OC 1386–87 νοστῆσαι . . . τὸ κοῖλον Ἄργος
           OT 151–52 lyr. ἀγλαὰς ἔβας Θήβας
Eur.   *Andr.* 402–03 ἀφικόμην Φθίαν
           Andr. 801 lyr. Εὐρώπαν ἀφίκεσθαι
           El. 274 Ἄργος . . . μόλῃ
           El. 432 lyr. ἔβατε Τροίαν (ἔβατε LP: ἔμβατε λ)
           El. 1254 ἐλθὼν . . . Ἀθήνας
           Hel. 30 Σπάρτην ἀφίκεθ᾽
           Hel. 846 Ἑλλάδ᾽ ἐλθών
           Hel. 929 Ἑλλάδ᾽ ἔλθω
           Hel. 1291 Ἑλλάδ᾽ ἔλθω
           Heracl. 250 Ἄργος ἐλθών
           HF 1285 Ἄργος ἔλθω
           Hipp. 974 Ἀθήνας τὰς θεοδμήτους μόλῃς
           Ion 1333 Ἀθήνας ἔλθ(ε)
           IT 26 ἐλθοῦσα . . . Αὐλίδ(α)
           IT 1449 Ἀθήνας τὰς θεοδμήτους μόλῃς
           Ph. 77 Ἄργος ἐλθών
           Ph. 408 ἦλθες Ἄργος
           Tr. 423 μολόντες Ἴλιον
           Tr. 883 πέμψομεν . . . Ἑλλάδα
           Tr. 1002 Τροίαν ἦλθες
           Tr. 1086–87 lyr. πορεύσει . . . Ἄργος
Eubulus 53.1 K. Θήβας ἦλθον (see above, p. 73)
           54.1 K Κόρινθον ἦλθον

Distribution of the Terminal Accusative in
Tragedy by Metrical Category

(Dubious examples of the construction are not shown.)

Lyric

Aeschylus   *Supp.* 556–58   Subtotal: 2
               PV 182–83

Sophocles	*Aj.* 607, 1192–94	Subtotal: 13
	Ant. 119–20, 804–05, 810–12	
	El. 163	
	OC 151–52, 669, 1576–77	
	OT 161, 176–77	
	Ph. 141, 1175	
Euripides	*Alc.* 872	Subtotal: 31
	Andr. 287, 801	
	El. 432, 708, 1194	
	Hel. 659	
	Heracl. 80–81, 362	
	HF 409–10, 652–53	
	Hipp. 157–58, 1102	
	Ion 95–96, 458, 702	
	IA 1520	
	IT 1125, 1138	
	Or. 982–84, 1490	
	Ph. 295, 638, 681, 1043–45	
	Supp. 621	
	Tr. 207–08, 841, 1086–87, 1110–11	
	fr. 1011	
		Grand total: 46

Iambic Trimeter

Aeschylus	*Ag.* 968	Subtotal: 12
	Pers. 709, 736, 809	
	PV 682, 708, 723–24, 735, 807	
	Supp. 238–40, 768, 955	
Sophocles	*Aj.* 249, 804	Subtotal: 24
	Ant. 1216	
	El. 32–33, 63–64, 893	
	OC 1–2, 89, 379, 643, 757–58, 1386, 1590	
	OT 434, 533, 637, 798, 912, 1178–79	
	Ph. 601, 1332	
	Tr. 58, 259–60, 329	
Euripides	*Alc.* 8, 545, 560	Subtotal: 67
	Andr. 3, 1085, 1265, 1277	
	Ba. 347, 847, 1286, 1354	
	El. 274, 917, 1254, 1271, 1281	

Hel. 105, 144, 596, 617, 846, 929,
   1092, 1291
Heracl. 250
HF 1285
Hipp. 29, 36, 974, 1530
Ion 1333, 1455, 1543–44
IA 1543–44
IT 26, 85, 341, 480, 521, 534, 1421,
   1449
Med. 7, 12, 681, 757, 771, 920–21,
   1143, 1384
Or. 1094, 1209, 1648
Ph. 5–6, 77, 112, 408
Rh. 223, 289, 432–33
Tr. 423, 434, 883, 952, 984, 1002
fr. 819.2

                                                Grand total: 103

Trochaic Tetrameter

Aeschylus	*Pers.* 159	Subtotal: 1
Sophocles	—	Subtotal: 0
Euripides	*Ion* 550	Subtotal: 1
		Grand total: 2

Anapests

Aeschylus	*PV* 284	Subtotal: 2
	Supp. 14–15	
Sophocles	*OC* 1769–70	Subtotal: 1
Euripides	*Andr.* 1168	Subtotal: 5
	Hipp. 233, 1371	
	IA 1627	
	Med. 13–14	
		Grand total: 8

Dochmiacs

Aeschylus	—	Subtotal: 0
Sophocles	—	Subtotal: 0
Euripides	*Hipp.* 841	Subtotal: 1
		Grand total: 1

3. The Local Dative

The local dative bears a strong, but incomplete, resemblance to the terminal accusative. Like that feature, it is an archaism well attested in epic and conspicuous in poetry of the classical period. It is also excluded from prose and colloquial language, though not as strictly as the terminal accusative. And the local dative is less semantically explicit than its pedestrian gloss, viz., the same word governed by an appropriate preposition.

In defining this differentia one must reckon with complications arising from the history of the dative. As all the grammars observe,[1] it is a syncretic case, embracing three functions:

1. The "designation of a person with an interest in the verbal action or an attitude toward it" (Schwyzer, *Gramm.* 2.139), what we usually call the "indirect object." This is its original, "proper" use in the parent language.
2. The designation of an instrument by which an action is performed, or (in the "comitative" use) the designation of persons or circumstances conceived as instruments that "attend" an action (cf. English "the general captured the town *with* his troops"). As means and manner are often indistinguishable, the "modal" dative also falls under the instrumental rubric. This range of meanings had been expressed by the Indo-European instrumental case before it became defunct.
3. The designation of place or time in which (the "illative" use), or place to or toward which (the "allative" use).[2] This function is inherited

---

1. E.g., Schwyzer, *Gramm.* 2.138; Humbert, *Synt.* §472.

2. I prefer "local" to "locative" as the wider term, since it avoids confusion with the morphological category. "Allative" and "illative" are convenient, but not especially familiar, or even unambiguous. "Illative" is sometimes used for what I call "allative": see *OED* s.v. In order to avoid confusion on *that* score, I have preferred "allative" to the more immediately comprehensible "directional." When there is movement toward and remaining in (or on) a thing, the allative/illative distinction is inappropriate: see, e.g., Eur. *Or.* 88 δεμνίοις πέπτωχ᾽ (δ᾽ ἐν Musgrave) with Benedetto's note (and cf. below, p. 91, on Aesch. *Ag.* 27–29).

from the locative case, formally preserved by a few words: πέδοι, χαμαί, οἴκοι. (The temporal dative is discussed separately below, on pp. 98–99.)

The first category of dative persisted far longer than the second, the second longer than the third (Humbert, *Synt.* §§490, 494). It is not surprising that the third category, the one in quickest retreat, shows the clearest genre conditioning.

Attention to context and common sense are normally sufficient to decide whether a dative belongs to the first or third category. For example, no one would suppose that the dative at Aristoph. *Nub.* 305 designates the celestial gods *qua* physical recipients:

οὐρανίοις τε θεοῖς δωρήματα.

At Pind. *I.* 6.41, however, the dative could not possibly be heard as an indirect object:

ὁ δ᾿ ἀνατείνας οὐρανῷ χεῖρας.

More troublesome are datives that seem simultaneously instrumental and local. It is indeed futile to assign a word to one category or the other when means and location are logically identical, as with verbs of hiding or burying:

Soph. *Ant.* 1254 κρυφῇ καλύπτει καρδίᾳ θυμουμένη

καρδία rec.

Similarly, Emp. 21 Wright (27 D–K).4:

. . . Ἁρμονίης πυκινῷ κρύφῳ ἐστήρικται.[3]

Where one hides a thing and with what one hides it are the same.[4] Nothing is gained by insisting on the distinction at Soph. *OC* 605 σφ᾿ ἀνάγκη τῇδε πληγῆναι χθονί, where the scholiast deems the dative instrumental, Jebb locative. On Pind. *P.* 1.78, ταῖσι [sc. battles at Salamis and Plataea] Μήδειοι κάμον ἀγκυλότοξοι,[5] Gildersleeve is right to see the locative and instrumental coexisting: "Not simply 'where,' but 'in and by which.'"

Words like κύκλῳ, μάχῃ, and ὁδῷ (sometimes called "prosecutives": see Schwyzer, *Gramm.* 2.162–63) tend, I think, to refer to a process more often than to a place, e.g., κύκλῳ = "encircling," not "circle." Only where

---

3. Cf. Hom. *Il.* 11.28 ἐν νέφεϊ στήριξε.
4. Some other passages with dative + verb of hiding or burying: Hdt. 2.130 ἡ βοῦς γῇ οὐκ ἐκρύφθη, Soph. *El.* 55, *Tr.* 556. But at Aristoph. *Th.* 885 ποῦ δ᾿ ἐτυμβεύθη τάφῳ; the dative is strictly instrumental, since ποῦ preempts the local sense.
5. For demonstrative pronouns as local datives see below, p. 95.

the run of the passage gives prominence to the physical terrain would I consider that those words were perceived as partly local. (Since ὁδῷ often suggests instrument, e.g., "We depart *by a route,*" or "by traveling," I would not follow Wilamowitz [ad Eur. *HF* 116] in calling Eur. *Ba.* 68–69 lyr. τίς ὁδῷ; τίς ὁδῷ; τίς / μελάθροις; ἔκτοπος ἔστω a "paradigm" [*Musterbeispiel*] of the local dative; here ὁδῷ uncharacteristically excludes any notion of instrument.[6]

Some examples can be explained by reference to parallel expressions where a preposition appears. We could not tell *a priori* whether the Greeks thought of ἀπορία as something one could sit in; how then could we decide between a locative and instrumental reading in Eur. *HF* 53–54?

> . . . ἐκ γὰρ ἐσφραγισμένοι
> δόμων καθήμεθ᾽ ἀπορίᾳ σωτηρίας.

Wilamowitz pronounces ex cathedra: "The dative has a locative, not instrumental, meaning." The prepositional expressions ἐν or εἰς + ἀπορία (attested by several authors: see Schwyzer, *Gramm.* 2.155, n. 1) give prima facie support to the local interpretation. But ἐν and εἰς do not inevitably carry local signification: thus we should confine ourselves to saying that the state of ἀπορία was used as the object of prepositions most often expressing a frankly spatial sense. Only to the extent that a Greek perceived, say, ἐν ἀπορίη ἔχεσθαι (Hdt. 9.98) as spatial did he interpret the dative in the Euripidean passage as spatial. But additional evidence that Wilamowitz's conclusion was correct can be drawn from the words ἐκ . . . ἐσφραγισμένοι δόμων, where a local sense seems at least possible.

ἀπορία lends itself to a locative interpretation because it designates a zone (whether concrete or abstract) external to the person. Harder to analyze, and significant in determining the provenience of usage, are nouns that refer to strictly internal emotional states. The coexistence of the dative alone and preposition + dative does not prove that the dative alone of such words was perceived as locative. Consider, for example, the pair ἐν ὀργῇ vs. ὀργῇ. Fairbanks ("Dative Soph.," p. 102) lists instances of the latter at *Ph.* 368 and *OT* 405 under the rubric "locative of condition expressing subjective emotion":

---

6. The datives are almost certainly instrumental at Soph. *Tr.* 561 λαίφεσιν (parallel to κώπαις ἐρέσσων in the same line), *pace* Fairbanks, "Dative Soph." p. 112, and at *Tr.* 597 αἰσχύνῃ πεσῇ (so Ellendt, *Lex. Soph.* s.v. αἰσχύνη, who renders the phrase "turpiter te dabis"; Jebb; and Kamerbeek, *pace* Bruhn, *Anhang* §51).

> κἀγὼ δακρύσας εὐθὺς ἐξανίσταμαι
> ὀργῇ βαρείᾳ . . .

> ἡμῖν μὲν εἰκάζουσι καὶ τὰ τοῦδ᾽ ἔπη
> ὀργῇ λέλεχθαι καὶ τὰ σ᾽, Οἰδίπου, δοκεῖ.

Sophocles himself does not attest ἐν ὀργῇ, but Thucydides has both: see 2.8.5 with Krüger's note. The use of οὕτως in the Thucydidean passage strongly suggests that the dative there is adverbial—οὕτως ὀργῇ εἶχον οἱ πλείους τοὺς ᾽Αθηναίους. This looks no different from 2.18.3: ἐν τοιαύτῃ . . . ὀργῇ ὁ στρατὸς τὸν ᾽Αρχίδαμον ἐν τῇ καθέδρᾳ εἶχεν. Therefore the existence of ἐν ὀργῇ in Sophocles would not necessarily rule out the prima facie adverbial character of the dative used alone.

It is, however, possible that some purely ornamental difference was felt. The two examples of adverbial ὀργῇ in Aristophanes both suggest the high style:

> ἐντεῦθεν ὀργῇ Περικλέης οὐλύμπιος
> ἤστραπτ᾽, ἐβρόντα, ξυνεκύκα τὴν ῾Ελλάδα.
> > > > > > > *Ach.* 530–31[7]

> ἀλλ᾽, ὦ τηθῶν ἀνδρειοτάτη καὶ μητριδίων ἀκαληφῶν,
> χωρεῖτ᾽ ὀργῇ, καὶ μὴ τέγγεσθ᾽ . . .
> > > > > > > *Lys.* 549–50[8]

But there is virtually no trace *except* in Thucydides of the construction with ἐν. Checking Aristophanes, Antiphon, Lysias, Isocrates, Isaeus, Demosthenes, and Plato, I find only one such example, Dem. 1.16 ἐν ὀργῇ ποιεῖσθε, as against seventeen instances of the dative alone as an instrumental, adverb, or object of a verb.

More can be said about (ἐν) ἐλπίδι/ἐλπίσι, another alleged locative use, e.g., at Soph. *Tr.* 137–38 lyr.:

> ἃ καὶ σὲ τὰν ἄνασσαν ἐλπίσιν λέγω
> τάδ᾽ αἰὲν ἴσχειν·

Sophocles himself provides the pedestrian gloss at *Ant.* 897–98: ἐν ἐλπίσιν τρέφω φίλη / . . . ἥξειν πατρί. Also, the group of authors scanned for ἐν ὀργῇ tends to confirm the locative sense of the dative in the *Trachiniae* passage. The five instances of ἐν ἐλπίδι/ἐλπίσι suggest a sphere of expectation rather than a modal or adverbial use.[9] The bare dative at Pl. *Lg.* 5.732d4, ταύταις ταῖς ἐλπίσι ζῆν, might be translated "live in these

---

7. Van Leeuwen: ὀργῇ = ὀργισθείς.
8. Van Leeuwen: "ornate diction."
9. Antiphon 2.γ.6; Isoc. 6.5, *Ep.* 2.11; Pl. *Phil.* 36a8, *Lg.* 4.718a5.

hopes," but the other Platonic (or pseudoplatonic) use of the dative with ζῆν (*Alc.* 1.105a7, ἐπὶ τίνι . . . ἐλπίδι ζῇς) and the drift of the passage favor "in accordance with these expectations," a nonlocative use.

The "dative of accompanying circumstance" is another nebulous subcategory of the instrumental dative that overlaps the locative (often in a temporal sense). Under the rubric "locative of condition expressing subjective emotion" Fairbanks ("Dative Soph.," pp. 102–03) lists such pairs as κακοῖς/ἐν κακοῖς, νόσῳ/ἐν νόσῳ, and σχόλῃ/ἐν σχόλῃ, as well as datives with ἐπί. Provided that adverbial, purely temporal expressions are eliminated, e.g., γαλήνῃ, Θεσμοφορίοις, and ellipses of ἡμέρᾳ, this disorderly group of datives does appear genre conditioned, but in a peculiar distribution.[10] As Fairbanks's list suggests, there are many examples in tragedy. The other locus is historiography: Herodotus has ἐπεὰν Βορέῃ ἀνέμῳ . . . ἐξανύσῃ νηῦς (6.139), Thucydides ἀτελεῖ τῇ νίκῃ . . . ἀνέστησαν (7.27.6), and Xenophon ηὐλίζεσθε ἐγκεχαλινωμένοις τοῖς ἵπποις (*An.* 7.7.6). I would hesitate to speak simply of an archaism of usage, as Kamerbeek does at Soph. *Tr.* 137. Since the category has such ill-defined boundaries, it is possible that expressions like κακοῖς and καιρῷ were understood as adverbial; if so, they would have a synchronous parallel in expressions not requiring a preposition, e.g., σπουδῇ, τῷ ὄντι, ἰδίᾳ, and σιγῇ. Military historians may also have been influenced to write ἀτελεῖ τῇ νίκῃ and the like by their habitual use of the bare dative to refer to "troops, ships, etc. as accompanying the leader" (K-G 1.434), and by the instrumental/locative μάχῃ. (See also n. 18, below.)

Where the presence or absence of a locative sense was more than a grammarian's conundrum, Greek writers seem to have taken some care to avoid ambiguity. For instance, it would make a difference, indeed it might mar the account, if the audience thought that Hippolytus was heading for the messenger or any other person at Eur. *Hipp.* 1178–79:

> ὁ δ᾽ ἦλθε ταὐτὸν δακρύων ἔχων μέλος
> ἡμῖν ἐπ᾽ ἀκτάς . . .

Hippolytus' sense of isolation is explicit at 1184: πόλις γὰρ οὐκέτ᾽ ἔστιν ἥδε μοι, and though he does conduct business with the attendants (1183–84: ἐντύναθ᾽ ἵππους . . . δμῶες), it is merely of the practical sort. Thus Barrett's comment transcends the pedantic: "ἐπ᾽ ἀκτάς tells us where he came, ἡμῖν is dative of interest . . . as the dat[ive] seems always to be with uncompounded verbs of coming (e.g. Th[uc.] 1.107.7 ἦλθον δὲ καὶ Θεσσαλῶν ἱππῆς τοῖς Ἀθηναίοις κατὰ τὸ ξυμμαχικόν, the Ath[enian]s also had a detachment of Th[essalian] cavalry come to join them)."

---

10. Fairbanks says that lyric uses are relatively more common in Sophocles.

At Soph. *Ant.* 1232 the difference between allative and instrumental is more than a grammarian's quibble. Describing Haemon's angry rebuff of his father's supplication, the messenger says

πτύσας προσώπῳ κοὐδὲν ἀντειπών.

Jebb regards the dative as "an instance of the boldness with which poetry could use a simple dative to express the object to (or against) which an action is directed . . ." Prose would have πτύσας εἰς (or ἐπὶ) πρόσωπον. Mazon[11] claims that this reading is grammatically illegitimate: the dative must, he thinks, be instrumental with the subject of the participle. In support of this interpretation he cites 653, but that line shows only that a character could speak of spitting without indicating an object. I would not give up the allative reading, which seems perfectly suited to Haemon's passionate rage, without an unambiguous parallel showing πρόσωπον as instrument.

The semantics of the verb found with a dative suspected of local sense are not an entirely reliable criterion. Fraenkel addresses this problem in his remark on Aesch. *Ag.* 27–29:

. . . δόμοις
ὀλολυγμὸν εὐφημοῦντα τῇδε λαμπάδι
ἐπορθιάζειν . . .

Here too the grammatical interpretation makes an important difference to our understanding of the sense. Fraenkel prefers to discard the locative interpretation because δόμοις as a *dativus ethicus* permits us to explicate (following Karsten): "*domi, ut domum quasi participem faciat gaudii sui.*" He argues: "the locative dative of common nouns is normally found with verbs of tarrying, sitting, lying, laying down, and so on, although collocations like E. *Phoen.* 931ff. θαλάμαις . . . σφαγέντα are found here and there." (Fraenkel does not mention it, but in that passage the local sense is guaranteed by the relative adverb οὗ.) In my view, the grammar cannot be fixed by reference to the use of δόμοις or the sort of motion implied by the verb. The crucial point is, instead, peculiar to this text: the persistent personification of the House in the *Agamemnon*.[12] The locative reading is not wrong; it is simply less connected with a poetic theme. Similarly ambiguous uses of δόμοις enrich the meaning at *Ag.* 717–19 lyr.:

ἔθρεψεν δὲ λέοντος ἴ-
νιν δόμοις ἀγάλακτον οὔ-
τως ἀνὴρ φιλόμαστον

11. *Rev. de Phil.* 25 (1951): 14.
12. Discussed (and perhaps exaggerated) by John Jones, *Aristotle and Greek Tragedy* (London, 1962), sec. 2, chap. 3.

and *Ch.* 885:

Κλ. τί ἐστὶ χρῆμα; τίνα βοὴν ἵστης δόμοις;

Hearing the first, the audience might suppose that the house was just a temporary holding pen for the lion cub; at *Ag.* 732 they learn that the house is more intimately involved—αἵματι δ᾽ οἶκος ἐφύρθη. The *dativus localis* now looks like a *dativus incommodi* as well. The second example of δόμοις recalls *Ag.* 27–29, for there too the voice is raised in and for the house. The audience has been trained, so to speak, to understand Clytemnestra as asking what the cry portends for generations of men inhabiting the house of Atreus.[13]

The *Oresteia* is not, of course, the only tragedy in which δόμοι suggests a family line as much as the structure in which they live. In Sophocles, for example, there are instances of the dative that a locative interpretation (proposed by Fairbanks, "Dative Soph.," p. 97) would hobble:

   Ant. 1078–79 φανεῖ . . .
               ἀνδρῶν γυναικῶν σοῖς δόμοις κωκύματα.
   OT 1291 μενῶν δόμοις ἀραῖος, ὡς ἠράσατο.
   Tr. 893–95 ἔτεκ᾽ ἔτεκε μεγάλαν ἁ
            νέορτος ἅδε νύμφα
            δόμοισι τοῖσδ᾽ Ἐρινύν.[14]

On the same ground, we must reject Fairbanks's locative interpretation of πόλει ("Dative Soph.," p. 98); it is certainly more than a geographical unit at Soph. *Ant.* 657, where Creon declares

       ψευδῆ γ᾽ ἐμαυτὸν οὐ καταστήσω πόλει.

And at Soph. *OT* 164–67 lyr.:

       εἴ ποτε καὶ προτέρας ἄτας ὕπερ
         ὀρνυμένας πόλει
       ἠνύσατ᾽ ἐκτοπίαν φλόγα πήματος,
       ἔλθετε καὶ νῦν.

---

13. The house is also named in the collocation ἐν + δόμοις seventeen times in the trilogy, not every time with an unmistakable suggestion of the family of Atreus. At 1312, for example, the fate of Agamemnon and Cassandra is singled out.
14. Local meaning is possible at Soph. *Tr.* 840 lyr., where the concrete sense is aided by the verb ἀΐσσουσαν (Nauck: ἀΐσσόντων codd.), but the general run of thought favors the "true" dative. Fairbanks is probably justified in calling δόμοις at *Tr.* 950–51 lyr. a local dative. At 943 the Nurse, concluding her report, says τοιαῦτα τἀνθάδ᾽ ἐστίν, then proceeds to speak of the impossibility of reckoning on the future. The Chorus repeats the antithesis; this promotes a local interpretation. On δόμοις at Soph. *OT* 422, declared a local dative by Jebb, see Silk, *Interact.*, p. 143, n. 4, who construes the word with ἄνορμον in the next line on the ground that it is an "intrusive 'equivalent'" to νηΐ" (Silk explains the term "intrusion" at *Interact.*, pp. 23–24).

It is not easy to categorize the dative here—Kamerbeek can name four different possibilities, all better than "locative"—but the attempt is unnecessary. As a residual case, the dative is bound to elude grammarians. Yet no Hellenist, I imagine, will find πόλει unintelligible in its context, or even vaguely mysterious. Since the locative function is not likely to impress itself on a hearer, and the other dative functions present in this passage appear in nonpoetic Greek without a preposition, the use of πόλει does not here constitute a differentia.

Local Dative and Verbal Prefix

As with the terminal accusative, we must distinguish as best we can between legitimate examples of the feature and datives that the Greek ear would take with the prefix of a compound verb. Of course this difficulty arises only with verbs whose first element can, as a freestanding preposition, govern the dative case. On this ground, compounds with ἀντί and πρό do not compromise the status of apparent local datives at Soph. *Ph.* 830 ὄμμασι . . . ἀντίσχοις (locative or "true" dative) and at Eur. *Supp.* 51–52 lyr. δόμοις προθέμαν (see Collard).

ἀνά is not so straightforward: in tragedy it is attested with the dative only in lyric passages, but I am not sure that this alone would be sufficient reason to detach the prefix from the pertinent datives in dialogue, e.g., at Soph. *Tr.* 767 ἱδρὼς ἀνῄει χρωτί and Eur. *Supp.* 322 τοῖς κερτομοῦσι γοργὸν ὄμμ' ἀναβλέπει. Instead, we should rely on the fact that no motion is implied in the combination ἀνά + dative (LSJ s.v. B). Similar reasoning protects the status of the allative dative at Pind. *I.* 6.41 ἀνατείναις οὐρανῷ ("to heaven") χεῖρας: the genre permits ἀνά as preposition to govern the dative case, but the combination would make no sense in the passage.

ἐν and ἐπί govern the dative throughout all genres of Greek literature, and the meaning of the prefix in verbal composition is, semantically, very broad indeed. Consequently, verbs compounded with ἐν and ἐπί make the classification of datives found in their presence very uncertain. At Aesch. *Ag.* 27–29 (see above, p. 91) Wecklein cannot be proved wrong in his theory of the passage, which joins δόμοις to ἐπορθιάζειν. Fairbanks ("Dative Soph.," p. 98) cannot be proved right in seeing a local dative at Soph. *OC* 1488 τί δ' ἂν θέλοις τὸ πιστὸν ἐμφῦναι φρενί; (*if* that is what Sophocles wrote: see below, p. 94). The expression may be paralleled by Hdt. 3.80.3 φθόνος . . . ἐμφύεται ἀνθρώπῳ, where a local dative is impossible unless we declare an exception to the exclusion of the feature from prose.

πρός also gives headaches. The semantic range of its compounds is often wide enough to accommodate datives of varying semantic function. προσπίπτω, -πίτνω illustrates the problem. When this verb (in its first form) means "attack," it governs a dative that could not have been understood as locative; but a dative can be so taken if the verb means "supplicate," for that action involves a nonhostile falling to or at the knees. At Soph. *Ph.* 485 προσπίτνω σε γόνασι the problem is twofold: does the prefix govern the dative (this would discharge the locative interpretation of γόνασι), and whose knees are meant? It is possible in Greek to say "fall before the knees of another person," his knees being designated by the dative, but then that person is named in the genitive case.[15] The involuted expression at Eur. *Ph.* 293 γονυπετεῖς ἕδρας προσπίτνω and the accusative pronoun designating the person supplicated strongly support reading γόνασι as a local dative. But at Pl. *Ep.* 7.349a, where the person supplicated, not just a part of him, is indicated by the dative, there is no physical sense. That, I think, is postponed until the second clause, and expressed in quite different syntax: προσπεσὼν δ' αὐτῷ ὁ Θεοδότης λαβόμενος τῆς χειρὸς ἐδάκρυσέν τε καὶ ἱκέτευεν.

πρόσημαι is similarly problematic. At Soph. *OT* 15–16 and *OC* 1158 it appears with βωμῷ/βωμοῖσι. These datives can be understood as local or as governed by the prefix without altering the plain meaning of the text. In any case, πρός implies anything but hostility. At Aesch. *Ag.* 1191, on the other hand, the nuance is very much affected by the grammar: the Furies ὑμνοῦσι δ' ὕμνον δώμασιν προσήμεναι. Insist on a local dative, and you lose a stronger reading, "besieging the chambers" (so Verrall, followed by Fraenkel, Page, and Lloyd-Jones in his translation). Cassandra's promise to speak directly (1178–79) should discourage us from arguing for any pleasing ambiguity in this speech.

Text

Textual uncertainty threatens rather less than 10 percent of the instances of the feature (or plausible candidates) that I have examined. Some of these have in fact been called into question by editors against partial or unanimous manuscript evidence. A few examples:

Aesch. *Ch.* 48 lyr. πεδῷ M πεδοῖ Dindorf
Soph. *Tr.* 564 ἣν μέσῳ πόρῳ codd. ἣ 'ν Cobet
   Tr. 730 οἴκοις codd. ("true" dative?) οἴκοι Wakefield
   OC 1488 ἐμφῦναι φρενί codd. ἐμφῆναι ξένῳ Wunder[16]

15. Eur. *Hec.* 737, *HF* 986, *Or.* 1332.
16. But cf. Soph. *El.* 174, where the older manuscripts have ἐν, the *recentiores* the local dative, and Hermann comes to the aid of the construction with preposition expressed.

Copyists were familiar with the local dative; they could read many possible instances as some other sort of dative *not* requiring a preposition; and ἐν could be interpolated without adding a syllable only by aphaeresis, which was not always possible. For these reasons, the number of local datives that have vanished in scribal transmission is probably quite low.

Provenience

One usage is common to the archaic and classical periods and many genres: pronouns in the dative case that function as local adverbs. Starting with Homer we find, for instance, ἄλλῃ = "elsewhere" (*Od.* 22.140) and ᾗ = "in which place" (*Il.* 12.389); in Bacchylides τᾷδε = "here" (13.55 S); in Parmenides τῇ = "thither" (B 1.4 D-K); in Herodotus τῇ τε ἄλλῃ = "here and elsewhere"; in Aeschylus τῇδε = "here" (*Supp.* 201); in Aristophanes τῇδε = "here" (*Ach.* 204 lyr.); in Plato τῇδε = "here" (*Lg.* 958d); and in one of the *Carmina Popularia* τίς τῇδε = "who's there?" (879.2 Page). I will make no further mention of this variety of local dative or of the "prosecutives" (see above, p. 87).

Homer shows an abundance of local datives, both allative and illative. Especially common are ἀγρῷ, δόμῳ, and πόντῳ, but body parts and proper nouns are also attested in this function (see Chantraine, *Hom.* §§86, 106–12). Chantraine points out that the bare local dative is already meeting stiff competition from the preposition ἐν. In the classical period the local dative is far more popular with the tragedians than with the lyric poets. In Bacchylides I have found, excluding place names, only one clear example, δόμοις at Dith. 17.11 S. Another possibility is ναυσί at 1.115 S, which is much more likely to be instrumental. Pindar had more use for the local dative: candidates include two instances of οὐρανῷ (*I.* 6.41, *N.* 10.58), πόρῳ (*O.* 1.92), βάσσαισι (*P.* 3.4), νόῳ (*P.* 1.40), and κόλποις (*O.* 6.31).

The local dative is almost entirely absent from prose. Nearly all the attested examples are with a few place names, e.g., Πλαταιαῖς, Ἐλευσῖνι, Μαραθῶνι. Humbert (*Synt.* §491) remarks that "these datives have the rigidity of adverbs: one cannot say *Λακεδαίμονι 'at Sparta' as one says Μαραθῶνι, nor *Συρακούσαις 'at Syracuse' as one says Πλαταιαῖς." Conversely, the combination of ἐν + any of the favored place names is of doubtful legitimacy (unless, in the case of Marathon and Salamis, the battles there are mentioned in tandem). The meter guarantees one exception, Aristoph. fr. 413K διὰ τοὺν Μαραθῶνι τροπαῖον. Possible exceptions include virtually the same phrase at Aristoph. *V.* 711 τοῦ 'ν Μαραθῶνι τροπαίου (where the nu is transmitted but not metrically indispensable) and Isaeus 5.42 ἡ Ἐλευσῖνι μάχη (see Wyse). The only

instance in Aristophanes of a local dative place name other than
Μαραθῶνι occurs at *Lys.* 1299 lyr. τὸν Ἀμύκλαις σιόν, but this is sung by
a Laconian. Lyric poets and tragedians could omit the preposition with any
place name, but only Euripides was an aficionado of the construction.[17]

There are so few examples of the local dative with common nouns in
prose that it is hard to say what to make of them. As an intransitive,
πελάζω is used a few times by Herodotus, Plato, and Xenophon with
simple datives that might be interpreted as allatives (LSJ s.v.). But from
the examples cited by LSJ I would eliminate all but one, Xen. *An.* 4.2.3
πελάσαι . . . τῇ εἰσόδῳ. In the others, the dative designates persons or
animals with an interest in the movement, and in Pl. *Smp.* 195b ὅμοιον
ὁμοίῳ . . . πελάζει, the dative can be explained by the general tendency
of words expressing similarity to be constructed with that case. Thuc. 3.33
uses γῇ as an allative: γῇ ἑκούσιος οὐ σχήσω ἄλλῃ ἢ Πελοποννήσῳ.
Similarly, 3.29.1 and 7.1.2. But the collocation occurs several times more
often with the preposition (see Classen). Tantalizing because the same
noun appears in a text that might be even earlier is [Xen.] *Ath. Pol.* 1.15:
ἔστι δὲ πάσῃ γῇ τὸ βέλτιστον ἐναντίον τῇ δημοκρατίᾳ (add. ἐν Stephanus).[18]

To my knowledge, Empedocles furnishes no examples of local datives.
In Parmenides I have noted only two instances, neither of them at all
secure, B.8.14 D-K Δίκη χαλάσασα πέδῃσιν (D-K translate "in den
Fesseln lockernd," but an instrumental interpretation is also possible) and
B.12.5–6 πέμπουσ' [sc. τόκος and μίξις] ἄρσενι θῆλυ μιγῆν τό / τ' ἐναντίον
αὖτις ἄρσεν θηλυτέρῳ, where each gender is beneficiary as well as destination.

Herodotus is also devoid of examples, but the construction is frequently
attested in the Hippocratic corpus (see Langholf, *Syntakt. Hipp.*, pp. 91–
92). Langholf points out that in some passages the dative to which a local
meaning can be given can also be read as instrumental, "true," dative, i.e.,
indirect object, or as falling under the regime of a preposition in an earlier
clause. But we find this sort of syntactical ambiguity everywhere, and there

---

17. Detailed examination of place-name usage: A. Wannowski, *Syntaxeos anomalae
Graecorum pars de constructione, quae dicitur, absoluta deque anacoluthis, huc pertinentibus,
etc.* (Leipzig, 1835).

18. A possible bare dative of circumstances in a Delphic inscription: τοῦτα δὲ τοὶ ταγοὶ
ἐπιτελεόντων καὶ τῷ δεομένῳ συναγόντων (Schwyzer, *Dialect. Epigraph.*, no. 323.B.23).
W. Vollgraff says that τῷ δεομένῳ is the archaic equivalent of ἐν τῷ δεομένῳ, "if the
necessity arises," a phrase that appears on an inscription of the mid fifth century establishing
relations among Argos, Knossos, and Tyllisos ("Le decret d'Argos relatif à une pacte entre
Knossos et Tylissos," *Verhand. Nederland. Akad. van Wetensch. Afd. Letterk.* n.r. 51.2
[1950]: 27). There too the construction without ἐν is possible if one reads (with Chatzidakis
and others) θέσθον τοὶ δεόμενοι, but this violates Argive orthography (Vollgraff, pp. 16, 26).

are enough unproblematic examples to certify the existence of the phenomenon in the Hippocratic corpus. In Langholf's examples anatomical words predominate: τῷ ἐγκεφάλῳ, τῷ βρέγματι, κτλ. But the construction with words not designating body parts is also attested. At *Epid.* 5.212.21–22 the dative is allative (I transcribe Langholf's apparatus): ἔπεσε (ἔπεσε VIR: ἔπεσε ἐν Gal. in cit. Diff. resp. 7, 955 K.) σκληρῷ χωρίῳ ὕπτιος. At *Epid.* 7.5.452.9 it is illative: ψῦξις δὲ τοῦ σώματος ὡς ὕδατι κειμένῳ.[19] But as with the jussive infinitive, one needs to bear in mind the unusual character of the medical writings (see above, pp. 11–12). It is certainly possible to see this usage in medical shorthand as evidence that a local dative may have been an occasional feature in hurried colloquial speech; it is far less likely that the doctors were using the local dative as a poeticism meant to sweeten arid clinical descriptions.

It would obviously be imprudent to assemble a statistical table showing the distribution of the local dative in tragedy, the one genre where the feature is often encountered: there is no sense in counting examples that straddle the boundaries between local and instrumental, local and indirect object. What follows, therefore, is only a rough estimate.

Of the three tragedians, Aeschylus certainly shows the fewest examples, whether one reckons by absolute numbers or proportion. To that extent I agree with Sideras, *Aesch. Hom.*, p. 235. He is not correct in saying that the construction is "most common in Euripides, not seldom in Sophocles." My data are, admittedly, most complete for Sophocles (owing to Fairbanks's article); nonetheless I feel secure in attributing to Sophocles a fondness for the local dative of common nouns equal to Euripides'.

The tragedians exhibit the feature about twice as often in iambic trimeter as in lyric. Given the overall ratio of lyric to trimeter, roughly 1:4, a lyric passage is about twice as likely to contain an example. There are virtually no examples in the other meters of tragedy.

Gildersleeve (ad Pind. *P.* 1.40) remarks that "the range . . . [of the local dative] is narrower even in poetry than is commonly supposed." This strikes me as misleading, unless his contemporaries entertained wild ideas on the construction. From the examples discussed in this chapter it should be clear that plausible candidates for the category take in a respectable variety of nouns: regions of the earth, ocean, and sky; humans, in both their physical and mental aspects; human habitations; and abstractions. Gildersleeve's sense of the construction may be skewed by his notion that the local dative is "cold" in comparison with the "warm personal dative"

---

19. In Attic, proper usage is λοῦσθαι ὕδατι (instrumental, I think, considering Greek sanitary alliances), but λοῦσθαι ἐν πυέλῳ (a more luxurious bath, justifying the notion of place): see Kock ad Aristoph. fr. 107.

("Probs.," p. 21), and by his great enthusiasm for Pindar's exploitation of the prepositions ἐν and σύν, which in combination with the dative case touch or overlap territory occupied by the bare local dative (*Pind.,* pp. xcvi–xcvii).

Aristophanes has a few (surprisingly few) common-noun local datives in quotations from tragedy.

> *Ra.* 1317–19 lyr. = Eur. *El.* 435–37 lyr.
>
> . . . ὁ φίλαυλος ἔπαλλε δελ-
> φὶς πρῴραις κυανεμβόλοις.
> (Possibly a *dativus commodi,* a species of "true" dative.[20])

> *Ra.* 1403 = Aesch. fr. 38 = 446 Mette
> ἐφ᾽ ἅρματος γὰρ ἅρμα καὶ νεκρῷ νεκρός[21]

At *Th.* 1054–55 lyr., within the parody of Euripides' *Andromeda*, the dative is probably to be glossed ἐς νέκυας:

> . . . αἰόλαν / νέκυσιν ἐπὶ πορείαν.

(So Victor Coulon, "Aristophanes, Thesmophoriazusen 1015–1055," *RhM* 100 [1957]: 194.)

There is also a probable illative dative at Aristoph. *Nub.* 272, part of a high-style (though not paratragic) invocation of the Clouds:

> εἴτ᾽ ἄρα Νείλου προχοαῖς ὑδάτων χρυσέαις ἀρύτεσθε πρόχοισιν.[22]

Temporal Dative

Boundaries of gauze, not adamant, separate the temporal dative from the local and instrumental. Words with a primary temporal sense tend, in Greek, to suggest material space and matter. Gildersleeve writes (*Pind.,* p. xcviii), "the Greek considers Time as an attendant"; we may add, the Greek also may consider Time an arena, sometimes constructed from

---

20. So Denniston, commenting on the Euripidean original: "πρῴραις . . . if local, ought to mean 'on the prow': too bold, surely, for the boldest dolphin." But the allative, not illative, use is in question here.

21. Stanford: "a local dative . . . (but M has νεκρῶν) or else it depends on the ἐπὶ in the next line in A[eschylus]'s play—ἵπποι δ᾽ ἐφ᾽ ἵπποις ἦσαν ἐμπεφυρμένοι." As tragedy often attests similar expressions, e.g., Eur. *Hel.* 195 δάκρυα δάκρυσι, I strongly incline to the local interpretation, despite the two flanking ἐπί's. (Admittedly the tragic examples [collected at K-G 1.444] show the dative coming after the other case of the same word, but cf. Hom. *Od.* 7.121 ἐπὶ σταφυλῇ σταφυλή.)

22. Here too the local dative has been challenged: see H. Hommel, "Aristophanes über die Nilschwelle," *RM* 94 (1951): 320–21, answered by Dover ad loc. I cite also Hermippus 62K δεξιᾷ = "on the right" as a very slim possibility of a local dative in Old Comedy, but the text and interpretation are insecure. For τάφῳ at Aristoph. *Th.* 885 see above, p. 87, n. 4.

human deeds (e.g., μάχη, δεῖπνον) or circumstances of a certain type (e.g., βλάβαι, συντυχίαι). Any of these words can be employed in the dative and interpreted as temporal.

An instrumental interpretation makes the absence of a preposition entirely insignificant as a syntactical differentia. A temporal interpretation has a slightly less decisive effect: omission is only a predominantly, not exclusively (or very nearly exclusively), poetic feature. Consequently, I will offer here only a brief summary of the standard accounts (K-G 1.444–47; Schwyzer, *Gramm.* 2.158–59, 162–63, 169–70, 458; Humbert, *Synt.* §493). Emphasis on the notion "time *within* which" generally favors the expression of ἐν in prose. The bare dative is freely used by poets; in prose it is normal, but not inevitable, for lunar dates and recurring events, notably festivals. The presence and type of adjectival attribute with the dative condition the inclusion of ἐν, but not according to simple principles and not with any clear relation to genre.

APPENDIX 3a.
THE ABLATIVAL GENITIVE

Existing discussions seem to me to deal quite adequately with the one important poeticism in the use of the genitive case: the expression of origin by means of the case alone. I cite in particular T. D. Goodell's article "The Genitive Case in Sophocles"[1] and J. W. Poultney's exemplary study, *The Syntax of the Genitive Case in Aristophanes.*[2] I will, therefore, confine myself to a very brief account, largely drawn from these works.

The specifically poetic use of the genitive resides in its employment as a "whence" case of nouns with concrete referents and simplex verbs. The historical explanation for the differentia recalls what we have seen in the dative. The Greek genitive is a syncretic case, reflecting in part the function of the Indo-European ablative, the case designating origin and separation. At a very early stage prepositions and verbal prefixes began to supplement this function, particularly when the point of origin of the verbal process was concrete: already in Homer the case ending alone hardly ever suffices to indicate origin. As Schwyzer observes (*Synt. Arch.*, p. 7), the ablatival genitive with uncompounded verbs of motion often met

---

1. *TAPA* 15 (1884): 5–35.
2. See also K-G 1.393–401; Bruhn, *Anhang* §41; Humbert, *Synt.* §§462–65.

in tragedy (e.g., Soph. *OT* 152 lyr. *Πυθῶνος ἔβας*) is an archaism that cannot be explained as an epicism.[3]

Instances of this differentia in lyric poetry are few (see Gildersleeve, *Pind.*, p. xcii). In Parmenides I cite B8.10 D-K *τοῦ μηδενὸς ἀρξάμενον*; I have seen no examples in Empedocles. The grammarians cite Hdt. 2.80 (narrative) *εἴκουσι τῆς ὁδοῦ*, but this seems to be unique, and perhaps to be explained by the long-standing habit of the particular verb (see n. 3). Poultney shows no examples of the differentia in a long list of ablatival genitives with compounded verbs (*Genitive Aristoph.*, pp. 113–19), thus eliminating it from fifth-century colloquial Greek and paratragedy. A few simplex verbs designating the removal of a thing from a person (e.g., *ἁρπάζω*) appear with the victim in the genitive case, and this might look like an exception, though one of restricted semantics. But the genitive can also be interpreted as a possessive (Poultney, *Genitive Aristoph.*, pp. 119–91: in fact, nearly all the verbs he lists are compounds with prefixes that can govern the genitive).

Within tragedy, the one genre where this differentia is at all frequent, the distribution shows no concentration in lyric portions. Goodell's statistics (pp. 17–20) indicate that the genitive of separation with six simplex verbs of motion (*ἄγω, ἀείρω, ἁμαρτάνω, ἀμπλακεῖν, βαίνω, μολεῖν*) occurs ten times in dialogue and twice in lyrics.[4]

Like several other differentiae, this one turns on the interchange of abstract and concrete terms in relation to the rules of routine Greek. The poetry of our period had the option of extending the pedestrian rule that permitted the use of an ablatival pure genitive of nouns with intangible referents to tangible referents. As elsewhere, I understand this manipulation as a process operating strictly within the system of signs. I cannot believe that *Πυθῶνος* in the Sophoclean lyric was interpreted as referring to a locale of purely mental existence.

The "genitive of agent" is a species of ablatival genitive sometimes regarded as a poeticism. I would accept it neither as designating an agent nor as a differentia. Goodell[5] lists twelve instances, including one from Aeschylus. Five consist of genitive + alpha-privative adjective.[6] Except perhaps for Soph. *OC* 1521 *ἄθικτος ἡγητῆρος*, all of these suggest intan-

---

3. Schwyzer exaggerates a little. The genitive at *Od.* 18.10 *εἶκε προθύρου*, for example, must be ablative of the *Ausgangspunkt* with simplex verb.

4. Goodell reckons in Soph. *OC* 226 despite the presence of *ἔξω*, arguing (rightly, I think) that "from the freedom with which Sophokles uses the ablatival genitive with simple verbs of motion, it appears on the whole more probable that *ἔξω* was secondary in his mind."

5. P. 22. Several of his citations are ill chosen (see next note).

6. *Aj.* 910 lyr. *ἄφαρκτος φίλων*, *OC* 1521 *ἄθικτος ἡγητῆρος*, *Ant.* 847 lyr. *φίλων ἄκλαυτος*, 1034–35 *μαντικῆς ἄπρακτος* (not a proper example: the genitive is obviously no agent), *Ph.* 867–68 *ἐλπίδων ἄπιστον* (again, not a genitive of agent).

gible separation; perhaps for that reason prose could also use the bare
genitive with adjectives formed this way, e.g., ἄπαις. Separation is also a
semantic factor in such instances as Soph. *Ph.* 3 πατρὸς τραφείς: Goodell
compares *Aj.* 557 ἐξ οἵου 'τράφης.

A residue of four examples of "genitive of agent" remains in Goodell's
list. In three, the transitive verbs corresponding to the passive participle
are regularly construed with genitive-case objects: Soph. *Aj.* 1353 τῶν
φίλων νικώμενος, *El.* 344 κείνης διδακτά,[7] *Tr.* 934 ἐκδιδαχθεὶς τῶν κατ'
οἶκον, *Ph.* 1066–67 φωνῆς προσφθεγκτός. The locution in the *Electra*, for
example, is the other side of μου μανθάνεις (Pl. *Phil.* 51b). Insofar as the
notions of superiority and subjugation are construed with genitive-case
objects in prose, the expression κακῶν δυσάλωτος (Soph. *OC* 1722–23
lyr.) is explicable without recourse to a "genitive of agent."

Finally, whatever the grammatical explanation of these locutions, there
is reason to doubt that they were restricted to elevated poetry. Schwyzer
(*Synt. Arch.*, p. 8) notes the attestation in Attic prose of the expression ὁ
ἐρώμενός τινος, and other instances of the *genetivus auctoris* with passive
participles in Koine, and even modern Cypriot. I am not sure, therefore,
that ὑπό + genitive was the invariable pedestrian gloss of the examples
from the tragic stage.[8]

---

7. Page's emendation, δίδαγμα, is adopted by R. Dawe in his Teubner text.
8. Several putative instances of "genitive of agent" in Herodotus are more likely posses-
sives (see Stein ad 1.109.1, 2.18.3, 91.13 [*pace* Schwyzer, *Gramm.* 2.119]).

4. Voice

The ancient grammarians drew a functional distinction between verbs showing active and passive meanings (ἐνέργεια and πάθος respectively). On a formal level, verbs at the two poles may be unlike: ἐνέργεια embraces both λύω and αἰτιάομαι. Likewise, verbs of dissimilar morphology, e.g., the second perfect active διέφθορα "I have lost my wits" and the aorist middle ἐποιησάμην, were made to coexist in a vast gray area designated by Dionysius Thrax (pp. 48–49 Uhlig) as

. . . μεσότης . . . ποτὲ μὲν ἐνέργειαν ποτὲ δὲ πάθος παριστᾶσα.[1]

Modern terminology reduces the conflict of form and function somewhat by allowing intransitives like διέφθορα to stand with other verbs of obviously active formation. But like the Greek grammarians who used the term ἀποθετικά, we apologize for the passive form of verbs employed with an active meaning (say, by calling them "deponent," i.e., laying aside the passive meaning indicated by the morphology).[2] Also perplexing (though the ancient grammarians, as far as I know, say nothing about it) are voice variations within a single verb (present δέρκομαι vs. aorist ἔδρακον) and between verbs of similar meaning (ἱκάνω vs. ἱκνέομαι). Our understanding of the morphology and syntax of voice has made considerable advances in this century, especially since Hittite was added to the body of comparative material,[3] but on the stylistic side of the question there has been less progress.

---

1. The category includes both intransitives and verbs that can in different contexts either take an object or be used passively.
2. On the ancient theories see Wackernagel, *Vorl.* 1.120–21; Hirt, *IG* 6.198–200; Schwyzer, *Gramm.* 2.222–23.
3. Especially important are Benveniste, "Actif et moyen dans le verbe," *Prob.*, pp. 168–75, and C. Watkins, *Indogermanische Grammatik*, vol. III/I (Heidelberg, 1969), p. 67 and passim.

Minor Differentiae of Morphology and Lexicon

The origin of certain poetic differentiae in voice is plain enough. Many variations from prose usage are direct reflections of poetry's greater richness of morphology and lexicon. There are, for example, no syntactic implications per se in the intransitive character of second aorists and second perfects in poetry where prose has only the first aorist and first perfect of the same verb, still less if the verb is altogether alien to prose.[4] The tragedians use κλύω as a passive, but surely it was felt as a lexical substitution for ἀκούω.[5] Still, we can say that the willingness to substitute synonyms in a grammatical category that shows lexical restrictions in prose, or, more generally, to extend the precedents of ordinary language, is part of poetry's more abstract perception of linguistic phenomena.

A construction common to poetry and prose is ποιοῦμαι + a noun derived from a verb. A typical use is λόγους ποιούμενοι for λέγουσιν (Pl. R. 527a), where the periphrasis serves to allow fullness without repetition. Though this type of periphrasis substitutes for both active and middle verbs, only the middle ποιοῦμαι is used, never the active ποιῶ. Poetry, on the other hand, uses both active and middle of τίθημι in a similar periphrastic construction:

Aesch. Ag. 1059 μὴ σχολὴν τίθει
Soph. OT 134 ἔθεσθ᾽ ἐπιστροφήν

Poetry has a precedent for both voices in Homer. Prose does without this use of τίθημι/τίθεμαι—and so the option of selecting only the active—because it does not use the verb in the meaning "make" or "create" (see LSJ s.v. C). Why poetry does not use ποιῶ + noun on the analogy of τίθημι + noun I can only guess.[6]

The semantic compression of middle and passive uses, which obtained in the aorist tense before the creation of distinct passive forms, has left few relics in our period. Even in Homer, only the older sorts of aorist middle are used as passives, never the relatively recent sigmatic aorists (see Palmer, "Hom.," p. 145).[7] The second aorist middle participle of κτείνω

4. Examples at K-G 1.97–99.
5. LSJ s.v. κλύω III.
6. Perhaps ποιῶ is avoided because it was felt to suggest that the thing designated by the noun would be, as it were, created or executed for the world. The middle, by contrast, suggests that the noun designated a sphere within which only the subject of the verb is active; once the subject withdraws from this action, the signifié of the noun vanishes, except as abstraction. τίθημι might work where ποιῶ does not because poets tolerated, even welcomed, the notion of the signifié as existing before and after the verbal action and so available to be "put into position"; and this is a nuance τίθημι, but not ποιῶ, will bear.
7. Od. 8.35–36 may be an exception: κούρω δὲ δύω καὶ πεντήκοντα / κρινάσθων κατὰ δῆμον. A scholiast sees the verb as passive, ἐπιλεχθήτωσαν κατὰ γειτονίαν, as does

appears with passive function a few times in fifth-century poetry but never in prose, to judge from Veitch and LSJ:

Aesch. *Pers.* 923 lyr. ἥβαν Ξέρξᾳ κταμέναν

Cratin. 95K φθονερὸν ἀνθρώποις τόδε
κταμένοις ἐπ᾿ αἰζηοῖσι καυχᾶσθαι μέγα.

Also at Pind. fr. 203S, if we accept Wilamowitz's unnecessary emendation:

ἄνδρες θήν τινες ἀκκιζόμενοι
νεκρὸν ἵππον στυγέοι-
σι λόγῳ κτάμενον ἐν φάει, κρυφᾷ δέ
σκολιαῖς γέννσσιν ἀνδέροντι πόδας ἠδὲ κεφαλάν.

κτάμενον Wilamowitz κείμενον codd.

Since Homer uses several moods of the second aorist middle as passive, the restriction in our period to the participle is fairly strong evidence for regarding these examples as lexical, not syntactical, archaisms. That is, κτάμενος was felt more as an adjective, "dead by a violent act," than as the more verbal "slaughtered," which is a condensed version of ὃς ἀπέκτατο. The dative Ξέρξᾳ, which is to be construed with the participle in the example from the *Persae,* is no obstacle to this view: we can as easily call it a "dative of reference" as a "dative of agent" (the latter a dubious category anyway).

Also to be explained as a lexical phenomenon is the passive use of the second aorist middle of ἔχω in both simple and compounded forms. Such a use appears in Homer, choral lyric, Ionic prose, tragic dialogue, and even Attic prose.[8]

I think that in both verbs the susceptibility to the passive use bears some relation to the deficiency of aorist passive forms. θνήσκω and its compounds regularly supply the passive of κτείνω in several tenses: Homer and Herodotus show several passive forms of κτείνω itself, but, in Attic, Thuc. 3.81 ἐκτείνοντο is unique, and presumably an Ionicism. The aorist passive ἐκτάθην is attested only two times, both in Homer. Similarly, ἐσχέθην was not in use before or during the classical period.[9] With no competition from aorist passives, the aorist middle would more easily function as a passive.

From the Homeric evidence one might expect that sigmatic aorist

---

Schwyzer, *Gramm.* 1.757, but Merry and Riddell think "the voice is middle, and has an indefinite plural subject unexpressed."

8. Barrett, ad Eur. *Hipp.* 27, states: "In no other verb [than ἔχω and its compounds] does Attic use an aor. mid. as pass." Unless by "Attic" he means Attic prose, the participial use of κτείνω in Aeschylus and Cratinus counts as a minuscule exception.

9. See Veitch and LSJ s.vv.

middles would never be used as passives, yet there are several possible instances in post-Homeric poetry. Our oldest example, which may antedate the classical period, comes from Simonides' poem on the fleecing of the athlete Crios:

> ἐπέξαθ᾽ ὁ Κριὸς οὐκ ἀεικέως
> ἐλθὼν ἐς εὔδενδρον ἀγλαὸν Διὸς
> τέμενος.
>
> 507P

In his partial quotation of this passage at Aristoph. *Nub.* 1356 Strepsiades replaces the aorist middle with the aorist passive ἐπέχθη, which shows that Aristophanes did not think Simonides' verb carried a middle meaning, e.g., "had himself a haircut."[10]

The passive sense is less certain in some Pindaric uses of στεφανόω in the aorist middle participle, e.g., *O.* 7.15–16:[11]

> . . . ὄφρα πελώριον ἄνδρα παρ᾽ Ἀλ-
> φειῷ στεφανωσάμενον
> αἰνέσω . . .

Kühner-Gerth (1.118), who are determined to show that the sigmatic aorist is totally inhospitable to passive uses, explicate the participle as "he who acquired the crown for himself" (*coronam sibi peperit*). But this interpretation may blur the distinction between the achievement, which is the athlete's own doing, and the concrete recognition of his victory, which is an act performed by others. Our knowledge of the specifics of the crowning ceremony at Olympia is too limited to settle the question.[12] Nor can we be certain whether the passive function appears at Soph. fr. 535.5P anap. = 492.5N (see Wackernagel, "Misc.," p. 311) or Aristoph. *Nub.* 1006.

---

10. For the interpretation of the poem see D. Page, *JHS* 71 (1951): 140–41. Strepsiades is paraphrasing, not quoting, the poem: (ἐ)κέλευσα ᾆσαι Σιμονίδου μέλος, τὸν Κριὸν ὡς ἐπέχθη. The diction is conversational, but Aristophanes probably would have made the same alteration in an original lyric of his own.

11. Schwyzer, *Gramm.* 1.757, n. 1, interprets the participle as a passive. Other examples are at *O.* 7.81, 12.17, *N.* 6.19.

12. Since Pindar is calling to mind a literal crowning, I think it fair to suppose that the K-G interpretation suggests an Olympic victor crowning himself. It would follow that the victor would be described as indecorously behaving like Napoleon at *his* coronation, *if* we knew for certain that an official of the games actually placed the crown of olive on the victor's head, as *O.* 3.11–14 says. But it is not unthinkable that a Greek athlete crowned himself: this appears to be what is depicted in the well-known relief in the National Museum at Athens (no. 3344). But on a *psykter* by Oltos (Metropolitan Museum, acquisition no. 10.210.18) and a calyx krater by Euphronios (Berlin F 2180) an older man crowns a young athlete. Ancient notices of the olive crowning are not clear on the point (see Σ ad Pind. *O.* 5.8, Pausanias 5.7.7,

Some of the remarks made above on κτείνω apply here too. We have a verb singled out for unusual treatment; hardly any other verbs could be so used. The participle is favored (though the indicative makes one appearance with passive function: *O.* 7.81), a form that can be interpreted as more adjectival than verbal.[13]

It is easier to reject alleged instances of sigmatic aorist middles with passive function in prose. A few examples: at Antiphon 3.*a*.1, Gernet in the Budé and Maidment in the Loeb understand τῶν ψηφισαμένων as "decrees," i.e., things voted:

τὰ μὲν ὁμολογούμενα τῶν πραγμάτων ὑπό τε τοῦ νόμου κατακέκριται ὑπό τε τῶν ψηφισαμένων, οἳ κύριοι πάσης τῆς πολιτείας εἰσίν·

Decleva Caizzi shows that the participle can be translated as a masculine, "judges," without harming the antithesis.

We could decide whether the aorist middle of τάσσω/τάττω had passive force in Thucydides and fifth-century Athenian inscriptions if we knew for certain whether there was such a thing as self-assessment by subjects of the Athenian empire. In their discussions of the rubric first appearing in the tribute list for 434/3, πόλεις αὐταὶ φόρον ταξάμεναι, the authors of *ATL*[14] argue that Thuc. 1.101.3 constitutes evidence against taking the middle as passive:

Θάσιοι . . . τρίτῳ ἔτει πολιορκούμενοι ὡμολόγησαν Ἀθηναίοις τεῖχός τε καθελόντες καὶ ναῦς παραδόντες, χρήματά τε ὅσα ἔδει ἀποδοῦναι αὐτίκα ταξάμενοι καὶ τὸ λοιπὸν φέρειν, τήν τε ἤπειρον καὶ τὸ μέταλλον ἀφέντες.

No one denies that this assessment was made under severe duress; but that does not rule out a self-assessment by the Thasians, even if the Athenians had full power to accept or reject it. The generally fierce regulations for Chalcis include the phrase καὶ τὸν φόρον ὑποτελῶ, ὃν ἂν πείθω Ἀθηναίους (*GHI* 52.25–27), apparently a reference to a judicial procedure allowing a tribute-paying ally a chance to propose the amount, or at least try to persuade the Athenians to lower the amount recommended by the assessors.[15]

5.15.3). We are told, however, that the *palm* crown was placed in the victor's hand (see Paus. 8.48.2).

13. Wackernagel (*Hom.*, p. 91n) is convinced that the aorist middle of πράσσω is used as a passive at Pind. *P.* 4.243 ἔλπετο δ᾽ οὐκέτι οἱ κεῖνόν γε πράξασθαι πόνον. He argues against Schröder, who reads the infinitive as active, that οἱ is meaningless if Jason is the subject of the infinitive and that the verb cannot mean "fulfill." Neither of Wackernagel's claims seems cogent.

14. *ATL* III, pp. 83–84.

15. See D. Kagan, *The Outbreak of the Peloponnesian War* (Ithaca, 1969), p. 127;

The same verb looks as though Plato gives it passive meaning at *R.* 416d:

τὰ δ᾽ ἐπιτήδεια, ὅσων δέονται ἄνδρες ἀθληταὶ πολέμου σώφρονές τε καὶ ἀνδρεῖοι, ταξαμένους παρὰ τῶν ἄλλων πολιτῶν δέχεσθαι μισθὸν τῆς φυλακῆς.

Since Socrates has invented the guardians and the details of their life, it is easy to think of them as merely receiving orders, rather than actively "agreeing to accept" the necessities of life as a wage. But at Hdt. 3.13 the aorist middle is quite clearly used to designate an assessment of tribute that, though not made with any pleasure, is still an act taken at the initiative of those who must pay:

οἱ . . . Λίβυες δείσαντες τὰ περὶ τὴν Αἴγυπτον γεγονότα παρέδοσαν σφέας αὐτοὺς ἀμαχητὶ καὶ φόρον τε ἐτάξαντο καὶ δῶρα ἔπεμπον.

To the conservatism of the aorist middle as a passive in an admittedly small number of poetic texts we can add two closely related areas of genre distinctiveness:

1. The intransitive use by Attic poets of many aorist middles; prose authors avoid these in favor of the aorist passive (K-G 1.118).[16]
2. The preference of poetry for middle aorists in deponent verbs, and of prose for the aorist passive (K-G 1.119).

Attic in all genres is conservative in having resisted the wholesale replacement of aorist middles (especially in -σάμην) by aorist passives in -θην. In the fifth and fourth centuries Ionic and Doric show ἐγενήθην (Epicharmus and Archytas of Tarentum), but Attic attests only ἐγενόμην until the time of New Comedy (Philemon). Antiphon used ἀπελογήθην in the more Ionic language of the *Tetralogies,* but ἀπελογησάμην in speeches for delivery in Athens.[17]

If the development of -ην and -θην aorists was too old to make much difference in our period, the distinct future passive in -θήσομαι is too young. According to V. Magnien, it does not occur in Homer, the Ho-

---

ML pp. 86, 141, 198; Gomme at Thuc. 1.101.3; G. E. M. de Ste. Croix, *The Origins of the Peloponnesian War* (London, 1972), p. 104, n. 42. At Thuc. 1.99.3 the run of the sentence seems to me to imply that οἱ ξύμμαχοι initiate, and not merely accept, a substitution of specific tribute payments for ships.

16. The converse also appears: tragedians, but not prose authors, sometimes wrote the aorist passive of ἵστημι (simplex and compound) instead of the second aorist middle. The precedent is found in Homer, Sappho, and Pindar: for examples see Groeneboom ad Aesch. *Pers.* 206.

17. Meillet, *Aperçu,* pp. 240, 298. Meillet overstates the case: there are a number of aorist passives in Attic of our period, used both intransitively (e.g., Pl. *Phd.* 89c11–12 εὐλαβηθῶμέν τι πάθος μὴ πάθωμεν) and transitively (e.g., Aesch. *PV* 53 ὡς μὴ σ᾽ ἐλινύοντα

meric hymns, Hesiod, Sappho, Alcaeus, Theognis, Pindar, and Bacchylides; in the three tragedians there are about seventy occurrences, in Aristophanes about thirty. Though Herodotus shows only eight verbs in -θήσομαι, Attic prose adopted the tense rather quickly: Lysias holds forty-three instances.[18] Gildersleeve ("Probs.," p. 125) regards the -θήσομαι future as carrying a "sophistic" flavor; however, an examination of all the attestations in Herodotus, tragedy, and Aristophanes convinces me that this is not the case. But its distribution among the formal sections of tragedy is peculiar: with the exception of κριθήσεται at Eur. *Supp.* 601, the first future passive never appears in lyrics. Apparently the novelty of the tense and its absence from the tragedians' lyric exemplars are responsible for the restriction.[19]

Tragedy often gives a passive signification to the future middle (Jebb furnishes a short list at *OT* 672), but so does prose of the fourth century. A marked contrast between poetry and prose is evident in only a few words, such as καλοῦμαι and λέξομαι, which are preserved with passive meaning only in tragedy—even older prose uses λεχθήσομαι (Wilamowitz ad *HF* 582).

Differentiae of the Active Verb[20]

Prose tends to discriminate against simplicia by selecting normally transitive verbs for intransitive use, i.e., without an explicit direct object. This category includes elliptical expressions such as ἐλαύνειν (sc. ἵππον) and αἴρειν (sc. ἄγκυραν), for the original objects were truly forgotten within our period: Xenophon could write ἐλαύνων ἀνὰ κράτος ἱδροῦντι τῷ ἵππῳ (*An.* 1.8.1). One might, however, disregard such uses as *sui generis* and specially appropriate to historians, and so reduce the number of simplex verbs in prose considerably. Ad hoc ellipses are another matter. Cucuel (*Antiph.*, pp. 68–69) claims that the absence of an expressed complement of a transitive verb "expresses an action considered in itself, an abstraction

---

προσδερχθῇ πατήρ). For the growth of forms in -θην see also Rutherford, *NP*, pp. 186–93; Wackernagel, *Vorl.* 1.139; Fraenkel ad *Ag.* 1498. Intransitive ἐστάθην (see n. 16) recalls the active ἔσστα used passively at *SIG* 56.43 (Argos fifth century): see Bechtel, *Gk. Dial.* 2.504, LSJ s.v. ἵστημι.

18. *Les formes du futur grec* (Paris, 1912), p. 375 (totals), pp. 347–75 (list of attestations lemmatized by simplex verb). In the Septuagint -θήσομαι outnumbers -σω!

19. Gildersleeve writes: "All such new formations are in a large sense stylistic. We are no longer in an Homeric world, a Pindaric world; we are among the sophists, the sophists of the stage as well as the sophists in the forum." I intend to publish elsewhere my evidence for rejecting Gildersleeve's interpretation.

20. Krüger, *Att.*, pp. 147–52, *Poet.*, pp. 80–83; Gildersleeve, "Probs.," pp. 124–26; K-G 1.90–91; A. Marguliés, "Verbale Stammbildung und Verbaldiathese," *KZ* 58 (1931): 81; Schwyzer, *Gramm.* 1.291–92, 2.224–26.

made from the object on which the verb is exercised." This is perhaps an overblown way of putting it, since the unexpressed objects in his examples are for the most part definite persons or things easily supplied from the context (e.g., Antiphon 5.29 ἠρεύνων sc. σημεῖα vel sim.), or the potential objects of actions sanctioned or forbidden by the law (e.g., 2.β.2 ἀποκτείναντα sc. ἄνθρωπόν τινα vel sim.). Somewhat different are the absolute uses found only or predominantly in poetry, which are prompted by a need for generalization, as in Eur. Or. 667

$$\text{ὅταν δ' ὁ δαίμων εὖ διδῷ, τί δεῖ φίλων;}$$

Here we may speak of abstraction in the sense of nonparticularity, or of a verb easily replaced by an adjective or noun, say, εὐεργέται; but in passages like Antiphon 5.29 the brachylogy cannot be regarded as conceptually different from the longer form.[21]

The origin of this genre difference in the treatment of compound and simplex verbs is reasonably certain, though all discussions I have seen omit either the synchronic or diachronic ingredients of the explanation. Many transitive compounds arose from verbs that as simplicia were intransitive. Although the consolidation of preverb and verb sometimes turned transitive to intransitive (e.g., ἄγω/ὑπάγειν in the sense of "withdraw," or Latin peto/suppeto), the more common result was the conversion of intransitive to transitive. By being attached to a preverb, the "verbal concept acquired a direction toward a goal or otherwise a narrower relation to a nominal concept" (Wackernagel, Vorl. 2.180).[22] A splendid illustration is the rebuke delivered by Cleisthenes of Sicyon to Hippocleides, ἀπορχήσαο τὸν γάμον (Hdt. 6.129.5).[23] Ceteris paribus, the compound verb is more explicit than the corresponding simplex. This makes the compound more amenable to absolute use in prose than the relatively unfocused simplex. Put another way, the absence of a direct object to complement a compound creates (or in some cases revives an original) intransitiveness by a sort of inversion of the historical process that made intransitive simplicia into transitive compounds.[24] Poetic language, however, uses fewer compounds and interprets them somewhat differently: it repeats the prefix as a

21. Omission of the object is frequent in Greek—see K-G 1.96, 2.561.
22. Cf. the tendency of compounding to turn a verb active in the simplex into a middle; again, the reverse occurs, but less frequently (Wackernagel, Vorl. 1.128, 2.178–79).
23. The simplex can also be transitive: Herodotus writes, ὁ Ἱπποκλείδης . . . ὀρχήσατο Λακωνικὰ σχημάτια (6.129.3), but here the object is internal. If Cleisthenes had been charmed by Hippocleides' dance, he could not have congratulated him with ὀρχήσαο τὸν γάμον, "You have danced yourself a marriage."
24. Compounds, both active and middle, achieve what we may call, borrowing Benveniste's formulation (see above, n. 4), a positioning of the subject in the process; simplicia do not. See J. Vendryes, "Le mode de participation du sujet," BSL 44 (1948): 10–11.

preposition with the nominal object less often than prose (Smyth §1654) and continues to use preverbs *in tmesi* (Wackernagel, *Vorl.* 2.173–74). Consequently it never developed the prosaic contrast whereby the compound became more suitable to intransitive use.[25]

One unexpected active form, apparently a fossil of great antiquity, seems virtually excluded from *Kunstprosa*. παῦε for παύου is, according to Schwyzer (*Gramm.* 2.224), a remnant of a verb system without the later, thoroughly attested Indo-European opposition of active to middle. When παῦε is used absolutely it behaves just like other imperatives which, being not much more than exclamations, have little need of nice voice distinctions (see Jebb ad *OC* 1751). Distinctions of number and person can be superfluous as well: see Wackernagel, *Vorl.* 1.106, where he remarks that second-person singular commands to a group of unspecified persons are especially frequent in drama; but this fact reflects merely the abundance of the royal retinue and that characters and audience do not care which servant executes an order. The only instance of παῦε in prose comes at Pl. *Phdr.* 228e, in a colloquial exchange;[26] its several occurrences in comedy (some with genitive complements) cannot be counted as parodistic. Clearly the active must have flourished in casual speech. But the finite use at Eur. *Hel.* 1320 lyr., ἔπαυσε πόνων (unless we must emend with Murray to πόνον), cannot be paralleled and may be a high-style extension of the normal-language precedent.[27] Intransitive ἔγειρε, "wake up" (for the expected ἐγείρου) at Eur. *IA* 624 and, past our period, in Aesop and the New Testament, cannot be proved colloquial, though nothing appears more likely, especially as groggy early-morning utterance.[28] I am less confident in guessing at the status of ἀνακάλυπτε at Eur. *Or.* 294, for the word is attested only one other time in the appropriate sense (Xen. *HG* 5.4.6, as a middle participle).

Gildersleeve has offered a roundabout explanation for the residue of active verbs used where the middle is normal: "The middle has more color, more feeling than the active, and we might be tempted to see in Pindar's use of εὑρεῖν where we might expect εὑρέσθαι (P. 2.64), a certain aristocratic contempt of effect" (*Pind.*, pp. ci–cii).[29] Passages like the following,

25. It should be mentioned that there is doubt over the intransitive use of βάλλω: see Fraenkel ad *Ag.* 534. K-G (1.95 Anmerk. 1) mention the poetic mixing of transitive and intransitive uses of the same verb, but I know no examples from our period.

26. Krüger, *Att.*, p. 149 (§52.2.6) cites this passage after remarking on "παύειν as an intransitive especially in the imperative, not quite certainly [*doch nicht eben*] in Attic prose."

27. The shortened form παῦ, as at Men. *Sam.* 96, also befits an everyday phrase.

28. Wackernagel (*Vorl.* 1.122) reports Von der Mühll's conjecture that the first ἔγειρε at Aesch. *Eum.* 140 is intransitive.

29. Similarly, δρέπει is "colder" than δρέπεται (ad. *P.* 1.49), and διδάξασθαι "only a more intense διδάξαι, 'getting up scholars'" (ad *O.* 8.59). But in a less impressionistic

where feeling is not lacking and the middle is the *more* common voice, make me doubt Gildersleeve's formula:

χοὔτως ἐδήχθη τοῦτο τοὔνειδος λαβὼν
ὥσθ᾽ ὅρκον αὐτῷ προσβαλὼν διώμοσεν /
ἦ μὴν . . .

Soph. *Tr.* 254–56

(Jebb notes that the active of διόμνυμι is rare, except in the perfect.)

Middle for Active: Dialect and Lexicon[30]

The poetic repertory includes a fair number of middle forms eschewed by Attic prose. A trio of familiar linguistic forces account for the difference, but we cannot hope to fix their relative weights with any precision.

A most general explanation lies in the gradual decline of the middle voice. The middle survives in Modern Greek (with reduced scope), but on the whole it lost ground to both active and passive forms. So if we knew nothing else, we could say that if active and middle forms of a verb coexist and there is no gross difference in meaning between them, the middle is more archaic, and we could conclude that poetry retains the old without denying itself the new. But this is by no means a reliable criterion. Numerous verbs known only in active forms in their earliest attestations later develop middle and passive forms (and, sometimes, meanings), e.g., Homeric ἐντρέπω vs. Herodotean ἐντρέπομαι (see Wackernagel, *Hom.*, pp. 130–34; *Vorl.* 1.129–30). The active forms of some verbs appear on Attic inscriptions older than those showing the middle, e.g., γέγονα is attested before γεγένημαι (Meisterhans, *Inschrift.*, pp. 192–93).

Fortunately we know more. Dialect preference is clearly of major importance since, as with variations in number, Ionic and poetic uses converge. Voice variations from Attic can be found in many areas, for instance, Achaean ὁμόσασθαι for Attic ὁμόσαι (Bechtel, *Gk. Dial.* 2.885),[31] and not even nearby cities speaking the same dialect always agree. From Datis' masturbatory ditty at Aristoph. *Pax* 289–91 it appears that proper selection of voice could serve as a shibboleth for Attic speakers:

---

moment (ad. *P.* 1.48) Gildersleeve's eye is on denotation, not connotation, and he contrasts εὑρίσκομαι "gain" and εὑρίσκω "find."

30. See Krüger, *Poet.*, pp. 85–88; K-G 1.101–02; Stahl, *Verb.*, pp. 59–60; Schwyzer, *Gramm.*, 2.232–33.

31. Conversely, Bechtel (*Gk. Dial.* 2.886) compares West Locrian διομόσαι and Attic διομόσασθαι.

νῦν, τοῦτ᾽ ἐκεῖν᾽, ἥκει τὸ Δάτιδος μέλος,
ὃ δεφόμενος ποτ᾽ ᾖδε τῆς μεσημβρίας·
" Ὡς ἥδομαι καὶ χαίρομαι κεὐφραίνομαι."

χαίρομαι for χαίρω looks like a most forgivable mistake, since the other two verbs might lure one into an analogical middle. Moreover, it may not have been a barbarism but a legitimate dialect variant (see LSJ s.v. χαίρω). In any case, it is far less blatant than the solecisms perpetuated by the sniveling Phrygian of Timotheus 791.150ff. Page, Ἑλλάδ᾽ ἐμπλέκων Ἀσιάδι φωνᾷ.[32] But Soloi and Parnassus are sometimes neighbors, and I take it that to alter the customary voice of a good Attic word from active to middle is to give the word a dialectal flavor. That flavor was Ionic. Bechtel (Gk. Dial. 3.246–48) finds that writers of Ionic, like the other Greeks, mix their voices, but more important, he attributes to them a "strong tendency" to use the middle. Significantly, the double-voice verbs are generally not found in Attic prose as either actives or middles (one important exception is discussed below). In Schwyzer's list (Gramm. 2.232) of poetic doublets we find the following distribution:[33]

Intransitives

σπέρχω. Poetic and in Ionic prose; Attic has compounds with ἐπι- and κατα-, but these are not used in the middle.
βρέμω. Poetic.[34]
ἱμείρω. Epic, Ionic, and tragic; never in Attic prose, except for Pl. Cra. 418d, where the active is etymologized.
πέλω. Poetic and Aeolic, Doric, and Ionic prose. Its use in Aristophanes (Pax 1276) is epic parody.
ἀΐσσω. Poetic, chiefly epic word, rarely found in prose (one citation each from Herodotus and Isaeus; two from Plato, one of which is from the probably spurious Alcibiades I; once in the Hippocratic corpus). Aristophanes attests the verb 12 or 13 times (at Nub. 1299 ἄξεις seems correct), only in the active. Some instances, both simplex

32. See Wackernagel, Vorl. 1.123–24. If Ἰάονα γλῶσσαν (149) meant Ionic, rather than simply Greek, as suggested by 146–67, we would have had a contradiction of Bechtel's dictum (see below). But from the Asian point of view, of course, Ionian = Greek.
33. LSJ is the main source, supplemented by Veitch. Schwyzer is surely right to say that the double inflection has metrical advantages.
34. It is curious that all three uses of the middle in our period have depersonalized subjects: Pind. N. 11.7 λύρα . . . βρέμεται καὶ ἀοιδά, Aesch. Sept. 348–50 lyr. βλαχαὶ δ᾽ αἱματόεσσαι / τῶν ἐπιμαστιδίων / ἀρτιτρεφεῖς βρέμονται (the isolation of the cries is accentuated by the enallage), Aristoph. Th. 997–98 lyr. μελάμφυλλά τ᾽ ὄρη δάσκια πετρώδεις τε νάπαι βρέμονται.

and compounded, *may* reflect its currency in everyday language, e.g., at *V.* 988 and *Ra.* 567, but elsewhere the context provides evidence of poetic flavor, e.g., at *Nub.* 996 (see Dover's remark on his conjecture of a tragic word at 995), *V.* 837 (where the prosody of ἰπνόν suggests paratragedy: see MacDowell), and *Ra.* 468 (where the overall level of expression is highly pathetic).

Transitives

ἐρέω/ἔρομαι. The first is epic; the second is used in both poetry and prose.

κολάζω. This verb has a *narrower* voice range in poetry. Tragedy uses only the active, but "the future active is confined to prose, . . . the future middle is in prose and Comedy" (Veitch).

λοιδορέω. Active only in tragedy; prose and Aristophanes use active and middle.

μέλπω. Poetic.

πειράω. Both poetry and prose.

λάμπω. "Found chiefly in poetry and [sic: ?including] comedy, though the present and imperfect occur in Xenophon (middle) . . . Plato [one citation, *Phdr.* 250d], Aristotle . . . and later prose, and aor. in Hdt. 6.82 (v.l.)" (LSJ).

φημί. Both poetry and prose.

αὐδάω. "This verb is almost exclusively Epic, Lyric, and tragic. We think it occurs once only in prose, Her. 2.57, and twice in comedy" (Veitch);[35] "Never in good Attic prose" (LSJ).

κλαίω. Both poetry and prose.

ἀγαπάζω. Epic and lyric form of ἀγαπάω.

The impersonal μέλεται, which Schwyzer mentions, of course corresponds to the frequent impersonal active of Attic prose, but it is rare. A more common poetic usage (also in Hippocrates) is the middle with a personal subject, a construction Attic prose does not allow with the active (LSJ s.v.).

Thus the liberty of dual voice inflection is partially sunk in lexical distinctiveness.

---

35. One citation is to Aristoph. *Ra.* 369 anap. (366 in Veitch), a warning to the uninitiated to make way for the sacred procession, but the text is uncertain. Coulin prints: τούτοις αὐδῶ καῦθις ἐπαυδῶ καῦθις τὸ τρίτον μάλ᾿ ἐπαυδῶ.

Middle for Active: Semantics[36]

The middle is emphatic insofar as its positioning of the subject within the process *can* invite reflection on the subject's attitude to the action. Schwyzer (exaggerating a little) contrasts πολιτεύω "I am a citizen" to πολιτεύομαι "I am a citizen of deepest sentiments and devotion; not just in name do I play the part of citizen." Mere action can be contrasted to action more intimately connected to the subject and so more specifically motivated. A poet often makes this kind of point by employing the middle voice: for two Sophoclean examples see Kamerbeek's remarks on τιμωρουμένης at *El.* 349 and προυβάλου at *Ph.* 1017. *A priori* the middle is the more psychological or subjective voice, and so better adapted to expressive language.[37] But this principle has been greatly exaggerated and made into a genre differentia.

Specifically to be rejected as a grammatical concept and as a genre differentia is the category of "dynamic" middle, a use of the voice that is said to convey greater intensity than the active. Stahl's definition runs:

> The intensive or dynamic middle designates an activity that demands the resources [*Mittel*] or powers of the subject, whereby the general meaning attaches to itself an urgent or willful [*angelegentlichen oder absichtlichen*] action. [*Verb.*, p. 57]

Two pages later he weakens the concept:

> Since, strictly speaking, every activity is simultaneously an expression of power, the use of the dynamic middle is extended, indeed sometimes to the extent that between middle and active either only an unimportant difference exists, as between ὁρᾶσθαι/ἰδέσθαι and ὁρᾶν/ἰδεῖν . . . or an imperceptible one, as in ἐφίεσθαι/ἐφιέναι. . . . Hence it is at the same time comprehensible that in individual verbs the medial uses are confined to one area of literature.

The *Iliad* and the *Odyssey* use actives and middles to describe the same event,[38] a mixture of voice no one is prepared to explain as a shuttling between subjective and objective modes of narration. The concept of a dynamic middle, even when offered in diluted form (as in the second quotation from Stahl), will not clarify the deviations in question. Gildersleeve and Wackernagel (*Vorl.* 1.127) are quite right to disdain it. Gilder-

---

36. The phenomenon of semantically unexplained voice alternations is too widespread to allow Hermann Grosse's conclusion that such variations in lyric, tragedy, and Herodotus are intentional imitations of Homeric usage (*Beiträge zur Syntax des griechischen Mediums und Passivums* [Dramburg, 1899], p. 13).

37. See K-G 1.111.

38. E.g., *Il.* 2.781 γαῖα δ' ὑπεστενάχιζε and 784 ὡς ἄρα τῶν ὑπὸ ποσσὶ μέγα στεναχίζετο γαῖα (from Chantraine, *Hom.* 2.173).

sleeve calls it the "drip-pan middle, the πανδέκτης-middle, the middle that is put at the bottom to catch the drippings of the other uses as the ablative is put to catch the drippings of the other cases."[39] Even Schwyzer, who is relatively hospitable to the notion of a dynamic middle, says, "A difference with respect to emotion or a double marking [*Doppelcharakterisierung*] once existed, e.g., νήχειν:νήχεσθαι and similar verbs, whose contents equally lie in the sphere of the subject. How long this very old difference between active and middle was felt as still alive is difficult to say." This formulation is harmless, i.e., it will not encourage fanciful distinctions, provided we adjust it to say that the distinction died earlier than the beginning of attested poetry. We can exclude only such distinctions as may arise from the association of deviant uses with particular styles of language. It is possible, for instance, that συμφέρεται standing where συμφέρει is normal provoked a faint suggestion of the divine hand because the middle occurs in several oracular pronouncements (see Dover ad Aristoph. *Nub.* 594). This is far from saying that the middle voice per se makes the verb connote greater will than the active.

A clear example of error springing from *a priori* assumptions about the middle voice is Bénard's interpretation of ἰδεῖν vs. ἰδέσθαι in Herodotus.[40] He alleges that "*ἰδεῖν* is said of a perception of an object which impinges on our vision; one uses ἰδέσθαι when one wishes to indicate attention or effort." He explains the voice of ἰδόμενοι φεύγοντας (Hdt. 6.14.3) as marking the subjects' concentrated reconnaissance of their enemies. But the same attentiveness can be accommodated by the active, as at 4.119.4:

ἢν μέντοι ἐπίῃ καὶ ἐπὶ τὴν ἡμετέρην ἄρξῃ τε ἀδικέων, καὶ ἡμεῖς οὐ πεισόμεθα. μέχρι δὲ τοῦτο ἴδωμεν, μενέομεν παρ᾽ ἡμῖν αὐτοῖσι·

Again, there has been an unwarranted extrapolation from the positioning of the subject within the verbal action. Perception and cogitation may be distinguished by uses of the active and middle voices respectively, but it is gratuitous to assume that the former is somehow more arduous or exciting than the latter. Kühner-Gerth (1.101–02) more accurately speak of the middle as allowing no spatial separation between subject and object, which explains the affinity toward the middle of deponent verbs that "express a mental activity," like θεάσασθαι or ὀλοφύρασθαι. They point out that Attic prose uses the middle of ὁράω in compound forms, mostly of men-

---

39. *AJP* 29 (1908): 277. A. Marguliés (*KZ* 58 [1931]: 116–18) is also hostile to the "dynamic middle."

40. L. Bénard, *Essai sur la signification et l'emploi des formes verbales en grec d'après le texte d'Hérodote* (Paris, 1889), p. 99.

tal vision; only Xenophon uses προσοράομαι in the literal sense (no surprise here). We can say that the prefix, in altering the meaning of the verb, justifies the "interiority" of the middle.[41]

I excuse myself from an examination of certain middles assembled by Kühner-Gerth (1.109–10) that contain "only a faint hint that the action is carried out to the advantage or disadvantage of the subject." A poetic usage, they maintain, especially frequent in Homer, is the middle "used of a transaction that falls to one person to perform, though it is executed at the order of another, or to another person's advantage or disadvantage." To think that Sophocles makes Heracles order Hyllus and his retinue αἴρεσθε sc. ἐμὲ ἐς πυράν, with the middle to convey the nuance "as is your duty," is to imagine the speaker throwing his verbal voice like a ventriloquist.[42]

41. περιοράω is something of an exception, since it appears in the active when it means "allow," but in the middle with its more literal meaning.

42. Tr. 1255. It is acutely discouraging that one cannot test a supposed instance of Sophoclean preference for the middle, προὐδιδάξατο at Tr. 681. Pace LSJ s.v. διδάσκω, the usage of classical prose is not certain: see Dover ad Aristoph. Nub. 783 and his general remark ad 368; and Riddell, "Plat. Id." §87b.

5. Subjunctive, Optative, and ἄν

In this section we consider differentiae of both the subjunctive and optative moods as they center on the presence or absence of ἄν. I will refer to this word as a "modal particle" for convenience in exposition, though the propriety of the term is controversial. Many scholars have interpreted ἄν as a word that alludes to circumstances surrounding the designated verbal process. The particle is sometimes translated "in those circumstances" or "in that case." As A. O. Hulton remarks, it is in conditional sentences that a reference within the apodosis to certain circumstances is clearest: the circumstances are stipulated by the protasis.[1] Following Gonda we may define verbal mood as "a means of intimating the speaker's view or conception of the relation of the process expressed by the verb to reality" (*Moods*, p. 6). The choice of an oblique (i.e., nonindicative) mood suggests that the speaker regards the process as something other than actual, for instance, it may be something he presents as a possibility. If he alludes to conditions under which this thing is possible, his stance toward the process in question is not altered: the process itself is no more or less a possibility for being narrowed down in the universe of possibilities.

According to this description, ἄν is no modal particle. But it is misleading to insist on a nonmodal interpretation of the word when its association to a mood becomes fixed. The mechanically reproduced ἄν's of subordinate subjunctive clauses in Attic prose surely were not perceived as pointing to circumstances every time they were used. These ἄν's I would rather call stylistically required concomitants of a mood. ἄν's with secondary tenses of the indicative, on the other hand, are more than concomitants: they mark the difference between facts and potentials, and so fully deserve the designation "modal." And it would be perverse to deny modal function to ἄν when it points to the mood represented by an infinitive or participle. The propriety of the term must be decided separately for each

1. "ʺAν with the Future: A Note," *CQ* 51 (1957): 140, n. 1.

construction, and only after an examination of relevant genre and lexical features. We cannot learn anything useful from a general classification of the term.[2]

Perhaps more than other aspects of genre-conditioned syntax, the use or omission of the modal particle has been interpreted as marking a psychological difference between authors of poetry and of prose. For example, Kühner-Gerth (1.231) promote the idea that the greater receptivity of poetry to the potential optative without the modal particle reveals the impracticality of poets, their imagination soaring over the particulars of reality:

> Whereas the optative without *ἄν* expresses a visualization [*Vorstellung*] per se, without any regard to the relationships and conditions under which the realization could take place, the optative with *ἄν* expresses the visualization together with a consideration of these relationships and conditions. . . . That in poetic language the use of the potential optative without *ἄν* is preserved longer than in prose is entirely natural. The poet's freer mode of vision [*Anschauungsweise*] expresses a purely subjective judgment not concerned with the actually existing relationship of things. The prose writer, by contrast, who keeps the actual situation in mind to a greater degree, shows in his expression too a regard for the relation of his thoughts to reality.

To determine whether *ἄν* is present or absent in a given piece of Greek, especially in prose texts, is a ticklish problem once one leaves the shallow waters of elementary rules. *ἄν* is a small word: its interpolation or omission is often, on internal grounds, equally probable. Inevitably, one's view of the text is guided by a theory of moods and particles more than the theory is guided by the text. Still, there are better and worse ways to travel around a circle. A diachronically informed argument, taking into account the movement of usage from Homeric to Hellenistic times, explains some of the phenomena of the classical period only by extrapolation; but it seems certain to me that language is immune from sudden, catastrophic changes, and this implies that assumptions of continuity and gradual change are not gratuitous. The vagaries of textual corruption, particularly where we are denied metrical criteria, permit us to say virtually nothing about certain

---

2. A. C. Moorhouse favors the term on the ground that "*ἄν* and *κε* supplement the use of the subjunctive and optative moods, and even become an indispensable unit in the modal expression. In Attic, to take just one example, the optative preserves its potential use as a normal rule only when *ἄν* is associated with it" ("A Reply on *ἄν* with the Future," *CQ* 53 [1959]: 78). His example points to a reason for caution: if one starts off thinking that the particle is obligatory with potential optatives, one risks prejudging its omission as semantically disreputable.

transmitted ἄν's; our expectations of what is possible Greek, on the other hand, are not mere guesswork.

Over the last hundred years discussions of the semantic force of the subjunctive and optative moods have revolved mainly around one issue, whether they express properly modal or temporal ideas.[3] Modal theories differ in either attributing a unified meaning to each mood, say, "will" and "wish" respectively, or dividing the terrain of each mood between two more or less strictly demarcated uses, "voluntative" subjunctive and "cupitive" optative on one side, "prospective" subjunctive and "potential" optative on the other. Similarly, temporal theories juggle the future, making either the subjunctive a future and the optative present and timeless, or both moods futures. For our purposes, only one aspect of these general theories of mood is important, namely, the role of the modal particle.

We may take as representative of current thinking two recent investigations, both as it happens written by Dutch scholars, J. Gonda's *The Character of the Indo-European Moods* and C. J. Ruijgh's *Autour de "TE épique."* Their points of departure are quite different: Gonda canvasses evidence from ancient and modern Indo-European languages and, despite the title of his book, the expression of verbal mood in many non–Indo-European languages as well, whereas Ruijgh is interested in the Greek moods and tenses as they illuminate epic τε. Further, their conclusions diverge considerably. Nevertheless, both interpretations attribute a secondary role to the modal particle in the expression of mood.

Speaking in terms of the greatest generality, Gonda defines the essential notion of both subjunctive and optative as modes by which one presents a verbal process not as a fact occurring in the world but rather as mentally entertained. The difference between subjunctive and optative is that the latter carries with it an additional nuance, the possibility that the process will not take place.

> The optative, it would appear to me, enables the speaker to introduce the elements of visualization and contingency, the latter being, in my opinion, the main character of this mood. In using this form the ancient Indo-European took, with regard to the process referred to and which existed in his mind, the possibility of non-occurrence into account; he visualized this process as non-actual: it is possible, or it is wished for, or desirable, or generally advisable or recommended and therefore individually problematic, or even imaginary, its realization

---

3. The history of the dispute is traced by Gonda, *Moods,* passim, and G. Calboli, "I modi del verbo greco e latino," *Lustrum* 11 (1966): 235–58.

is dependent on a condition or on some event that may or may not happen. [*Moods*, pp. 51–52]

On the subjunctive he writes:

Its general function may, if I am not mistaken, have been to indicate that the speaker views the process denoted by the verb as existing in his mind or before his mental eyes, or rather: as not yet having a higher degree of being than mental existence. The subjunctive, in other words, expresses visualization. A process in the subj[unctive] represents a mental image on the part of the speaker which, in his opinion, is capable of realization, or even awaits realization. There is, however, no question of contingency. Whether the speaker expects this realization, desires it, fears it, orders or hopes it or whether he merely sees it before his mental eyes, is a matter of indifference. [*Moods*, pp. 69–70]

In Gonda's presentation the semantic value outlined for each mood can undergo further specialization by a variety of means: the influence of context, word order, conjunctions, intonation, the meaning of the verb, and so on. The modal particle is, then, only one of many elements capable of narrowing the fundamental meaning of the mood, e.g., making an optative more or less potential or cupitive (*Moods*, pp. 52, 70–71).

Ruijgh is rather more schematic and influenced in his presentation by the distinctions of classical Greek. In his temporal interpretation of the moods he places far greater stress than Gonda on the semantic influence of *ắv*:

the subjunctive indicates in principle that the realization of the process exists in the thought or desire of the subject . . . and that it is expected in the future. With the particle *ắv* the subjunctive designates a process existing in the desire (voluntative use). It is very difficult to define the value of the particle *ắv*. Roughly, one could say that it indicates that the realization of the process depends on the realization of certain conditions; it has, then, the force of a weak "if such should be the case," or "possibly." The difference between "subjunctive with *ắv*" and "subjunctive without *ắv*" is easily explained. Since as a rule a first-person subject is less inclined in expressing a desired process to underline that his desire cannot be realized except after the realization of certain conditions, the absence of *ắv* is not surprising. ["*TE* épique," §242]

The optative, according to Ruijgh (§§223, 252), differs from the subjunctive in that the process conceived or desired "is not quite expected in the future." It largely resembles the subjunctive in that the presence or absence of ἄν signifies, respectively, that the process exists in the mind (the potential use) or in the desire (the cupitive use). At first glance this précis of Ruijgh's views might make it appear that he thinks of ἄν as a word endowed with decisive, if hard to translate, semantic value; but he does, of course, acknowledge that in Homer the modal particle is not yet obligatory with the prospective subjunctive (§48) or noncupitive optatives (§§252, 257). Further, he observes that the occurrence of ἄν and κεν with the subjunctive to indicate the future is especially frequent with verbs lacking a proper future tense form (§248); and he conjectures that the absence of ἄν from subordinate clauses with the optative (but see below, pp. 123–24), despite the existence of this type with κε in Homer, shows a preference to do without the particle because its presence in the apodosis sufficiently marked the period as conditional (§253). These are important matters because they indicate the susceptibility of ἄν to lexical and combinatorial influences. We see, then, that even that theory of moods which integrates ἄν most fully into its scheme cannot systematize it fully.

ἄν: Homeric and Attic Patterns

As compared with Attic prose, Homeric usage of the subjunctive and optative is fluid, and more nearly resembles the general description of the moods presented by Gonda. In semantic terms, however, there are only three principal areas of difference:[4]

1. Homer, but not Attic prose, employs the subjunctive in independent clauses traditionally translated as future indicatives, e.g., *Il.* 1.262 οὐ γάρ πω τοίους ἴδον ἀνέρας οὐδὲ ἴδωμαι "for I never saw such men nor will I see [them]." (Gonda, who does not think that the futurity of the event is necessarily implied by these "prospective" subjunctives, prefers to translate, "I don't expect to see, I can't fancy them being seen again" [*Moods*, p. 75].)

2. Homer attests the optative for unfulfilled wishes in the present, as in *Il.* 16.722 αἴθ᾽ ὅσον ἥσσων εἰμί, τόσον σέο φέρτερος εἴην "Would that I were as much stronger than you as I am weaker."[5] But Attic, unlike Homer, uses εἴθε and εἰ γάρ with past tenses of the indicative for present and past wishes.

---

4. Palmer ("Hom.," pp. 149–53) gives a concise list with examples.

5. Palmer ("Hom.," p. 151) says that this construction is limited to the fixed expression ὡς ὄλοιτο, but as far as I know this expression (and indeed all uses of the simplex ὄλλυμι within our period) appears only in poetry; further, the two instances I have found in a cursory search, Soph. *El.* 126–27 lyr. and Eur. *Hipp.* 407–09, refer respectively to the future and the past.

3. The potential optative with or without ἄν or κε(ν) may be used in Homer for unreal events in both present and past time, e.g., *Il.* 9.515 εἰ μὲν γὰρ μὴ δῶρα φέροι "If he were not bearing gifts," and *Il.* 5.311 καί νύ κεν ἔνθ᾽ ἀπόλοιτο ἄναξ ἀνδρῶν Αἰνείας "Aeneas would have perished." Attic expresses these counterfactuals only with ἄν and the imperfect (for present time) and the aorist (for past time) indicative. (Homer attests the past form but probably not the present.)[6]

It is notable that none of these divergences turns simply on the presence or absence of the modal particle. Only the third involves the particle at all, and there the mood of the verb is different in the two constructions. Furthermore, ἄν in Attic usage is not a certain thing (see below, esp. p. 134).

I have called these "semantic" rather than "syntactic" differences, thereby risking some circularity of argument: they are instances of differences in meaning more fundamental than variations in the rules governing the joining of clauses in hypotaxis. The differences between Homeric and Attic usage in this regard are the consequence of the semantic differences already discussed and a growing rigidity in Attic prose.

The Attic prose rule distributes the modal particle (only ἄν, of course) and subjunctive and optative moods between independent and dependent clauses as follows:[7]

Independent Clauses	Dependent Clauses
subjunctive	subjunctive + ἄν
optative + ἄν	optative

In conditional sentences this distribution takes the following form:

Apodosis	Protasis
subjunctive	εἰ + ἄν + subjunctive
optative + ἄν	εἰ + optative

This pattern of complementary distribution adequately describes a large percentage of Attic prose instances of these two moods and the modal particle. Leaving aside for the moment extremely rare and textually controversial constructions, there are three sorts of expressions that do not fit the pattern:

1. The so-called "pure optative" or "cupitive" without ἄν in main clauses expressing a wish. This construction, which is met rather less often

---

6. Palmer, "Hom.," p. 165.
7. The chart shows only the constellation of these three elements, and does not apply to constructions in which ἄν is never used with one of the moods, e.g., clauses of fearing, where ἄν is never joined to the subjunctive.

than one might suppose, has special lexical and semantic tendencies. Most instances are introduced by εἴθε or εἰ γάρ; simple εἰ, attested twice in tragedy (Soph. *OT* 863 lyr., Eur. *Hec.* 836), never appears in the prose of our period. Cupitives lacking these introductory words are most often preceded by vocatives, say ὦ Ζεῦ, or fall within a very limited lexical range: συνενέγκοι and νικῴη are especially frequent. (For examples of the cupitive see *GMT* §§722–27, K-G 1.226–28, Schwyzer, *Gramm.* 2.320–21.) The point is that there were means other than the absence of ἄν to mark a main clause optative as cupitive. (On possible instances of cupitives *with* the modal particle see Gonda, *Moods*, pp. 143–44.)

2. Final clauses, particularly those introduced by ἵνα or μή and followed by the subjunctive. The predominance of ἵνα over other conjunctions is of great importance because it has virtually ousted the other final particles in Herodotus, Aristophanes, the orators, and Plato (whereas Thucydides and Xenophon prefer ὅπως: *GMT* §§311, 313). The statistics for the various final particles (assembled from Weber's study in Goodwin, *GMT,* appendix III) show the predominance in orators of ἵνα over its competitors, and particularly over ὅπως ἄν and ὡς ἄν. Demosthenes, for instance, has ἵνα eighteen times more often than ὅπως and sixty-three times more often than ὅπως ἄν. (These statistics are confirmed by Amigues, *Subord.,* pp. 99–101.) In inscriptions, on the other hand, ἵνα is attested only twice, and ὅπως without ἄν followed by the subjunctive does not appear until 343 B.C. (Meisterhans, *Inschrift.,* pp. 253–54; Kühner-Gerth [2.385] regard ἄν as a mark of official cautiousness). The inverse relation of ἵνα to ὅπως ἄν does not, however, hold in Aristophanes or Plato. Simple μή in negative final clauses, though far less frequent than final particle + μή and very scarce in the orators, does occur some forty times in Attic prose (see *GMT* §315). The strict exclusion of ἄν from the company of ἵνα extends back to Homer and seems to have spilled over in large measure to ἵνα meaning "where" (see K-G 2.386–87, *GMT* §325 with note, Schwyzer, *Gramm.,* 2.674. Explanations for this phenomenon do not seem to me very convincing—see, e.g., *GMT* §311; Ruijgh, *"TE épique,"* §243). It takes no special pleading to interpret the violation of the scheme of Attic prose as inherited from the earliest language and reinforced by the predominance of ἵνα over those conjunctions that are followed by ἄν. (Exceedingly unusual in Attic writers, with the exception of the "half-Attic Xenophon," are the final constructions with ὡς ἄν and ὅπως ἄν + optative: see Goodwin, *GMT* §§329.2, 330, appendix IV, and Amigues, *Subord.,* chap. 3. These two must count as violations of the pattern.)

3. Intrusions of the potential optative into subordinate clauses are well attested. Fourth-century prose holds a number of passages in which ἄν joins the optative in the protasis of a condition, e.g., Dem. 21.212:

εἰ δ᾽ οὗτοι χρήματ᾽ ἔχοντες μὴ πρόοιντ᾽ ἄν, πῶς ὑμῖν καλὸν τὸν ὅρκον προέσθαι;

Goodwin (ad loc.) calls this "not an uncommon construction," but he exaggerates (lists at K-G 2.482–83, *GMT* §506, Schwyzer, *Gramm.*, 2.327). Schwyzer (2.685–86), who calls the normal Attic distribution, as in εἰ δυναίμην, ποιοίην ἄν, a "regressive arrangement" for the protasis, seems on safe ground in denying that the late-appearing Attic construction is connected with Homeric κε(ν) + optative. Though it is true that the "illegitimate" εἰ κε(ν) + optative appears to result from a purely mechanical contamination in the Delphic enfranchisement texts,[8] the Attic construction seems semantic. Since the ἄν does not follow immediately after the εἰ, which we would expect if the construction were mechanically imitative of subjunctive protases, grammarians are right to see a true potential optative, one taken into the apodosis to suggest that the conclusion of the condition depends not on a simple supposition but on a supposition whose truth or falsity is itself dependent on conditions contemplated by the speaker.[9]

The rule assigning ἄν to the subjunctive verb of indefinite relative clauses appears nearly absolute in prose (K-G 2.426), but the bare optative is far less rigorously required. Where the transmitted texts have such indefinite clauses with the optative and the modal particle, editors have been tempted to make unnecessary emendations, e.g., at Thuc. 7.48 ἐξ ὧν ἄν τις εὖ λέγων διαβάλλοι, where Stahl reads διαβάλλῃ. But only the optative without ἄν that refers to general or repeated past actions is common in prose (K-G 2.427–28). The optative, whether with or without the particle, in relative clauses not referring to the past is infrequent or very scarce in Attic prose. Kühner-Gerth offer the following specifics:

1. The construction without ἄν used as an equivalent of an ordinary potential optative + ἄν is found only in poetry (2.429).
2. The construction used as an equivalent of εἰ + optative is found occasionally in prose, but Xenophon is overrepresented in this category (2.429).
3. The construction with ἄν used as a potential optative has twenty-two citations (2.430–31).
4. The construction used as an equivalent of εἰ ἄν + optative, as in the

---

8. M. Lejeune, *Observations sur la langue des actes d'affranchissement delphiques* (Paris, 1939), §§16–18.

9. Wyse (ad Isaeus 5.32) argues that an analysis of several examples "in which the optative with ἄν after εἰ is intelligible and right" shows that the condition is present, not future. On Homeric εἰ + κε(ν) + optative (only once εἰ + ἄν + optative) see Ruijgh, "*TE* épique," §257.

"potential optative protasis" just discussed, is sporadically attested (2.431).

To a great extent, the pattern of complementary distribution holds for the modal transitions of *oratio obliqua* constructions in secondary sequence. It is exceedingly common for an optative to represent a subjunctive verb in a dependent clause of the *oratio recta* form, and, in conformity with the pattern, the *ἄν* that accompanied the subjunctive is dropped (for the rare instances in which the modal particle is retained see K-G 2.549, *GMT* §§692, 702, Smyth §2626). Now it is true that optative representations of the bare subjunctives in indirect questions and in clauses of fearing do not acquire an *ἄν*. This fact shows, I think, that the optional modal change was felt to emphasize the hypotaxis of the entire utterance, including the subjunctive clause that in the original form appears independent of the introductory verb (see Schwyzer, *Gramm.* 2.675). Logically enough, the optative was not used to represent either bare indicative in unreal protases or any indicative apodoses with *ἄν*; that would have introduced wholesale semantic mischief into *oratio obliqua*. (An optative + *ἄν* in *oratio recta* is never represented by a bare optative, simply because the omission of the modal particle was treated as the concomitant of the modal shift, not as a separable transformation.)

By contrast with Attic prose, Homeric usage allows the following combinations within a conditional clause that are forbidden or rare (according to which view one takes) in Attic prose:

εἰ + subjunctive in protasis: *Il.* 22.86 εἴ πεϱ γάϱ σε κατακτάνῃ

εἰ + *κε(ν)* + optative in protasis: *Il.* 5.273 εἰ τούτω κε λάβοιμεν

ἄν + subjunctive in apodosis: *Il.* 2.488 πληθὺν δ᾽ οὐκ ἂν ἐγὼ μυθήσομαι οὐδ᾽ ὀνομήνω

optative in apodosis: *Il.* 4.18 ἤτοι μὲν οἰκέοιτο πόλις Πϱιάμοιο ἄνακτος

Several conclusions, and one difficult question, emerge from this survey of Homeric and Attic prose usage. The constellation of subjunctive, optative, and the modal particle shows far more regularity in Attic prose. To this truism we may add that the three main modal differences between Homer and Attic prose (see above, pp. 121–22) have occurred without significant alteration in the use of the modal particle. To recapitulate, both the Homeric subjunctive used like a future indicative in independent clauses and the optative of present unfulfilled wishes required no *ἄν* or *κε(ν)*, and the conterfactual optative with the modal particle was discarded in favor of another construction, also with *ἄν*, but with a different mood. Except in this last instance, the semantic role of *ἄν* is negligible in the Attic system. Thus we can say that complementary distribution of *ἄν* in independent and dependent clauses with the subjunctive and optative is a semantically superfluous element in a scheme of stereotyped expressions. Or better, ἄν in this constellation is not primarily a marker of verbal mood. It would, however, be incautious to deny the particle any power to contribute nuance by its presence or absence (see addendum at end of chapter).

The stereotyping is not perfectly symmetrical. With the exception of final clauses, the assignment of ἄν to subjunctive dependent clauses and its absence from independent clauses are virtually complete (see, e.g., K-G 2.426 on relative + bare subjunctive); a morphological sign of this inflexibility is evident in the many contractions of words introducing subjunctive dependent clauses with ἄν, e.g., ἐάν, ἄν, ἤν, ὅταν (word order is also a factor here: see below, pp. 127–28). That the optative shows more variation is not surprising, since the mood is entering a decline. Within the classical period the existence of two sets of personal endings in many tenses is symptomatic; and the rapidity of decline can be seen in the comparative statistics for Aristophanes and Menander assembled by Poultney ("Synt. Comedy," pp. 370–73). (Not many centuries after our period the mood survives only in the *expression glacée*, μὴ γένοιτο.) Though I view the regularization as largely a mechanical process, the intrusion of potential optatives with ἄν into dependent clauses seems to me rather different. The "softened assertions" associated with "Attic urbanity"[10] are not originally, or exclusively, Attic, but they are a pronounced stylistic mannerism. That these potential optatives did not seep into everyday Attic as frequent, unconscious replacements for the indicative is made highly probable by their total absence from prose inscriptions (Meisterhans, *Inschrift.*, p. 248). Rather they are refinements easily adopted by *Kunstprosa*.

The semantic debasement of ἄν is well under way in the classical period. The ἄν in κἄν has lost so much of its grammatical force that it can stand before the indicative, as at Pl. *Men.* 72c κἄν εἰ πολλαὶ καὶ παντοδαπαί εἰσιν, ἕν γέ τι εἶδος τἀυτὸν πᾶσαι ἔχουσι. It appears with weakened modal significance in ὡσπερανεί, as at Pl. *Grg.* 479a φοβούμενος ὡσπερανεὶ παῖς τὸ κάεσθαι, where ὥσπερ might be substituted. Similarly, Koine Greek forces ἄν into unnatural association with all tenses of the indicative (even the perfect) following relatives (LSJ s.v. ἄν IV), ὅταν, and ἐάν. In Modern Greek κανείς ("anyone") the ἄν is a fossil. A comparable mechanical expression in English is the common "the fact that" when substituted for "that." In this expression the meaning of "fact" has become so degraded that one often hears it used for suppositions that the speaker is anxious to impugn. A New Jersey politician under indict-

10. Lammermann, *Urbanität*, pp. 58–64.

ment once told the press: "The fact that I am guilty of embezzlement and extortion I emphatically deny!"

The influence of word order on the employment of ἄν is great indeed. In his famous 1892 article, "Über ein Gesetz der indogermanischen Wort-stellung," Wackernagel investigated the ancient tendency of ἄν to take the second position in a clause, following immediately after introductory and emphatic words. In subordinate clauses with the subjunctive it is displaced from this position only by γάρ, γε, δέ, μέν, -περ, τε, and occasionally δή ("Gesetz," p. 379). The postpositive position is preserved most consistently after certain words: two such are οὐκ and ὅστις, and rather than break either of the two combinations Demosthenes wrote (18.206):

οὐκ ἔσθ᾽ ὅστις ἂν οὐκ ἂν εἰκότως ἐπιτιμήσειέ μοι.

ἄν post ὅστις S et L: om. cet.

Wackernagel ("Gesetz," p. 387) shows that ἄν adheres to its traditional place with special tenacity in subordinate subjunctive clauses; its position in subordinate clauses with other moods is far less restricted. He argues that this difference reflects the freer position of ἄν in main clauses:

> In classical Greek ἄν + subjunctive occurs only in subordinate clauses; therefore, what would have drawn ἄν away from its traditional place? In contrast, ἄν + indicative and ἄν + optative are not merely more frequent in main clauses than in subordinate clauses but also are frequently carried over from the main clauses. Necessarily, the customary positions that ἄν had in main clauses had to be carried over to the subordinate clauses in question. ["Gesetz," p. 392][11]

There is an analogous difference between relative clauses beginning with pronouns whose case is determined by their own clause and those in which the introductory pronoun is assimilated to the case of its antecedent. Most of the latter show ἄν following directly after the pronoun, whereas in the former the position of ἄν is variable. To Wackernagel this is an effect of the closer bond between main and subordinate clause created by the assimilation of the pronoun ("Gesetz," p. 390). Also, ἄν does not take postpositive position after a pronoun that introduces a main clause, e.g., Lysias 2.34 ὁ τίς ἰδὼν οὐκ ἂν ἐφοβήθη; ("Gesetz," p. 391).

The semantic function of ἄν increasingly drew the particle into close

---

11. We can rephrase the argument: subordinate clauses, the class to which subjunctive + ἄν is limited in classical Greek, regularly begin with a small repertory of words, e.g., εἰ, ὅς, ἕως, ὅταν. These are precisely the words immediately after which ἄν almost invariably follows. This accounts for the rigorously postpositive placement of ἄν in subordinate clauses in the subjunctive. Independent clauses have an immensely greater range of opening words, and therefore show ἄν in its traditional, postpositive position far less often.

proximity with words or word groups that it qualified, but not necessarily at the expense of the postpositive placement. Uneconomically, perhaps, ἄν may be repeated. Wackernagel interpreted the repetition as

> a compromise between the traditional impulse to have ἄν near the beginning of the sentence and the need that arose in the classical language to bring the particle near the verb and other portions of the clause. ["Gesetz," p. 399]

The repetition of ἄν becomes much less frequent in the fourth century, and is particularly rare in the orators. Wackernagel attributes this trend to the weakening of the tradition that favored the postpositive placement of ἄν ("Gesetz," p. 402). (G. L. Cooper III proposes, quite plausibly, I think, that within one semantic field an idiom of word order that postpones εἰ + ἄν in conditional protases with the subjunctive has the effect of generating an additional ἄν [= εἰ + ἄν]: "On the Supposedly Otiose ἄν at Demosthenes, 20,17," AJP 92 [1971]: 307–11.)

We have now sketched the background against which one can better judge both the unquestioned attestations of the "omitted ἄν" and the disputed examples. Insofar as there is no compelling semantic need for the modal particle, its occasional absence from a construction in which the rules of one sort of Greek, namely, Attic prose, require it should not be rejected out of hand, or necessarily explained as a literary reminiscence, or twisted into semantic curiosities.

Wackernagel explains the absence of ἄν where it was expected as simply a relic of an old usage: since ἄν has no cognate in other Indo-European languages, it is clear that the word is an innovation of Greek (*Vorl.* 1.236–37; Schwyzer [*Gramm.* 2.558] is, however, receptive to the proposal that ἄν is inherited from Indo-European and cognate with Latin *an* and Gothic *an*.) But since the innovation, if such it is, has won a predominant position as early as Homer, it seems most unlikely that the omission of ἄν in our period was recognized as an archaism per se. We have no reason to believe that Greek speakers of the fifth and fourth centuries could distinguish more or less archaic uses in Homer. On the other hand, a special aura must have surrounded constructions that deviated from even the poetic norm. (If Forbes and Palmer are correct in deriving ἄν from a false division of οὐ κάν [Palmer, "Hom.," pp. 90–92], the very word, and not just its semantic force, is a latecomer. That derivation has, however, been challenged: see D. J. N. Lee, "The Modal Particles ἄν, κε(ν), κα," AJP 88 [1967]: 45–56.)

The Potential Optative without ἄν

At the opening of this chapter I quoted Kühner-Gerth's description of the omitted ἄν as a mark of a poet's "freer mentality." I doubt that they quite approve of this quality of mind, for they would exclude it from Attic soil though recognizing it in Homer, Hesiod, Pindar, and Theocritus (K-G 1.226). In this program they are joined by many scholars. The instruments of ξενηλασία are two, textual emendation and an attempt to segregate apparent examples as somehow semantically different from "real" potentials. A review of some of the passages allowed or rejected by Kühner-Gerth and others will show, I believe, that the case against bare potential optatives is largely *a priori*.

Text and Provenience

Even the most skeptical will admit that Homer sometimes uses a bare optative with a potential sense, e.g., at *Il.* 15.45:

$$αὐτάρ τοι καὶ κείνῳ ἐγὼ παραμυθησαίμην.$$

The inclusion of ἄν at *Il.* 9.417 makes no perceptible difference (Chantraine, *Hom.*, p. 216):

$$καὶ δ᾿ ἂν τοῖς ἄλλοισιν ἐγὼ παραμυθησαίμην.$$

Because they show οὐ rather than μή, examples in the negative confirm that we are dealing with a potential, not a cupitive:

> *Od.* 14.122–23 ὦ γέρον, οὔ τις κεῖνον ἀνὴρ ἀλαλήμενος ἐλθὼν
> ἀγγέλλων πείσειε γυναῖκά τε καὶ φίλον υἱόν . . .

Even in Homer, however, the construction with the modal particle is far more common (Schwyzer, *Gramm.* 2.324).

Lyric

Enemies and friends of the potential optative without ἄν agree that the construction needs least defense in those types of poetry furthest removed from ordinary conversational Attic. Thus even Stahl (*Verb.*, p. 299), the most stiff-necked opponent of the construction, admits two examples from the lyrics of tragedy, though he is reluctant to allow any in dialogue. He tolerates the omission of ἄν at Aesch. *Ch.* 594–95 lyr.:

> ἀλλ᾿ ὑπέρτολμον ἀν-
> δρὸς φρόνημα τίς λέγοι . . .

To my knowledge, this reading has never been challenged. Stahl also allows Soph. *Ant.* 604–05 lyr.:

> τέαν, Ζεῦ, δύνασιν τίς ἀν-
> δρῶν ὑπερβασία κατάσχοι;

(Wecklein outdid Stahl as a regularizer of texts with his conjecture σὰν *ἄν*.) The epic possessive pronoun *τεός* is found in Pindar, Aeschylus (lyrics), and has been conjectured at one lyric passage each in Sophocles and Euripides (Müller is more accurate than Jebb in reporting the provenience of the word). Euripides does use *δύνασις* in dialogue at *Ion* 1012, but the *Ion* is not an early play, and we can regard the word as distinctly poetic at the time of the production of the *Antigone*.

Stahl's rejection of two other possible examples in lyric seems justified:

Aesch. *Ag.* 1163 doch.　*νεογνὸς ἀνθρώπων μάθοι·*

ἂν ἀίων· Karsten: *ἀνθρώπων* codd.

Schwyzer (*Gramm.* 2.325) accepts the transmitted reading, which presents the potential optative without *ἄν*, but the paleographic argument for Karsten's emendation seems strong (see Fraenkel). An occurrence of the construction in dochmiacs would, of course, be significant evidence of its stylistic status.

Soph. *OC* 1565–67　　　*πολλῶν γὰρ ἀνταλλαγὰν*
πημάτων ἱκνουμένων
πάλιν σφε δαίμων δίκαιος αὔξοι.

ἀνταλλαγὰν Buechler: *ἂν καὶ μάταν* codd.

Here the construction exists only as a conjecture.

Tragic Dialogue

The case against the construction is sometimes very weak:

Aesch. *Supp.* 727　*ἴσως γὰρ ἢ κῆρύξ τις ἢ πρέσβη μόλοι*

ἂν Burges: *ἢ* M

The repeated disjunctive *ἢ* of the manuscript requires no defense; the sole motive for the emendation evidently is to avoid the bare potential optative in dialogue.

At Soph. *OC* 170 the choice is between two unusual constructions, the potential optative without *ἄν* or a third-person deliberative subjunctive:

θύγατερ, ποῖ τις φροντίδος ἔλθοι;

ἔλθῃ A rec: *ἔλθοι* L rec

It is true that the subjunctive here, in Oedipus' mouth, would anticipate the mood of Antigone's question at 310:

ὦ Ζεῦ, τί λέξω; ποῖ φρενῶν ἔλθω, πάτερ;

(*ἔλθοιμι* would not scan.) But third-person deliberative subjunctives are comparatively much rarer in tragedy than the same construction in the first person: the only other example listed in *GMT* §289 and Kühner-Gerth 1.221–22 is *Aj.* 403 (which Harl rewrites as a potential optative without ἄν).

Stahl rejects the construction at Eur. *Hipp.* 1186:

$$καὶ\ θᾶσσον\ ἢ\ λέγοι\ τις\ .\ .\ .$$

Barrett remarks, "This ἢ λέγοι τις has no exact parallel, but seems inevitable. . . . There is certainly no easy remedy to hand: V's ἢ λέγει τις is evidently false, and conjecture can do no better than ἢ λόγοισιν (Wecklein . . .) and ἢ λέγειν τιν᾽ (Burges)." Many languages express the idea of rapid action by some idiomatic, non-high-style phrase: English, "before you could say Jack Robinson"; Italian, "In un batter d'occhio."[12] I would guess that θᾶσσον ἢ λέγοι τις is likewise drawn from colloquial speech.

If one follows the manuscripts, there is something of a parallel at Eur. *Andr.* 929:

$$πῶς\ οὖν\ τάδ᾽,\ ὡς\ εἴποι\ τις,\ ἐξημάρτανες;$$

πῶς οὖν ἂν εἴποι τις τάδ᾽ Pflugk: ὦδ ἐρεῖ τις Nauck

Both Stevens (ad loc.) and Barrett (ad *Hipp.* 1186) are dubious, adding to their fundamental doubt about the bare potential optative an objection to ὡς (Stevens: "hardly makes sense"; Barrett: "scarcely tolerable"). Murray accepted the transmitted reading. I am not sure it is impossible that Hermione is identifying πῶς οὖν τάδε ἐξημάρτανες; with the word ὡς ("thus") as familiar in content or formulation.

Eur. *IT* 1055, like the example from Aeschylus quoted at the beginning of this subsection, has a bare potential optative with ἴσως.

$$τὰ\ δ᾽\ ἄλλ᾽\ ἴσως\ ἄπαντα\ συμβαίη\ καλῶς.$$

Verrall places a dash after ἴσως, thereby producing an aposiopesis and a cupitive optative; Markland's ἴσως ἂν πάντα is less dramatic. I feel more confident in rejecting the former, though it was adopted by Murray. As we know it from the orators, aposiopesis suggests that the speaker has interrupted his thought, finding it somehow intolerable. Here the break proposed by Verrall would make the audience believe that Orestes was either despondent or impatient when considering the escape. Neither emotion seems appropriate after he has made the women's complicity the keystone of his tactics—ἑνὸς μόνου δεῖ, τάσδε συγκρύψαι τάδε (1052).[13]

12. C. Pekelis, *A Dictionary of Colorful Italian Idioms* (New York, 1965), p. 133.

13. "Where first two, then one, were condemned to die, there are now three who are threatened with death in the service of Apollo's rescue plan, yet all are now perfectly confident" (A. P. Burnett, *Catastrophe Survived* [New York, 1971], p. 59).

A few other iambic trimeter passages are discussed below, in the section titled "Semantic Reinterpretations."

Comedy
There is by no means an abundance of possible examples, but neither are they so few or so dubious that we can follow Stahl in barring them from the genre altogether. Stahl discusses only Attic comedy, but our list should start with Epicharmus 21 Kaibel:

> πρᾶτον μὲν αἴ κ᾽ ἔσθοντ᾽ ἴδοις νιν, ἀποθάνοις.

We may, in fact, have the potential optative without the modal particle early in our period, in Doric and in comedy.[14]

Stahl would alter the text of three comic fragments of the fifth and fourth centuries:

> Cratin. 370K "τίς δὲ σύ;" κομψός τις ἔροιτο θεατής . . .

Stahl conjectures κομψός ⟨σ᾽ ἄν⟩ τις ἔροιτο.

> Philetaer. 13.4K   θνητῶν δ᾽ ὅσοι
> ζῶσιν κακῶς ἔχοντες ἄφθονον βίον
> ἐγὼ μὲν αὐτοὺς ἀθλίους εἶναι λέγω·
> οὐ γὰρ θανὼν δήπουθεν ἔγχελυν φάγοις,
> οὐδ᾽ ἐν νεκροῖσι πέττεται γαμήλιος.
>
> οὐκ ἄν Dindorf: οὐ γὰρ codd.

The run of the passage seems to me to call for words introducing an explanation: "I say they are wretched because when you're dead you cannot . . ." With οὐκ ἄν the explanatory sentence stands as a bald, almost disconnected continuation.

> Amphis 20.4K στρέφοιθ᾽ ὅλην τὴν νύκτα, μηδὲ ἓν πλέον
>
> στρέφοιτ᾽ ἄν ὅλην Jacobs: τὴν νύκτ᾽ ἄν οὐδὲ Meineke

Meineke's is the superior emendation, for the article is expected; but Meineke himself commented, ". . . fortasse recte omittitur particular hoc loco."[15]

In Aristophanes I know of three possible instances:

---

14. Admittedly one could argue that the κα of the protasis is to be carried over to the apodosis, but I am not aware of any parallel instance of perseveration from a subordinate to a main clause (cf. pp. 140–41). The text has been disputed: see Kaibel's *apparatus*.

15. It would help us evaluate the text if we could be sure that οὐδέ was the correct negative conjunction. Unfortunately, μηδέ can also be defended.

Αν. 180 Ἐπ. πόλος; τίνα τρόπον;
Πι.   ὥσπερ εἴποι τις τόπος.

ἄν post ὥσπερ add. Dobree

An extra syllable is not metrically required. This passage joins Eur. *Hipp.* 1186 and *Andr.* 929 in presenting the bare potential optative with τις and a verb meaning "speak" in a short parenthetical phrase (Stahl omits this example.)

> *Lys.* 839–41: σὸν ἔργον εἴη τοῦτον ὀπτᾶν καὶ στρέφειν
> κἀξηπεροπεύειν καὶ φιλεῖν καὶ μὴ φιλεῖν,
> καὶ πάνθ᾽ ὑπέχειν πλὴν ὧν σύνοιδεν ἡ κύλιξ.

ἤδη Dobraeo auctore Dindorf (1837): εἴη R ἐστὶ S

Stahl is content with the manuscript reading εἴη, for it looks to him like a cupitive. But it is certainly inappropriate to make Lysistrata sound almost desperately wistful at this moment of crisis. Myrrhine's answer, ἀμέλει, ποήσω ταῦτ᾽ ἐγώ, seems to me the sequel of a courteous command; σὸν ἔργον with either ἤδη or ἐστί is rather more peremptory than a potential optative. Whether σὸν ἔργον is solemn (Sandbach ad Men. *Dys.* 630) or colloquial (Stevens, *Colloq. Eur.*, pp. 39–40) is difficult to say. I lean toward the Sandbach view. Stahl omits *Pl.* 438, where the tone is para-tragic, or at least solemn.

> ἄναξ Ἄπολλον καὶ θεοί, ποῖ τις φύγοι;

φύγῃ (corr. ex -οι idque ex -ει R) RV: φύγοι Φ

As at Soph. *OC* 170, both subjunctive and bare potential optative have manuscript authority.

Prose
IONIC
At Hdt. 3.127.3 Darius asks:

> ὑμέων δὴ ὦν τίς μοι Ὀροίτεα ἢ ζῶντα ἀγάγοι ἢ ἀποκτείνειε;

ἄν post τίς add. Schaefer

Stahl prints, but does not justify, the insertion of the modal particle. (For the semantic consequences of accepting the text as transmitted, see below.)

According to Stahl there are two possible examples in Hippocrates (1.95.2; 1.132.1). In the first he simply adds an ἄν; the text of the second is variously transmitted, a fact Stahl welcomes as sanctioning his dismissal of the manuscript with the bare potential optative.

ATTIC

The manuscripts of Thucydides hold no example of the construction (Stahl, Dessoulavy).[16] But Stahl's collection of examples in orators from Antiphon (in both *Tetralogies* and speeches for court delivery) to Hypereides, Plato, and Xenophon, not one of which he accepts as genuine, numbers over sixty. As Humbert puts it, "The rather large number . . . suggests caution" (*Synt.* §199). Stahl, aware that his list might lure the reader over to the other point of view, argues that ἄν is sometimes falsely interpolated (e.g., at Plat. *Lg.* 719b) and that superior manuscripts do not report the construction. I am more impressed that the only example he attempts to discredit on specifically philological grounds survives the attack:

Is. 1.36 οὐκ οὖν ἄρα ὑπὲρ ἡμῶν μᾶλλον ἢ ὑπὲρ σφῶν αὐτῶν εἶεν εἰρηκότες;

Stahl insists on substituting ἄν for οὖν because he believes that οὖν ἄρα is an "unexampled combination." But Denniston (*Part.*, p. 43) lists two instances from Plato and one from Xenophon. (On οὔκουν vs. οὐκ οὖν see Wyse ad loc. and Denniston, *Part.*, pp. 439–40).

If one could see a pattern of some sort in the collected examples, the probability that they are not random errors in transmission would rise considerably.[17] But these passages come from different subgenres of prose, and they also vary in tone and content. Since I see nothing poetical in them, I would not follow Dover in defending the omitted ἄν at Andoc. 2.19 on the ground that a poeticism would be appropriate at this period (rev. of Albini's ed., *CR* 76 [1962]: 35; cf. Wyse ad Is. 3.54: "The 'syntax of Parnassus' is out of place in a court-house."). I would rather say that "the addition of ἄν is not necessary,"[18] and not stipulate a general stylistic quality as conducive to the bare potential optative. There is, however, a concentration somewhat higher than one might expect of those words that attract ἄν into postpositive position (see below, pp. 141–42). Questions with forms of τίς or πῶς are well represented (nine instances are listed at K-G 2.230); I would not interpret these as semantically unified, i.e., similar because they are questions, since very few examples exist of questions formed without these words.[19] The significance of this lexical tendency is discussed below (pp. 134–42).

16. P. Dessoulavy, *De la particule ἄν dans Thucydide* (Neuchatel, 1895), p. 36. According to Dessoulavy, Thucydides holds 30 potential optatives in narrative and 144 in speeches, including the letter of Nicias (6.10–15). He does not include participles and infinitives with ἄν representing potential optatives.

17. This is a principle followed by A. C. Moorehouse in his work on another textual problem of enraging difficulty: "῎Αν with the Future," *CQ* 40 (1946): 2.

18. So Verdenius, "Notes on Plato's 'Phaedrus,'" *Mnem.* n.s. 8 (1955): 273.

19. Dem. 21.35, for instance, is exceptional among these bare potential optatives: ὁ τοιοῦτος πότερα μὴ δῷ διὰ τοῦτο δίκην ἢ μείζω δοίη δικαίως; (κἂν post ἢ add. Schaefer).

The best argument for allowing the omission of ἄν in prose is historical. Slotty (*Konj. u. Opt.,* pp. 85–86, 88–89) observes that the potential optative without the modal particle is widely, and securely, attested in Koine Greek of all types, whereas the construction with the modal particle is largely restricted to the more educated authors. It is difficult to believe that the more colloquial usage, the construction without the modal particle, erupted out of nothing in Hellenistic times. And if the bare potential optative was, as seems likely, a rather common element in colloquial Attic speech of the fourth century, its total exclusion from prose writing of the period would be surprising; other colloquial features certainly do appear in *Kunstprosa.* Still, I am inclined to see the growth in the number of prose examples in the fourth century as simply proceeding at a *slower* rate than the advance of the construction in colloquial Greek.[20]

Was the potential optative without ἄν colloquial or poetic in the fifth century? What I have already said in general about the possible examples in prose—that they are not noticeably poetic—is equally true of early and late examples. The high style (Pindar, tragic lyrics) did use the construction, but its nearly certain appearance in tragic dialogue and probable appearance in Old Comedy forbid our regarding it as markedly elevated. Its relative scarcity makes it difficult to classify as either a literary reminiscence or a colloquialism. Slotty (*Konj. u. Opt.,* p. 84) argues, rightly I think, that if the construction were borrowed from Homeric language, it would be used more frequently as a metrical expedient. And Aristophanes would exhibit far more examples if the construction had been heard every few minutes in the agora. I suspect, then, that in the fifth century the construction was not much more than a syntactical alternate to the usual form with ἄν, rare in all colloquial dialects and literary genres but excluded only from the most rigid and fastidious sorts of writing.

Semantic Reinterpretations: ἄν with Weakened Potential Force

Before examining the arguments whereby scholars have rejected the notion of potentiality in constructions without the modal particle, it is worthwhile considering how submerged the suggestion of potentiality in expressions *with* the particle can be.

The presence of ἄν does not guarantee that an optative is manifestly potential. Slotty (*Konj. u. Opt.,* pp. 142–43) lists seven passages in tragedy and comedy where a first-person optative with ἄν is used to express the speaker's assent to a command, e.g., Aristoph. *Eq.* 1107, 1110:

---

20. According to this view, Attic *Kunstprosa* of the fourth century was more resistant to colloquial speech than Slotty thinks (*Konj. u. Opt.,* p. 85).

Δη. ἀνύσατέ νυν, ὅ τι περ ποήσεθ᾽ . . .
Πα. τρέχοιμ᾽ ἂν εἴσω πρότερος.

The optative with ἄν is frequently used to give a command.[21] In Attic this construction is usually to be understood as more courteous than the imperative (Lammermann, *Urbanität*, pp. 72–78). The civility of the potential optative must derive, ultimately, from the notion that the person addressed might do otherwise than act as the speaker suggests. Wackernagel (*Vorl.* 1.237) points out that the construction could sometimes lose its genial nuance, as is clear from Aristophanes' rephrasing of a Hesiodic(?) maxim (338 M-W), μήτε δίκην δικάσῃς, πρὶν ἀμφοῖν μῦθον ἀκούσῃς:

ἦ που σοφὸς ἦν ὅστις ἔφασκεν· "πρὶν ἂν ἀμφοῖν μῦθον ἀκούσῃς
οὐκ ἂν δικάσαις."

V. 725–26

Bare Optative as an Imperative

It is important to realize that the slide from potential to imperatival force that we see here has occurred within a class of expression that has become conventional in one dialect. It does not imply that optatives can be freely interpreted as imperatives. There seems, therefore, little reason to follow Gildersleeve in his interpretation of two bare optatives in Pindar:

O. 3.44–45   τὸ πόρσω δ᾽ ἐστὶ σοφοῖς ἄβατον
κἀσόφοις. οὐ νιν διώξω. κεινὸς εἴην.

κεῖνος D^(ac): κενὸς ἄν Wackernagel: κενεὸς ? Schroeder

Gildersleeve comments: "κεινὸς εἴην: 'Set me down an empty fool' (if I do). There is no omission of ἄν."

P. 10.21–22   θεὸς εἴη
ἀπήμων κέαρ·

αἰεὶ Schneidewin: εἴη codd.

Gildersleeve: "θεὸς εἴη = θεὸς ἔστω. . . . Schneidewin's αἰεί is unnecessary, nor need we take εἴη as = εἴη ἄν. 'Let him that is free from heartache be a god.' 'Set him down as a god.'" Both examples are easily understood as potential optatives if we regard them as purely hypothetical,

---

21. Wackernagel, *Vorl.* 1.237. Orestes' order to Aegisthus at Soph. *El.* 1491, χωροῖς ἂν εἴσω σὺν τάχει, strikes some readers as bitterly ironical in its politeness (Lammermann, *Urbanität*, p. 76). With Slotty (*Konj. u. Opt.*, pp. 96–97) I refuse to see any sort of humor here.

contingent on states of affairs that Pindar clearly identifies: pursuit of τὸ πόρσω and being ἀπήμων κέαρ.

There are two credible instances in the *Oresteia* of bare optatives used as commands addressed to τις; they are identical in grammar, but dramatically rather different. Agamemnon wants his sandal removed:

> . . . ὑπαί τις ἀρβύλας
> λύοι τάχος, πρόδουλον ἔμβασιν ποδός.
>
> *Ag.* 944–45

Clytemnestra calls for an ax:

> δοίη τις ἀνδροκμῆτα πέλεκυν ὡς τάχος.
>
> δοίη Mˢ: δ***M: δότω Heyse
>
> *Ch.* 889

It is noteworthy that both speakers demand a quick response. Clearly these optatives were not felt as potential.

Bare Optative as a Cupitive

We have already considered two passages presenting bare optatives that some have called cupitives rather than potentials (Eur. *IT* 1055 [p. 131], Aristoph. *Lys.* 839–41 [p. 133]). The presence or absence of the modal particle is normally a functional feature distinguishing conditioned and unconditioned processes, respectively.[22] But just as it is true that ἄν stands with optatives expressing some aspect of the speaker's intention (which can neighbor, at least, on his desires), so it is also possible for the notion of condition to enter a clause lacking the particle and render an optative more potential than cupitive. This is, I believe, the correct explanation of Eur. *Ph.* 1200–01, which Kühner-Gerth (1.226) say can be interpreted as a wish:

> καλὸν τὸ νικᾶν· εἰ δ᾽ ἀμείνον᾽ οἱ θεοὶ
> γνώμην ἔχουσιν εὐτυχὴς εἴην ἐγώ.
>
> ἔχοιεν V et γρ. M

Murray's punctuation, a dash between ἔχουσιν and εὐτυχής, makes it appear that the chorus is deflected from completing a normal conditional apodosis. I would rather leave the condition uninterrupted, for it makes perfect sense for the chorus to say, "I would be lucky *if* the gods adopt a more favorable sentiment." There is something impious about breaking the connection between the gods' disposition and a human's fortune. The

22. Gonda, *Moods*, pp. 135–36.

next line, in fact, links divine will and human fortune: Jocasta says καλῶς τὰ τῶν θεῶν καὶ τὰ τῆς τύχης ἔχει (ἔχοι Μ).

A cupitive interpretation seems even less likely to be correct at Pind. *O.* 11.19–20:

> τὸ γὰρ ἐμφυὲς οὔτ᾽ αἴθων ἀλώπηξ
> οὔτ᾽ ἐρίβρομοι λέοντες διαλλάξαιντο ἦθος.

Here Gildersleeve's adherence to a theory of the optative as originally expressing wish makes little sense if synchronically interpreted: "διαλλάξαιντο: 'May change.' This is a survival of an abandoned use of the opt[ative], according to which the wish generated the thought." We cannot imagine a man confronted by a lion and wishing it would behave like a rabbit, then proceeding to regard such a transformation as even barely possible. It is abnormal for a wish to become a delusion.

In fairness to Gildersleeve, he does not bring in this genetic theory each time a bare potential optative occurs. For instance, he would accept as possible the addition of τάχ᾽ before εὕροις proposed by Bergk at *P.* 10.29–30:

> ναυσὶ δ᾽ οὔτε πεζὸς ἰὼν εὕροις
> ἐς Ὑπερβορέων ἀγῶνα θαυμαστὰν ὁδόν.

With τάχ᾽ we would have "the optative being used in the old potential sense." (Hermann proposed κεν, Moschopulos and Triclinius ἄν in different positions.)

Bare Optative as a "Remote Deliberative"

Aesch. *Ag.* 620 οὐκ ἔσθ᾽ ὅπως λέξαιμι τὰ ψευδῆ καλά.

Editors have let the reading stand because they recognize constructions introduced by ἔστιν ὅς (Homer), and ἔστιν ὅστις, ἔστιν ὅπως, and ἔστιν ὅποι in Attic poets as forming "a class by themselves" (Goodwin, *GMT* §241).[23] There are two examples in Aristophanes. *Th.* 871–73, part of the *Helen* parody, is tragic through and through:[24]

> τίς τῶνδ᾽ ἐρυμνῶν δωμάτων ἔχει κράτος,
> ὅστις ξένους δέξαιτο ποντίῳ σάλῳ
> καμόντας ἐν χειμῶνι καὶ ναυαγίαις;

I would not hesitate to call this particular sort of construction a feature of

---

23. See also K-G 2.429. Formally we are dealing with a type of dependent clause, but since the relative clause acts as a *de facto* subject, it is functionally independent.
24. See Rau, *Paratrag.,* p. 59 for particulars.

tragic syntax if it were not for the second Aristophanic example, *V.* 471–72:

ἔσθ᾽ ὅπως ἄνευ μάχης καὶ τῆς κατοξείας βοῆς
εἰς λόγους ἔλθοιμεν ἀλλήλοισι καὶ διαλλαγάς;

ἔλθοιμεν V: ἔλθωμεν RT

Here, if the syntax is tragic, it stands alone among words that look stylistically neutral.

Sidgwick (appendix I of his edition of the *Choephoroi*, pp. 80–81) includes examples of this sort as part of a larger set, one not formally stereotyped but semantically, and therefore grammatically, similar; in his view they are not really "conditionals without ἄν" (what I have been calling potentials without ἄν) but "deliberatives," or "dubitatives." They are optatives, rather than subjunctives (the mood one expects in deliberatives), because "the optative expresses the remoteness, not as usual . . . of *pastness,* but of possibility; the instinct is to express by optative something *more out of the question* than the subjunctive would have expressed." Unlike Goodwin and Kühner-Gerth, he admits as possible two prose examples, one a direct question, Dem. 21.35 πότερα μὴ δῷ διὰ τοῦτο δίκην ἢ μείζω δοίη δικαίως; (κἄν add. Schaefer), and one an indirect question, Pl. *Euthd.* 296e οὐκ ἔχω πῶς ἀμφισβητοίην (ἄν add. Heindorf).[25] Jebb (appendix on Soph. *OC* 170) endorses Sidgwick's position, adding that the optative "differs from this [the deliberative] subjunctive by expressing something more remote from the sphere of the practicable." He raises the criterion of practicability to a textual principle when favoring the insertion of ἄν at *OC* 1418 and *Ph.* 895.

This theory has little to recommend it. A strong refutation was made as long ago as 1894 by W. G. Hale.[26] Hale argues *inter alia* that the "wild impossibility" of propositions placed in this construction is simply not there. When Apollo asks Thanatos

ἔστ᾽ οὖν ὅπως Ἄλκηστις ἐς γῆρας μόλοι; (Eur. *Alc.* 52)

he is asking, "*Might* she then be spared?" and is not portraying Alcestis' imminent death as a certainty.[27] I would add that the Sidgwick-Jebb theory would make nonsense of Hdt. 3.127.3 (already quoted above, on p. 133). There the bare optative could not suggest that the assassination or capture

---

25. I do not see why Fraenkel (ad *Ag.* 620) says, "That passage would in any case belong to a different type."

26. "'Extended' and 'Remote' Deliberatives in Greek," *TAPA* 24 (1893): 190.

27. Though she does not speak of an omitted ἄν, Dale's comment is in accord with Hale's interpretation: "the opt[ative] is more tentative than the subj[unctive]."

of Oroetes was beyond the "sphere of the practicable," for if it did Darius would have scared off any volunteers. Hale also shows that in two instances (Aesch. *Ch.* 585–95; Eur. *Alc.* 48–52) potential optatives with *ἄν* establish the meaning of the constructions without the modal particle that follow.[28]

The use of the negatives *οὐ* and *μή* presents a further obstacle to the Sidgwick-Jebb theory. The deliberative subjunctive is negatived by *μή*, but negative examples of the alleged "optative deliberative" are almost invariably construed with *οὐ*, as at Pl. *Euthd.* 291e: *οὐ τὴν ὑγίειαν φαίης* (*ἄν* add Ast). We might say that the *οὐ* contributes to the idea that the verbal action is impractical, but this line of argument would make all potential optative clauses, not just "deliberatives," less hypothetical. The outcome would be to force together what the theory was meant to separate.

Some scholars have categorized interrogative forms with the bare optative where one would expect an *ἄν* as a subclass of the "remote deliberative" (e.g., Thompson ad Pl. *Meno* 97c); others leave at least those direct questions with no obvious proximity to deliberative subjunctives as true potential optatives (so K-G 1.230).[29] Scholars of the first group claim that these optatives are "exclamations, rather than interrogations." Both groups distrust the transmission of bare optatives in prose and tend to insert the particle or mentally carry it over from a preceding *ἄν*. I think we may safely call an expression interrogatory if it is followed by an answer, e.g., Pl. *R.* 352e:

> *ἔσθ᾽ ὅτῳ ἂν ἄλλῳ ἴδοις ἢ ὀφθαλμοῖς;*
> *οὐ δῆτα.*
> *τί δέ; ἀκούσαις ἄλλῳ ἢ ὠσίν;*
> *οὐδαμῶς.*

ἄν post ἀκούσαις add. Ast

Though it is clear that the question implies Socrates' expectation that his interlocutor will agree with him, it is still sufficiently like other interrogatives to be treated as such. It is less clear whether we have a true optative without *ἄν* or whether the *ἄν* of Socrates' first question persists long enough to be felt with *ἀκούσαις* (Thus LSJ s.v. *ἄν* D. IV. 1). Clear instances of perseveration of *ἄν* exist, e.g., Aesch. *Ag.* 1049.

---

28. Hale, "'Extended' and 'Remote' Deliberatives in Greek," pp. 193–94.

29. Thus K-G (1.230–31) call Eur. *IA* 523 *πῶς ὑπολάβοιμεν λόγον;* (*ὑπολάβοιμ᾽ ἄν* Markland) a potential optative, but not Theoc. 27.24 *καὶ τί, φίλος ῥέξαιμι;* The latter they call unique, as they approve the editors' insertion of *ἄν* into the other apparent examples. (K-G add a number of examples of alleged "deliberative optatives" in indirect questions, none of them in their view textually above suspicion.)

πείθοι' ἄν, εἰ πείθοι'· ἀπειθοίης δ' ἴσως.

Hermann (quoted by Fraenkel ad loc.) reasonably comments, "Recte omittitur ἄν in altero membro orationis, quod ita comparatum est, ut pro parte eius sententiae, cui additum est ἄν, haberi possit." But here the distance from one optative to another is very short indeed, and the potential sense is further aided by ἴσως. The tendency of prose writers to repeat ἄν seems to me evidence that it is a short-lived particle, unlikely to linger in the ear over the stretch we find in the passage from the *Republic*.[30]

Finally, let us consider, as we did at the opening of the section titled "Semantic Reinterpretations," another eccentric optative with the particle. What Ameis-Hentze say about πῶς ἄν + optative expressing a wish applies *mutatis mutandis* to "depotentialized" potential optatives: "Even in wish questions the interrogative word serves to express the possibility of the notion, so that the underlying idea is: in what way is it conceivable? is there no way at all by which you might bring it about? could you not somehow or other?"[31] It is perfectly possible to translate these expressions simply as wishes, but only by paying a price in nuance. Similarly, one can sometimes translate the bare optatives we have been considering as deliberatives or exclamations, but at the risk of losing the suggestion of contingency that clings to the optative mood.[32]

Word Order and the Omitted ἄν

From the strictly semantic point of view, there is no reason why the constructions οὐκ ἔστιν ὅστις, ἔστιν ὅποι, etc., should favor the potential optative without ἄν; nor is there anything about the meaning of interrogatives and negative sentences that renders the modal particle less necessary. Further, it is somewhat surprising that examples of the alleged "remote deliberative" in dependent clauses slightly outnumber those in independent clauses: Hale, who sees this distribution as a defect in the Sidgwick-Jebb theory, counts seven or eight examples in dependent and five in independent clauses.[33] The explanation for all these distributional features may lie in a phenomenon of word order.

To demonstrate one mechanical aspect in the employment of ἄν I have

---

30. Cf. A. H. Sommerstein, *BICS* 24 (1977): 79, who argues that the ἄν at Aesch. *Supp.* 1047 carries over to make the optative at 1050–51 potential. Blass (see Fraenkel ad *Ag.* 1328, n. 2) goes further than most in claiming that at Aesch. *Ch.* 595 one can supply the modal particle from the preceding strophe.

31. Quoted by Fraenkel ad *Ag.* 622.

32. Contingency seems detachable from the mood only in the stereotyped command, though there too it is often present (cf. above, pp. 136–37).

33. "'Extended' and 'Remote' Deliberatives in Greek," p. 187. As suggested above (n. 23), the distinction between dependent and independent clauses is not easily applied here.

summarized part of Wackernagel's study of enclitic word order (above, pp. 127–28). Wackernagel, of course, considers the placement of ἄν when it does occur in the text and the generation of extra ἄν's. But his observations have significance for the omitted ἄν as well. First, and most generally, the coexistence of the relatively more mobile ἄν and the traditional postpositive ἄν might have contributed to the omission of ἄν by diminishing the semantic value of the traditionally placed ἄν. That is, the semantic disadvantage of the postpositive ἄν position motivates the repetition of a functional, mobile ἄν, and in so doing, makes the postpositive ἄν increasingly dispensable.

More specifically, the constructions and words we have been discussing are among those that most consistently draw ἄν to its traditional position. On the syntagma οὐκ ἔστιν ὅστις, Wackernagel ("Gesetz," p. 386) observes that "where the main clause obtains its content from the subordinate clause, and thus the connection of the two clauses is especially close, the ἄν regularly follows directly after the relative." And ἄν rigorously assumes second position after τίς and πῶς ("Gesetz," p. 394). I offer the guess that as long as the postpositive placement of ἄν was a strong reflex of the language, an author or speaker would be discouraged from using ἄν once he passed the traditional second position in the clause. The option of constructing a potential clause without ἄν was always available, if rarely chosen. Whatever the motive for leaving out the modal particle, in my theory its omission became obligatory as soon as one failed to insert it as a postpositive; the mixture of defeating the strong expectation of ἄν in postpositive position and later supplying the particle was not tolerated. One might say that the postponed ἄν would appear later not quite as itself but as a vengeful and unwelcome ghost. We may add that if metrical convenience prompted the omission of ἄν, the advantage to poets in so doing lay more in the elimination of a syllable either long or short than of a short syllable, since one can rather easily make position with the ν; there seems to be no predominance of either short or long syllables in the spot where the ἄν is expected.

The Bare Subjunctive in Dependent Clauses

Fifth-century texts have considerably more examples of omitted modal particles in subjunctive dependent clauses than in optative independent clauses. This difference may be connected with the word-order phenomena discussed above (pp. 127–28, 141–42), but if so the effect is not uniform among genres and dialects. As compared with the bare potential optative, the provenience of dependent clauses (conditional, relative, and temporal) with the subjunctive but no modal particle is more certain: broadly, the omission of ἄν or κε(ν) is well attested in poetry but extremely rare in Attic prose. The main task of this section will be to give a more refined account of the construction's provenience and to investigate its origin and semantic force.

Archaism and Semantics

Since the modal particle was not obligatory in the earlier language, its omission in the classical period is, prima facie, an imitation of the older usage. In recent times scholars have been content to remark only on the apparent merely formal archaism of the construction. Homeric language is often specified as the model, e.g., "in the omission of ἄν poetry repeatedly follows the epic usage" (Groeneboom ad Aesch. *Sept.* 257). Most commentators of this persuasion, however, hedge slightly, e.g., "probably a Homeric survival" (Webster ad Soph. *Ph.* 764), "perhaps under epic influence" (Sideras. *Aesch. Hom.*, p. 241). I have not seen these qualifications defended, but I will argue that they are indeed necessary. Page (ad Eur. *Med.* 516–17) simply calls the bare subjunctive "a fairly common archaism," and this seems to me a more accurate statement.

Semantic interpretations, which reigned in the nineteenth century, have largely vanished. In my view they are worth reconsideration. The two most interesting, because they are the most easily tested, were formulated by Campbell and Gildersleeve. Campbell ("Lang. Soph." §27) held that "ἄν . . . is omitted . . . in hypothetical and relative clauses with the subjunctive . . . partly because the verbal inflexion is made to supply the meaning of the particle, and partly because of the poetical tendency to greater generalization." Gildersleeve treats the bare subjunctive in conditions as a phenomenon separate from relative and temporal clauses lacking ἄν; and he distinguishes between the Pindaric and Attic uses of the construction. The former he sees as an imitation of a Homeric preference for the bare subjunctive in generic statements.[34] On the tragedians he writes:

> εἰ with the subj[unctive] in Attic approaches in tone the harshness of εἰ with the fut[ure] ind[icative]. This is due in all likelihood to the exclusively imperative use of the pure subj[unctive] in Attic . . . we shall not go far wrong if in the particular condition we make the significance of the Attic conditional εἰ with the subj[unctive] = εἰ δεῖ w[ith] inf[initive] . . .[35]

---

34. "Pind. Synt.," pp. 436, 443.
35. Ibid., p. 442; cf. Gildersleeve, "On εἰ with the Future Indicative and ἐάν with the Subjunctive in the Tragic Poets," *TAPA* 7 (1876): 5ff.

We will soon evaluate these semantic theories by examining a number of examples. Here I will remark only that we should reject Gildersleeve's suggestion that the construction reflects the tone of the voluntative, or, as he says, "imperative" subjunctive. Unlike the bare subjunctive in protases, the voluntative subjunctive is restricted largely to the first person, especially the first-person plural (Goodwin, *GMT* §§256–58). This difference and the clear conditional force of εἰ would, I am sure, overwhelm any voluntative force persisting in the subjunctive from normal main-clause exhortations like ἔλθωμεν.[36]

At least as regards Pindar, Gildersleeve has incorporated the theory of Homeric imitation with a semantic interpretation. But it is not certain by any means that Gildersleeve was right to assume that Homeric usage included ἄν or κε(ν) when referring to a particular circumstance and omitted the particle in general assertions. For instance, no single event is described at *Il.* 1.166–67:

> . . . ἀτὰρ ἤν ποτε δασμὸς ἵκηται,
> σοὶ τὸ γέρας πολὺ μεῖζον . . .

The prevailing contemporary view, that the presence or absence of ἄν or κε(ν) in these dependent clauses in Homer has no clear semantic force, seems to me well founded.[37] If we deny the alleged distinction in Homer it follows that Greek writers of our period could not have meant the bare subjunctive in subordinate subjunctive clauses, *qua* archaism, to convey some special nuance. Even if one believes that the inclusion or omission of the particle is significant in every relevant Homeric passage, it is prudent to avoid the assumption that any tendency in later authors to employ these bare subjunctives in a certain way proves descent from an epic model. The Homeric legacy is simply too unclear to permit such a line of reasoning.

This is not to say that it is fruitless to investigate the etymology of the modal particles in Homeric subordinate subjunctive clauses. The problem is partly that one must look through a veil of discrepancies among the various types of clauses. Relative clauses, for instance, differ from the others in appearing more often *without* the modal particle (*GMT* §538).

---

36. Not that the nineteenth century was unanimous in seeing a semantic distinction here: see, e.g., Ellendt, *Lex. Soph.* s.v. εἰ 6; and Kamerbeek ad Soph. *El.* 770 is *more* interested in semantics than most twentieth-century scholars are.

37. See the criticisms of Monro and Chantraine by R. H. Howorth, "The Origin of the Use of *AN* and *KE* in Indefinite Clauses," *CQ* 49 (1955): 72–77. Howorth finds that "in Homer's temporal and conditional, as in his relative, clauses with the subjunctive, there is a strong tendency to put ἄν or κε if the reference is to the future, regardless of whether they are concerned with a particular case or not; and if they refer to the present or past, there is a weaker tendency for them to be without these particles" (pp. 76–77). Cf. also Gonda, *Moods*, pp. 139–42.

Further, the regularizing process, which culminated in the system of complementary distribution largely observed by Attic prose (see above, pp. 122–25), was well under way in Homeric language, producing contaminations like the Iliadic passage quoted in the last paragraph. Now, a semantic cause for the virtually obligatory inclusion of the particle in clauses with εἰ in later Greek (especially prose) can be devised, e.g., "a process which exists only in the mind of the speaker is dependent on certain conditions and circumstances in a larger number of cases . . . than actual or merely contingent processes" (Gonda, *Moods*, p. 176). But once leveling occurs, the original semantic motive for adding the particle to individual clauses is forgotten: the regularization is bound to deprive the particle of its semantic function. And the character of specific protases is by no means the only factor in the uniformization of subjunctive conditional clauses:

This development may to a certain extent be ascribed to the more vivid and distinct character of the εἰ clauses with the particle,—vivid constructions tending to be automatically reproduced—, to a tendency to differentiate between the contingent εἰ + opt[ative] and the construction under consideration and to a preference for an uniform εἰ, ἄν, ἐάν + subj[unctive] construction. [Gonda, *Moods*, p. 142]

Dialect

The association of the modal particle with subordinate subjunctive clauses is a Panhellenic feature, but Attic is more rigorous in this respect than several other dialects. Attic inscriptions show not one example of omitted ἄν in relative, temporal, or conditional clauses (Meisterhans, *Inschrift.*, pp. 236–37, 251–52, 255–56). The modal particle is, on the other hand, omitted in Cretan in conditional clauses employing the present subjunctive[38] introduced by ἤ (= εἰ), in Locrian, and in Doric treaty language (Thuc. 5.77.6, 8). Omission is also attested in relative clauses in Cyprian and Rhodian, and in Arcadian.[39] Literary attestations (other than in dactylic hexameter or elegiac poetry (include Sappho 31.7 L-P[40] and Simonides 542.28 P. We may add Alcman 56.1–2 P:

> πολλάκι δ᾿ ἐν κορυφαῖς ὀρέων, ὅκα
> σιοῖσι Fάδη πολύφανος ἑορτά . . .

---

38. Whereas it is obligatory with the aorist subjunctive (Stahl, *Verb.*, p. 296).
39. Bechtel, *Gk. Dial.* 1.381, 2.40; Stahl, *Verb.*, p. 296.
40. Also 30.7, 34.3, 98.3.

Though the meter of the poem is dactylic and some phrases may be borrowed from epic, he does here use the strictly Doric ὅκα.[41]

Most important, though, is the evidence of Ionic prose, which is partly epigraphic. An inscription from Erythrae reads:

ἦμ μὲν . . . , εἰ δὲ μή, οἷς θέλῃ. [Bechtel, *Gr. Dial.* 3. §315; Garbrah, *Erythrae*, pp. 135–36]

This is, of course, scanty evidence. Attestations of the construction in Ionic *Kunstprosa* are more abundant.

Stahl (*Verb.*, p. 296) observes that ἄν is optional in temporal clauses introduced by πρίν, ἐς ὅ, μέχρι, and ἄχρι in Herodotus and Hippocrates, and is actually excluded altogether from clauses beginning with πρότερον ἤ and πρὶν ἤ. Democritus writes μέχρι σμικρὰ ᾖ (278.4 D-K). Relative clauses are well attested with the bare subjunctive, e.g., Hdt. 1.216.1:

τῆς γὰρ ἐπιθυμήσῃ γυναικὸς Μασσαγέτης ἀνήρ, τὸν φαρετρεῶνα ἀποκρεμάσας πρὸ τῆς ἁμάξης μίσγεται ἀδεῶς.

τῆς . . . Μασσαγέτης om. R ἐπιθυμήσει CDPS[V]

It is not certain, however, whether conditional clauses with bare subjunctive protases are an Ionic feature. Stahl lists two examples from Herodotus. In the first (8.62.2) Themistocles says:

ἀλλ᾽ ἐμοὶ πείθεο. εἰ δὲ ταῦτα μὴ ποιήσῃς, ἡμεῖς . . . κομιεύμεθα ἐς Σῖριν . . .

ποιήσεις D P

Stahl favors ποιήσεις, as he thinks the verb should stand in the same mood as the preceding clause, εἰ μενέεις. It is probably wrong to insist on parallelism here. Themistocles' whole speech is vehemently expressed— the introductory words are λέγων μᾶλλον ἐπεστραμμένα; but the tone could well undergo some sort of modulation after ἀλλ᾽ ἐμοὶ πείθεο. There is urgency in the second example too: the κυβερνήτης says to Xerxes (8.118.3):

δέσποτα, οὐκ ἔστι οὐδεμία (sc. σωτηρία), εἰ μὴ τούτων ἀπαλλαγή τις γένηται τῶν πολλῶν ἐπιβατέων.

εἰ a P Const.: ἢν d

Both Herodotean examples, then, show the sternness that Gildersleeve sees in εἰ + future and εἰ + subjunctive conditional clauses.

41. The οι in ἔχοισα is probably a literary borrowing, not a genuine Doric form: see E. Risch, "Die Sprache Alkmans," *MH* 11 (1954): 34, 37.

Stahl strangely attributes Thucydides' numerous bare subjunctive temporal clauses to his alleged nearness to tragedy. This seems perverse, coming a few lines after an account of Ionic practice in these clauses. It is surely easier to regard these constructions as dialect borrowings; a temporal clause is an odd thing to send out in buskins when conditional clauses are hardly, if ever (see below, pp. 161–64), permitted to violate the rules of Attic prose.

Several other scraps of evidence from Attic milieus connect the construction to Ionic. The conditional form has been conjectured by Dover (ad Thuc. 6.21.1) in one clause of the decree, generally dated not later than 450, modifying judicial relations between Athens and Phaselis. Though it records a decree of the Athenian assembly, the Phaselites were ordered to pay for the inscription, and this explains why it was written in Ionic letters.

> [. . . . 8 . . . . , ε]ἰ μὲν καταδικάσ-
> [ηι . . . (IG i².16.18–19 = Meiggs-Lewis GHI 31)

Others restore καταδικάσει, but there are secure subjunctives at lines 15–16 and 20.[42] Homogeneity of mood would, however, be achieved at the cost of a variation in the opening word of each of these three clauses, for ἐάν is on the stone at 15 and is a probable restoration at 20, but it is impossible at 18. The variation ἐάν/εἰ seems to me more probable than an excursion into the future indicative. If there were to be a shift in nuance, it should occur at 20, where a fine of 10,000 drachmas is stipulated for transgressions of all the foregoing rules.

Two possible instances of bare subjunctive in temporal clauses occur in Antiphon: 1.29 πρὶν . . . ὧσι . . . καὶ γιγνώσκωσι and 2.α.2 οὐ πρότερον . . . ἤ . . . ποιήσωνται (ποιήσονται N). The first is accepted by Stahl, the second by Cucuel (Antiph., p. 102). Since the first speech falls in the relatively more Attic part of Antiphon's rhetorical work, it appears that Antiphon regarded these constructions as less blatantly Ionic than, say, -σσ- for -ττ- (see above, pp. 6–7, 10).

I conclude, then, that contemporary dialects, particularly Ionic, may have had a part in influencing poets to omit the modal particle in subordinate subjunctive clauses.

Empedocles, Parmenides, and the Homeric Model

In their hexameter poetry Empedocles and Parmenides adopt many

---

42. The second of these is mentioned by Wade-Gery, *Essays in Greek History* (Oxford, 1958), p. 181, n. 1.

features of Homeric style. If the bare subjunctive construction were perceived as an epicism by those authors, we could expect that they would make liberal use of it. But I find only one possible example of the type, εὖτ' ἐθέλῃσθα at Emp. 101 Wright (111 D-K).5, a reading transmitted by Clem. *Strom.* 6.30.2 (for the subjunctive verb form see Schwyzer, *Gramm.* 1.662) against all other accounts of the text, which have ἦν.

Pindar, Bacchylides, and the Homeric Model

Of those Greek authors who use the subjunctive in conditional clauses, Pindar is the only one who never includes the modal particle. His practice in regard to subjunctive relative clauses is roughly congruent with the distribution seen in Homer: the bare subjunctive predominates. Temporal clauses are also close to the Homeric pattern (cf. below, pp. 151–52).[43] The last two constructions may perhaps be Homericisms, but not the conditional clauses, as they differ from Homeric conditional clauses in two important respects. First, the protasis that predominates by a great margin is no subjunctive at all, but the indicative.[44] Second, Pindar eliminates the contrast between the two types of subjunctive protasis. Though we can hardly deny the possibility that he derived the bare subjunctive protasis from Homer, it is clear that Pindar establishes a *system* of conditional clauses peculiar to himself.

It might be argued that *Pythian* 4 indicates a Homeric origin for the omission of ἄν in subjunctive protases: in that epinician, which is written in dactylo-epitrites and has as strong an epic flavor as can be found in the Pindaric corpus, bare subjunctives account for two of the four conditional clauses.[45] But it can be said on the other side that bare subjunctives also occur in other meters, e.g., Aeolic (*N.* 7.12), that the dactylo-epitrite, used twenty-four times in epinicians, is too common a Pindaric meter to evoke especially strong epic association, and that in statistical terms we should be more impressed that the sole conditional clause in *Olympian* 7, a much shorter poem with no particularly epic tone, is a bare subjunctive.[46]

Bacchylides stands farther from the Homeric repertory of conditional clauses than Pindar. In his epinicians (all but three are in dactylo-epitrites)

---

43. *Pindar,* cvi–cvii. Gildersleeve lists seven relative clauses with the modal particle, six without.

44. Gildersleeve, *Pindar,* cvi–cvii and *TAPA* 7 (see n. 35). There are few unreal conditions; on these see D. C. Young's discussion of *P.* 1.1 ἤθελον . . . κε: *Three Odes of Pindar* (Leiden, 1968), p. 28, n. 2.

45. Following Gildersleeve's list.

46. *O.* 7.3. I think δωρήσεται must be a short-vowel subjunctive (so Boeckh and Gildersleeve), not a future indicative (so Veitch).

I have found four instances of *εἰ* + indicative,[47] one of *εἰ* + optative,[48] and none of *εἰ* + subjunctive, with or without modal particle. The latter is, in fact, totally absent from his preserved *oeuvre*, though *αἰ* + *κε* + subjunctive occurs in a "dithyramb" (17.64–65) that, though not lacking Homeric touches (e.g., *πόντονδε* at 94), is metrically remote from dactylic hexameter.[49] Thus Bacchylides can tell us nothing about the Homeric descent of the bare subjunctive protasis.

Relative clauses with bare subjunctive predicates are less sparse in Bacchylides, but their treatment is not clearly drawn from a Homeric model. There are three subjunctives without modal particle, and an equal number (or possibly one more[50]) with *ἄν*; no relative clauses with *κε(ν)* + subjunctive occur.

We see, therefore, that there is no strong evidence linking the subjunctive in dependent clauses in these two poets with the syntax they knew from Homer. Nor is there a treatment of these constructions that can be called a generic characteristic of epinician poetry of the early fifth century.

Tragedy and the Homeric Model

Tragedy, as well, does not seem to provide any cogent evidence that the construction was felt as an epicism. An argument against the epicism doctrine, *e silentio* but not negligible, is the nearly total absence of these constructions from "messenger," or better, "formal narrative" speeches, for these are generally regarded as a locus of mild epic flavor.[51] The only possible exceptions I have come across are the following:

Aesch. *Sept.* [818]820 ἔξουσι δ᾿ ἣν λάβωσιν ἐν ταφῇ χθόνα.
Soph. *Tr.* 250–51   τοῦ λόγου δ᾿ οὐ χρὴ φθόνον,
                γύναι, προσεῖναι, Ζεὺς ὅτου πράκτωρ φανῇ.

The bare subjunctive of the relative clause has been left unmolested by editors. The chorus addresses Lichas as *κῆρυξ* (227).

Soph. *Aj.* 760–61 ἔφασχ᾿ ὁ μάντις, ὅστις ἀνθρώπου φύσιν
                βλαστὼν ἔπειτα μὴ κατ᾿ ἄνθρωπον φρονῇ.

        φρονῇ Lᵃᶜ Πᶜ rec. Stob. ecl.: φρονεῖ LᶜA rec. Stob. flor.

---

47. 1.165, 4.11, 11.27, 13.199.
48. 5.190.
49. Campbell, *Lyr. Poetry,* pp. 434–35.
50. 7.8, 9.23–24, 16.117 (dithyramb in dactylic meter); ⟨ἄν⟩ at 5.193.
51. See Page ad Eur. *Med.* 1141, Dodds ad Eur. *Ba.* 765–68, 1066, Barrett ad Eur. *Hipp.* 1194; against epicism, L. Bergson, "The Omitted Augment in the Messengers' Speeches of Greek Tragedy," *Eranos* 52 (1954): 121–28. Dodds's remarks seem to be a sufficient answer to Bergson.

The reading is uncertain (Jebb: "here there is little to choose between indic[ative] and subjunct[ive]"). Moreover, the passage stands outside the messenger's narrative per se as it quotes the seer's words.

Soph. *OT* 1230–31   τῶν δὲ πημονῶν
                            μάλιστα λυποῦσ᾽ αἲ φανῶσ᾽ αὐθαίρετοι.

αἲ L^{ac}: αἲ ᾽ν (αἲ ἂν) L^cA rec.

Present general and future "more vivid" conditional clauses cannot be expected to abound in accounts of past events, but sententious remarks are very frequent,[52] and, as will be seen, a large proportion of bare subjunctives occur in gnomic statements. The two or three examples in formal narrative are therefore considerably fewer than we would expect.

A high incidence of the construction in lyric sections would suggest that it was perceived as highly elevated and, perhaps, as a Doricism. In fact, nonlyric uses are *more* common. This needs to be emphasized, since commentators and grammarians usually hint at or maintain the reverse. Groeneboom, for example, says that "the subjunctive after ἄν appears, under epic influence, not only in lyric sections . . . but also in dialogue" (ad Aesch. *Pers.* 791). Ellendt (*Lex. Soph.* s.v. εἰ 6) states that the bare subjunctive protasis is found especially in lyric parts of tragedy because it is a deviation from normal Attic. The figures, which take into reckoning many uncertain examples, are as follows. The list is not claimed to be exhaustive, but I warrant the omissions to be random, not tendentious.

Bare Subjunctive Protases in the Tragedians

	Iambic	Lyric	Anapestic	Trochaic
Aeschylus				
Conditional	3[53]	1[54]	2[55]	—
Relative	4[56]	—	—	—
Temporal	3[57]	2[58]	—	—
Subtotal	10	3	2	0
Sophocles				
Conditional	6[59]	2[60]	—	—

52. Especially to cap long speeches.
53. *Pers.* 791; *Ag.* 1327–29; *Eum.* 234.
54. *Supp.* 92.
55. *Ag.* 1338, 1339.
56. *Sept.* 257, [818]820; *Eum.* 211, 661.
57. *Supp.* 338–39; *Eum.* 338–39, 661.
58. *Ag.* 763–67; *Ch.* 360.
59. *Aj.* 496, 520–21; *Ant.* 710; *OT* 917; *OC* 508–09, 1442–43.
60. *OT* 198, 873–75.

Relative	8[61]	3[62]	—	—
Temporal	10[63]	3[64]	—	—
Subtotal	24	8	0	0
Euripides				
Conditional	2[65]	—	—	2[66]
Relative	4[67]	1[68]	—	—
Temporal	—	—	—	—
Subtotal	6	1	0	2
Totals for all tragedians by construction	40	12	2	2
Total of all constructions:	lyric: 12	nonlyric: 44		

Semantic Aspects

We return now to the question whether the omission of the modal particle in subordinate subjunctive clauses favors statements of general significance (the Campbell thesis) or of bleak necessity (the Gildersleeve thesis) or both. I confine my discussion largely to the relative and conditional clauses for a number of reasons. First, my strong impression is that temporal clauses do not undergo a change of connotation by losing the customary ἄν. The flavor would, of course, be different, but only on a formal level not affecting meaning. Second, the lexical effect complicates the issue: whereas εἰ is directly comparable to ἐάν, πρίν is not quite the same thing as πρὶν ἤ,[69] nor does the omission of ἄν with ὄφρα, a poetic word, have the same feel as the omission with a word common to prose and verse, like ἕως. The lexical problem is, in part, one aspect of the rather rapid change in temporal constructions in the classical period, e.g., the

61. *Aj.* 760–61, 1079–83; *Tr.* 250–51; *OT* 316–17, 1230–31; *El.* 770–71; *Ph.* 1360–61; *OC* 395.
62. *Aj.* 760–61; *Tr.* 1007–09; *El.* 1058–62.
63. *Aj.* 554–55, 742, 965; *Tr.* 148–49, 608, 946; *Ant.* 1023–26; *El.* 225; *Ph.* 764, 917.
64. *Ant.* 619; *El.* 225; *OC* 1224–27.
65. *IA* 1240; I include also *Rh.* 830, without thereby indicating any opinion on the play's authorship.
66. *Or.* 804–06, 1534.
67. *Alc.* 75–76; *Ion* 855–56; *Med.* 516–17; *El.* 972.
68. *Alc.* 978–79.
69. We must reckon, for example, with the movement of πρίν from adverb to conjunction: see J. Sturm, "Geschichtliche Entwicklung der Constructionen mit ΠPIN," *Beiträge zur historischen Syntax der griechischen Sprache* 3 (1882): 151–52.

emergence of the indicative and its increasingly strict association with negative assertions.[70] Third, the bare subjunctive in temporal clauses seems the least genre specific, since it is found in Ionicizing prose authors more often than the bare subjunctive in the other two types of clauses (see above, pp. 146–47).[71]

Pindar

I have not undertaken a close study of each instance of omitted ἄν in Pindar, but a cursory check confirms the conventional wisdom: he is scrupulous in avoiding the bare subjunctive for describing particular events. Most often, sentences containing bare subjunctive clauses prove to be plainly gnomic. The narrowest application I have seen (*O.* 3.11–14) describes any Olympic victor:

> ᾧ τινι κραίνων ἐφετμὰς Ἡρακλέος προτέρας
> ἀτρεκὴς Ἑλλανοδίκας γλεφάρων Αἰ-
> τωλὸς ἀνὴρ ὑψόθεν
> ἀμφὶ κόμαισι βάλῃ
> γλαυκόχροα κόσμον ἐλαίας . . .

Tragedy

As mentioned above (p. 143), Gildersleeve maintains that the conditional bare subjunctive had much the same harshness as εἰ + future indicative.[72] Comparing the εἰ + future indicative protasis to ἐάν + subjunctive, he holds that the latter enjoys "greater temporal exactness" but carries no "special tone."[73] Gildersleeve does not comment in these two articles on the relation of εἰ + subjunctive to ἐάν + subjunctive; his concern there

70. Cf. M. Griffith, *The Authenticity of 'Prometheus Bound'* (Cambridge, 1977), p. 191. As πρίν clauses are still in flux in the fifth century, I would hesitate to follow Griffith in looking to them for evidence bearing on the authorship of the work.

71. Gildersleeve, "Probs.," p. 140: "Nor are all spheres of ἄν to be judged alike, as we have seen in the case of ἕως and πρίν where the omission of ἄν may have offended the Attic ear as little as an occasional subjunctive would offend our own generation, which seems to be bent on the destruction of a mood that to most people is too vague to serve any useful purpose." Regrettably, there are but two short paragraphs reporting Gildersleeve's paper "On the Use of πρίν in the Attic Orators" (*PAPA* 12 [1881]: 23–24).

72. Gildersleeve triumphantly points out that the single, clear instance of εἰ with future indicative in Pindar, a poet with little to do with "gloom" or "menace," occurs in the paean on the solar eclipse, fr. 44 ("On εἰ with Future Indicative, or Statistics and Statistics," *The Johns Hopkins University Circular* 99 [June, 1892], n. p.). Sadly, his point relies on a discarded reading at line 13.

73. Ibid. Gildersleeve's 1892 paper is an answer to E. B. Clapp, "Conditional Sentences in the Greek Tragedians," *TAPA* 22 (1891): 81–92. The greater "temporal exactness" to which Gildersleeve refers has to do with the aspectual contrast (unavailable in the protasis with the future indicative) between present and aorist subjunctive (see Gildersleeve, "On εἰ with the Future Indicative . . . ," p. 7).

was with particular, not general, conditions, and in fact, general conditions are predominant in the bare subjunctive construction.

It is fruitful to examine the apodoses accompanying protases with and without the modal particle. The two types of protasis share several forms of apodosis, viz. potential optative, "timeless present," gnomic aorist, and imperative. The clear difference is that the future indicative often answers to ἐάν + subjunctive,[74] but rarely, perhaps never, to εἰ + subjunctive. The only possible exception I have seen is Eur. *Or.* 1534 troch (quotation in full: p. 158), where σῴζειν θέλῃ, the reading of M and A, is followed by κατόψεται.[75] What is excluded from the apodosis that goes with the bare subjunctive construction is precisely the tense usually excluded from the apodosis of general conditional sentences having ἐάν + subjunctive in the protasis. For example, contrast the apodoses with "future" and "generalizing" ἐάν's respectively, shown at Kühner-Gerth, 2.474–75; see also Goodwin, *GMT* §462, Smyth, §2295. This restriction points to a specialization of the εἰ + subjunctive type: formally considered at least, it resembles the normal form (with modal particle) used to express general hypothetical assertions.

But since there are some uses of the bare subjunctive form in particular conditions in tragedy (these will be cited below), we cannot explain the avoidance of the future indicative apodosis solely in terms of the rules of the normal construction. I think that the restriction was felt to point to the timelessness and certainly of the state of affairs that obtains if the circumstances specified by the protasis are fulfilled. The future indicative can express two sorts of propositions: (1) as a true indicative, "objective" statements about events that the speaker declares will occur imminently or in the more remote future (the prospective use) and (2) as a mood, statements of desire, intention, or necessity (the voluntative use).[76] Insofar as it is often difficult to distinguish these two elements, the modal sense can be compromised by the indicative, the indicative by the modal. I deduce that both the bare subjunctive protasis, whether with general or particular reference, and the ἐάν protasis in generalizations are meant to be free of this ambiguity.[77]

74. Canvassing the particular conditions assembled by Gildersleeve in his 1886 paper (see n. 35), I find that about one-half of the ἐάν + subjunctive protases are yoked to future indicatives in the apodoses. Future indicative apodosis sometimes, though less often, corresponds to εἰ + future indicative protasis, e.g., Soph. *El.* 465, *OC* 626–28.

75. Ignoring Aesch. *PV.* 1014, where the vvll. separate ἄν from πεισθῇς. Actually, ἔπεισι at 1016 would be a minor embarrassment, as εἶμι and its compounds sometimes function as presents in poetry (LSJ s.v. εἶμι I).

76. Schwyzer, *Gramm.* 2.290–93; Humbert, *Synt.* §§252–55.

77. I admit the possibility that the uses of the bare subjunctive form with particular references are merely secondary to more common generalizing uses, and derive their flavor from them.

We may test this theory as it applies to the bare subjunctive construction by examining individual examples in the tragedians, and at the same time consider the harshness of tone attributed to the construction by Gildersleeve.

AESCHYLUS

Of the tragedians, Aeschylus makes the most lavish use of the future indicative in protasis: Gildersleeve reckoned that this mood accounts for 73 percent of future conditions in his work as against 54 percent in Sophocles and 43 percent in Euripides.[78] Aeschylus uses the bare subjunctive no more than six times,[79] and he prefers to limits its use to statements of general application, though in this he is not as strict as Pindar. The two particular conditions he uses involve propositions whose validity extends beyond the dramatic situation. At *Pers.* 790–92 Darius answers the question, "How might we fare best in this situation (πῶς ἂν . . . πράσσοιμεν ὡς ἄριστα;)?"

> εἰ μὴ στρατεύοισθ᾽ ἐς τὸν Ἑλλήνων τόπον,
> μηδ᾽ εἰ στράτευμα πλεῖον ἦ τὸ Μηδικόν·
> αὐτὴ γὰρ ἡ γῆ ξύμμαχος κείνοις πέλει.

The expedition into Greece, expressed by the present optative, is but a plan; the numerical superiority of the Persian army, far from a hypothesis, is a fact, and a fact not only in 480 but a fact in 472 and a condition that all would assume was to endure pretty much forever. The ground for Darius' conviction—the protection afforded by the earth itself—is obviously a permanent advantage.

Eum. 232–34 holds the other apparently particular use. Apollo declares:

> ἐγὼ δ᾽ ἀρήξω τὸν ἱκέτην τε ῥύσομαι·
> δεινὴ γὰρ ἐν βροτοῖσι κἀν θεοῖς πέλει
> τοῦ προστροπαίου μῆνις, εἰ προδῶ σφ᾽ ἑκών.

ἤν Dindorf: ὃς προδῷ Weil

(The bare subjunctive protasis is contrary to the fact: this is, to my knowledge, unparalleled.) Betrayal of a suppliant by a god would subvert a religious premise of the greatest generality. Betrayal by a human would be inconsequential by comparison.

At *Ag.* 1338–42 anap. the construction exists only through the conjecture of two subjunctives.

---

78. "On εἰ with Future Indicative . . ." There is no simple relation between the frequency of εἰ + future to our construction.
79. Reported by Italie, *Index Aeschyleus* s.v. εἰ 7. C.

νῦν δ᾿ εἰ προτέρων αἷμ᾿ ἀποτείσῃ
καὶ τοῖσι θανοῦσι θανὼν ἄλλων
ποινὰς θανάτων ἐπικράνῃ . . .

ἀποτείσῃ Sidgwick: ἀποτείσαι Keck: -τίσει codd. ἐπικράνῃ Sidgwick: ἐπικράναι Keck: ἐπικρανεῖ FG, ἄγαν ἐπικρανεῖ Tr

Some emendation of the transmitted text is necessary to correct the
unmetrical ἐπικρανεῖ, and Fraenkel points out that the two verbs of the
apodosis ought to be syntactically parallel. Keck's brace of optatives seems
to me the inferior choice, for it would make the chorus sound foolishly
tentative, almost ostrichlike, only five lines before the cry of murder.
Assuming Sidgwick guessed right, the bare subjunctive is here used with
particular reference. The passage opens with gnomic reflections (τὸ μὲν εὖ
πράσσειν ἀκόρεστον ἔφυ, etc.) but soon focuses on Agamemnon.

The remaining examples are textually more secure. Both are found, as
Fraenkel observes (ad *Ag.* 1327–29), in "the context of a γνώμη." *Supp.*
92–93 lyr. is categorical but not ominous:

πίπτει δ᾿ ἀσφαλὲς οὐδ᾿ ἐπὶ νώτῳ,
κορυφᾷ Διὸς εἰ κρανθῇ πρᾶγμα τέλειον·

But at *Ag.* 1327–29, where only an iota is needed to restore the construction, the bare subjunctive introduces a thought most bleak:

ἰὼ βρότεια πράγματ᾿. εὐτυχοῦντα μὲν
σκιᾷ τις ἂν πρέψειεν, εἰ δὲ δυστυχῇ,
βολαῖς ὑγρώσσων σπόγγος ὤλεσεν γραφήν.

δυστυχῇ Victorius: δυστυχῆ codd.

SOPHOCLES

As is clear from the table on pp. 50–51, Sophocles is a devotee of the
bare subjunctive.[80] I suggest that his predilection for the construction
results from the merger of two tendencies of his style: the prevalence of
Ionicisms and the favoring of blended or analogically constructed syntax
(see Campbell, "Lang. Soph.," pp. 67–68, 87).

Conditional Clauses. All but two examples are frankly sententious:

Aj. 520–21 ἀλλ᾿ ἴσχε κἀμοῦ μνῆστιν· ἀνδρί τοι χρεὼν
μνήμην προσεῖναι, τερπνὸν εἴ τί που πάθῃ.

πάθῃ L rec: πάθοι Λ rec.

80. Even in satyr drama: *Ichn.* 145 (see Appendix B).

With the subjunctive, τερπνὸν εἴ που suggests that Ajax's pleasure may have been minimal; with the optative Tecmessa concedes more, that he may not have enjoyed even that small pleasure. This would, it seems to me, carry modesty beyond prudential limits. (John Herington suggests that the optative might be frequentative, the lapse into historical sequence excused by the appeal to Ajax's memory.)

> *Ant.* 710–11 ἀλλ᾽ ἄνδρα, κεἴ τις ᾖ σοφός, τὸ μανθάνειν
> πόλλ᾽ αἰσχρὸν οὐδὲν καὶ τὸ μὴ τείνειν ἄγαν.

κεἴ τις ᾖ rec: κεἴ τις εἰ L rec: κἤν τις ᾖ A Ven c

It is safe to assume that every syllable of the speech containing these lines meets the criterion of tact. What appears to be Haemon's hypothetical acknowledgment of a plausible exception to the rule—one might think that an indubitably wise man has no lessons to learn—is virtually the definition of a wise man. Creon is, of course, meant to identify himself with the ἀνήρ of the conditional clause. "Even if" must border on "since."

> *OC* 508–09   τοῖς τεκοῦσι γὰρ
> οὐδ᾽ εἰ πονῇ τις, δεῖ πόνου μνήμην ἔχειν.

πονῇ L Ricc b: πονεῖ ceteri

Unlike Tecmessa and Haemon, Ismene is not arguing a losing case. She has no reason to doubt that Antigone will heed her request to guard their father. The conditional clause concedes what is clearly true in her case, that the tendance of Oedipus is a great πόνος.

Also sententious is one lyric passage, *OT* 873–75:

> ὕβρις φυτεύει τύραννον· ὕβρις, εἰ
> πολλῶν ὑπερπλησθῇ μάταν . . .

εἰ] ἦν T

Two other examples in iambic trimeter are particular. *OC* 1442–43 is dismal: Antigone says to Polyneices

> δυστάλαινά τἄρ᾽ ἐγώ,
> εἰ σοῦ στερηθῶ.

A future indicative would certainly be appropriate here.[81]

OT 917 is variously reported by the manuscripts. Jocasta says of Oedipus that, unlike an ἀνὴρ ἔννους,

> . . . ἐστὶ τοῦ λέγοντος, εἰ φόβους λέγῃ.

εἰ Lᵃᶜ (ut videtur) rec.: ἦν LᶜA rec.: λέγοι Lᵃᶜ rec.: λέγῃ LᶜA rec.

---

81. Ellendt's note on this passage (*Lex. Soph.* s.v. εἰ 6) is obscure.

This cannot be a description of habitual cowardice: the dread reports of the present and the near future are at issue. Thus Jebb is right to reject the optative, "a statement of abstract possibility." Whatever construction most strongly suggests that messengers with fearsome tidings are en route is dramatically strongest.

Relative Clauses. There are only two instances in Sophoclean lyric. One is a complaint sung by Heracles and addressed to Hyllus:

> πᾷ ⟨πᾷ⟩ μου ψαύεις; ποῖ κλίνεις;
> ἀπολεῖς μ᾽, ἀπολεῖς.
> ἀνατέτροφας ὅ τι καὶ μύσῃ. (*Tr.* 1007–09)

The reference is particular: "You have stirred up[82] the pain that has fallen asleep." If there is any temptation to take the relative clause as general ("any and all pain"), it should be remembered that Heracles has just woken from sleep. Hyllus is charged with waking precisely those pains that have not yet woken with him.

In the other lyric example, *El.* 1060–61, the two coordinated relative clauses with bare subjunctive are part of a description of the customary *pietas* that birds offer their parents.

Among dialogue examples, only *OC* 395 refers to a particular person:

> γέροντα δ᾽ ὀρθοῦν φλαῦρον ὃς νέος πέσῃ.

πέσῃ codd: πέσοι Turnebus et edd. ante Brunckium

Oedipus is speaking of himself. Of course, the statement would hold for any man who meets calamity while young.

The remaining instances are found in generalizations. There is despondency each time, either in the sentence containing the relative clause or in the situation under discussion (the latter only at *Tr.* 250–51, where Lichas seeks to avoid opprobrium [see Jebb ad loc.]).

EURIPIDES

Conditional Clauses. There are, to my knowledge, only two possible examples, both in dialogue and both with particular references. At *Or.* 1534 troch. the bare subjunctive would be the syntactical parallel of an obviously minatory future indicative; I believe the parallelism of the two types of protasis is unique in tragedy, as is the future indicative apodosis.

---

82. The force of the perfect is: "so that it will always be awake."

εἰ γὰρ Ἀργείους ἐπάξει τοῖσδε δώμασιν λαβών,
τὸν Ἑλένης φόνον διώκων, κἀμὲ μὴ σῴζειν θέλῃ
σύγγονόν τ' ἐμὴν Πυλάδην τε τὸν τάδε ξυνδρῶντά μοι,
παρθένον τε καὶ δάμαρτα δύο νεκρὼ κατόψεται.

σῴζειν θέλει L P B: σῴζειν θέλῃ M A: σώσῃ θανεῖν V (sed εἶν in ras. v), γρ.
M γρ. B

Just possibly, the anomalous syntax is meant to reinforce the trochaic
rhythm in the representation of Orestes' excitement.

IA 1238–40 βλέψον πρὸς ἡμᾶς, ὄμμα δὸς φίλημά τε,
ἵν' ἀλλὰ τοῦτο κατθανοῦσ' ἔχω σέθεν
μνημεῖον, ἢν μὴ τοῖς ἐμοῖς πεισθῇς λόγοις.

ἢν Hermann: εἰ L P: εἰ . . . πείσῃ Elmsley: v. del Nauck

Iphigenia is in the extremity of desperation, but short of resigning herself
to death.

Relative Clauses. These are more numerous than conditional clauses and
are found in three metrical categories. All examples are sententious; with
the exception of *Ion* 856 and *Med.* 516, the contents are emotionally
neutral, or even optimistic:

Trochaic dialogue: *Or.* 806 (nisi leg. συντακεῖ [V])
Iambic dialogue: *Alc* 76, *Med.* 516 (nisi leg. ἢν [Clem. Alex., Stob.]),
               Ion 856, *El.* 972
Lyric: *Alc.* 978

Comedy
Conditional and Relative Clauses. I have no great confidence that Old
Comedy employed the bare subjunctive in either conditional or relative
clauses. In Aristophanes the number of candidates is few, and in all but
one case (*Ec.* 687–88) there is manuscript authority against the construction. Further, in only one instance did he incorporate the bare subjunctive
within an unmistakable parody of serious poetry, viz. *Av.* 928–30, a
takeoff on Pindar fr. 94B:[83]

δὸς ἐμὶν ὅ τι περ
τεᾷ κεφαλᾷ θέλῃς
πρόφρων δόμεν ἐμὶν τεῶν.

θέλεις ΜΥΓ: θέλῃς RVA

83. Some assign the fragment to the lyric *adespota.*

At *Eq.* 698–700 the bare subjunctive protasis is part of an oath spoken by Paphlagon and thrown back by the Sausage-Seller. The apodosis, moreover, is in the tense and mood avoided by the tragedians:

> **Πα.** οὗτοι μὰ τὴν Δήμητρ᾽ ἔτ᾽ εἰ μή σ᾽ ἐκφάγω
> ἐκ τῆσδε τῆς γῆς, οὐδέποτε βιώσομαι.
> **Πο.** εἰ μὴ ᾽κφάγῃς;

698 εἰ R: ἐὰν VΦ700 εἰ R: ἢν VΦ

At *Eq.* 805, where R and V agree on the subjunctive, the meter (recitative anapestic tetrameter) is one associated with exhortation, particularly in debates.[84] The evidence for bare subjunctive conditions in everyday Attic is thereby reduced to near invisibility. The protasis is again a future indicative (807: γνώσεται).

> εἰ δέ ποτ᾽ εἰς ἀγρὸν οὗτος ἀπελθὼν εἰρηναῖος διατρίψῃ,
> καὶ χῖδρα φαγὼν ἀναθαρρήσῃ καὶ στεμφύλῳ εἰς λόγον ἔλθῃ . . .

ἢν Dobree: εἰ codd: τρίψῃ RV: -τρίψει (εἰ in ras. Γ²) A² ΜΓ: -τρίψοι A¹: -θαρρήσῃ RV: -θαρρήσει (εἰ in ras. Γ²) A² Μ Γ: -θαρρήσοι A¹: ἔλθῃ RV: ἔλθοι (οι in ras. Γ²) Φ

The remaining three examples from complete plays of Aristophanes have in common a certain formality, in that they fall within lists:

> *Pax* 450–51   κεἴ τις στρατηγεῖν βουλόμενος μὴ ξυλλάβῃ
> ἢ δοῦλος αὐτομολεῖν παρεσκευασμένος,—

-λάβῃ, RVΓS: -λάβοι Meineke[85]

The speaker (Hermes, according to Zielinski's attributions) is here adding to a list of beneficiaries and victims of a prayer that Trygaeus begins at 433. Stahl (*Verb.*, p. 295) holds that an assimilation to the optative of wish (449: ἐσθίοι) is probable, but it is just as easy to suppose that the change of speaker at 449 does not interrupt the flow of conditional clauses at 444–45 and 447–48. These earlier protases (and, we might add, the relative clause at 440–41) are formed with indicatives, but as the passage in question is the last of the series it would be rash to insist on syntactical consistency.

> *Lys.* 580–81 anap.   τούς τε μετοίκους κεἴ τις ξένος ἢ φίλος
> ὑμῖν,
> κεἴ τις ὀφείλῃ τῷ δημοσίῳ, καὶ τούτους ἐγκαταμεῖξαι

84. White, *Verse* §§505–06.
85. Meineke marked his conjecture with a query: no sign of this caution exists in Stahl's reference.

κεῖ . . . ἦ Bergk[86]: κεῖ . . . ἦ ΡΓ: κῆν . . . ἦ Boissonade: ὀφείλῃ Γ: ὀφείλει R

Lysistrata is enumerating elements she would weave into the fabric of government at Athens. The construction is, though, but a conjecture.

Ec. 687–88 anap.　ὅτῳ δὲ τὸ γράμμα
　　　　μὴ 'ξελκυσθῇ καθ᾽ ὃ δειπνήσει, τούτους ἀπελῶσιν
　　　　ἅπαντες

The bare subjunctive is reported by all manuscripts, but Stahl (*Verb.*, p. 295) remarks that the writing of γράμμα in place of γράμμ᾽ ἄν would be a common sort of error. Blepyros' question (or statement: see Ussher) pertains to Praxagora's proposed system of chits, whereby citizens were to draw letters of the alphabet assigning them to various mess halls (684–86).

Finally, one Aristophanic *frustulum* recalls the penalty for failure to win one-fifth of the votes in a legal action:

Fr. 201K　εἰ μὴ μεταλάβῃ τοὐπίπεμπτον, κλαέτω

εἰ μὴ codd., οὐ μὴ Porson, Bekker ἦν μὴ Brunck

Since these four official-sounding examples have nothing to do with the practice of legal inscriptions, I regard them as enigmas.

Aside from Aristophanes, Old Comedy has, to my knowledge, only three other possible instances to show:

Cratinus 28K anap.　εἴ τις δ᾽ ὑμῶν κάλλει προκριθῇ
　　　　　　(Quoted at *Anecdota Graeca* 129.10 specifically to illustrate the omission of ἄν.

Crates 5K　εἰ σοφὸς ᾖ

Com. Fr. Adespot. K 360[87]　**A.** πρὸς θῆλυ νεύεις μᾶλλον ἢ 'πὶ τἄρρενα;
　　　　　　B. ὅτου προσῇ τὸ κάλλος, ἀμφιδέξιος.

ὅτου codd. ἵν᾽ ἄν vel ὅπου πρόσεστι κάλλος Kock

Temporal Clauses. There are even fewer examples of this type of bare subjunctive construction in Old Comedy. Here are all the possible instances known to me:

Aristoph. *Ra.* 1281–82　μή, πρίν γ᾽ ἀκούσῃς χἀτέραν στάσιν μελῶν
　　　　　　ἐκ τῶν κιθαρῳδικῶν νόμων εἰργασμένην.

86. According to Stahl (*Verb.*, p. 296), Bergk was here following Meineke.
87. = Plut. *Mor.* 766 = Trag. Adespot. 355N, variously regarded as comic (Kock), Sophoclean (Valckenaer), Euripidean (Cobet), or a tragic *adespotum* (Nauck). If comic, it may be from New Comedy.

(Van Leeuwen's note: "*ἄν*] inseruit Reisig,
Elmsley *μὴ μή, πρὶν ἄν γ᾽ ἀκούσῃς*, ne *ἄν*
particula anapaestum aperiat . . .")[88]

Aristoph. *Ec.* 628–29 anap.

*κοὐκ ἐξέσται παρὰ τοῖσι καλοῖς ⟨καὶ τοῖς μεγάλοις⟩
    καταδαρθεῖν
ταῖσι γυναιξὶν πρὶν τοῖς αἰσχροῖς καὶ τοῖς μικροῖς
    χαρίσωνται*

χαρίσονται R: *χαρί* Γ

(The indicative is unlikely. Goodwin, *GMT* §633 gives only one
example from Aristophanes, *Av.* 700.)

Aristoph. *Ec.* 750–52 *οὐ γὰρ τὸν ἐμὸν ἱδρῶτα καὶ φειδωλίαν
    οὐδὲν πρὸς ἔπος οὕτως ἀνοήτως ἐκβαλῶ,
    πρὶν ἐκπύθωμαι πᾶν τὸ πρᾶγμ᾽ ὅπως ἔχει*

πρὶν ἄν Porson

Cratinus 29 K *πρὶν παροῦσα διδάσκῃ*
(quoted with 28K: see above)

Com. Fr. Adespot. K 1235[89] *μὴ σπεῦδε γῆμαι, πρὶν τελευτήσαντ᾽ ἴδῃς.*

Prose
We have already discussed the prevalence of the bare subjunctive subordinate clause in Ionic prose and suggested that the Thucydidean and Antiphontean temporal clauses which omit *ἄν* are Ionicisms (pp. 146–47).
Conditional and relative clauses in Attic authors are attested so few times
that only the most guarded conclusions are possible.

I would set 399 as the *terminus ante quem* for the construction in Attic
prose, for our only strong candidates are found in Thucydides and Andocides 1.[90] Attic texts written thereafter do show a handful of possible
examples, but I am inclined to doubt them all for two reasons: (1) the total
number is small—some half-dozen conditions and ten relative clauses[91]
(2) the paleographic argument against the bare subjunctive in temporal
clauses is strong: in most cases a word beginning with alpha follows the
position where *ἄν* is expected.[92] Granted that temporal clauses are found

88. The objection to the anapest is a stringency not much believed in by more recent (i.e.,
twentieth-century) scholarship: cf. White, *Verse* §124.iv; Dover ad *Nub.* 876.
89. = Plut. *Mor.* 184b = Soph. fr. 601N. Again, the fragment may be from New Comedy.
90. MacDowell, *Andocides: On the Mysteries,* appendix J.
91. Stahl, *Verb.,* pp. 299–300.
92. Ibid. This is the sort of argument Stahl cannot use to impugn the potential optative
without *ἄν*.

only with the modal particle accompanying the subjunctive, the existence of the more recherché bare subjunctive in conditions and relative clauses is highly improbable.

The three examples from Thucydides are from speeches, which is probably not significant since less opportunity exists in narrative for the visualization of general conditions and future events. There are some points of contact with the pattern of usage seen in Aeschylus and Sophocles. At 6.21.1, the one conditional clause of the type, Nicias refers to a particular situation, but the envisaged circumstance is clearly undesirable:

πρὸς οὖν τοιαύτην δύναμιν οὐ ναυτικῆς καὶ φαύλου στρατιᾶς μόνον δεῖ, ἀλλὰ καὶ πεζὸν πολὺν ξυμπλεῖν, εἴπερ βουλόμεθα ἄξιον τῆς διανοίας δρᾶν καὶ μὴ ὑπὸ ἱππέων πολλῶν εἴργεσθαι τῆς γῆς, ἄλλως τε καὶ εἰ ξυστῶσιν αἱ πόλεις φοβηθεῖσθαι καὶ μὴ ἀντιπαράσχωσιν ἡμῖν φίλοι τινὲς γενόμενοι ἄλλοι ἢ Ἐγεσταῖοι ᾧ ἀμυνούμεθα ἱππικόν . . .

Hˢ (Parisinus gr. 1734), cj. Herwerden

Krüger (*Att.* §54.12. An. 3) accepts the bare subjunctive and maintains that in this construction "the idea of actuality or realization of the protasis predominates." This nuance would indeed fit Nicias' rhetorical ends nicely. In the atmosphere of this assembly he would overplay his hand with εἰ + future indicative, and yet he wishes to present the consequences of Sicilian unity against Athens as more than a mental projection. Perhaps ἐάν + subjunctive, and certainly εἰ + optative,[93] are too tentative. The suitability of the construction is slender evidence that Thucydides actually used it here, but my intuition is that he did. Many will, with Dover, find that "ἤν is tempting."[94]

A Spartan speech after the Athenian victory at Pylos contains two relative clauses with the bare subjunctive, both in general reflections and both in close proximity to the normal form with ἄν:

τοὺς δὲ λόγους μακροτέρους οὐ παρὰ τὸ εἰωθὸς μηκυνοῦμεν, ἀλλ᾽ ἐπιχώριον ὃν ἡμῖν οὗ μὲν βραχεῖς ἀρκῶσι μὴ πολλοῖς χρῆσθαι, πλέοσι δὲ ἐν ᾧ ἂν καιρὸς ᾖ διδάσκοντας . . . [4.17.2]

σωφρόνων δὲ ἀνδρῶν οἵτινες τἀγαθὰ ἐς ἀμφίβολον ἀσφαλῶς ἔθεντο (καὶ ταῖς ξυμφοραῖς οἱ αὐτοὶ εὐξυνετώτερον ἂν προσφέροιντο), τόν τε πόλεμον νομίσωσι μὴ καθ᾽ ὅσον ἄν τις αὐτοῦ μέρος βούληται μεταχειρίζειν . . . ἀλλ᾽ ὡς ἂν αἱ τύχαι αὐτῶν ἡγήσωνται· [4.18.4]

93. "The . . . condition . . . of the fancy. There is often an element of wish for or against, or hope, or fear" (Gildersleeve, *TAPA* 7 [1886]: 8).
94. In his school edition of the commentary (Oxford, 1965) Dover had written: "εἰ should be emended to ἤν."

One premise of Gomme's comment is that the construction in the first passage can be tolerated only by assuming a direct borrowing from poetry: "a trimeter scazon, as has been noted, and therefore, it is said, justifying the omission of ἄν. Since no hint is given that this is a verbal quotation, it would perhaps be better to insert ἄν in order to break the iambic rhythm." We cannot here assume the inadmissibility of a prosaic bare subjunctive relative clause without begging the question. And is it clear that the clause is too metrical for prose? An iambic rhythm is, according to Aristotle's well-known remark (*Rhet.* 1404a30–31), the closest to ordinary speech, and De Groot has demonstrated that Thucydides is nearly indifferent to prose rhythm, save for one favorite clausula (*A Handbook of Antique Prose-Rhythm* [Groningen, the Hague, 1919], pp. 21–29). Gomme's remark that there is no sign that a line of verse is being quoted is more secure: there are in fact no verse quotations in Thucydidean speeches. And choliambics, which are associated primarily with scurrilous poetry, seem singularly inappropriate to Spartan sobriety.

The second passage, a monstrous piece of Greek, presents a bare subjunctive with an ἄν. Normalizing the syntax would require either adding ἄν after οἵτινες and θῶνται or writing ἐνόμισαν. Curiously, editors have not made these suggestions, perhaps believing that after the interruption of καὶ . . . ἄν προσφέροιντο it would be easy for Thucydides to continue "as if οἵτινες ἄν had gone before" (Graves). There is also a chance of perseveration of the ἄν from the potential optative clause. I am unable to come to any conclusion about the true reading or rhetorical force of this example.

We have good reason to accept the transmitted text of Andocides 1.141:

. . . εἴ ποτέ τις αὐτοῖς ἢ τῶν ἐξ ἐκείνων τινὶ κίνδυνος γένηται ἢ συμφορά . . .

γένοιτο Dobree: γενήσεται Madvig

Poeticisms and Ionicisms occur here and there throughout Andocides (see p. 12), sufficient grounds to beware of emendations based solely on fourth-century Attic prose rules. And this passage from the peroration seems to me especially prone to purple embroidery. In §130 Andocides had used κληδών, he will use φιλότης at §145 and the phrase πᾶν πρόρριζον at §146; all three are poetic.[95] Albini[96] hears a "conversational

95. MacDowell, *Andocides*, p. 19; U. Albini, *Andocide: L'Orazione de Reditu*, pp. 29–30 lists additional Ionicisms. I observe that φιλότης appears in the Lysianic corpus only in the epideictic second speech.
96. *Andocide*, pp. 29–30.

tone" in the second clause of §141 (οὐδένας πώποτ᾽ ἐγὼ εἰπόντας οἶδα); I am not at all sure he is right about this phrase, and in any event the argumentation becomes more pointed by the time the clause in question comes around. The object of this section is to demonstrate "the foresight of And[ocides]'s ancestors in acting patriotically in order to save their degenerate descendant" (MacDowell ad loc. citing K. Jost). The argument would, I think, lose force if the fear of danger to later generations were expressed by a more abstract optative protasis. Madvig's future indicative is the better of the two emendations, but it seems to me quite unnecessary.

Addendum

In her thorough study *Les subordonnées finales par ΟΠΩΣ en attique classique,* Suzanne Amigues argues that ἄν strongly emphasizes the prospective sense of the subjunctive in final clauses introduced by ὅπως; she sees ὅπως + subjunctive as more abstract than ὅπως ἄν + subjunctive, i.e., the utterance calls less attention to the means or circumstances in which the process will come about (pp. 158–59, 163, 170–71).

I am not entirely persuaded that this nuance conditions the presence or absence of the particle, for several of the examples Amigues adduces to show that distinction or the distinction between voluntative and prospective subjunctive seem to me very much alike. Some instances: Aristoph. *Ec.* 116–17 ξυνελέγημεν ἐνθάδε, / ὅπως προμελετήσωμεν ἀκεῖ δεῖ λέγειν (p. 123) and Eur. *Heracl.* 335–38 κἀγὼ μὲν ἀστῶν σύλλογον ποιήσομαι, / τάξας δ᾽, ὅπως ἂν τὸν Μυκηναίων στρατὸν / πολλῇ δέχωμαι χειρί, . . . σκοποὺς / πέμψω (p. 150), both of which have the same subject in main and final clauses. Amigues cites the first to show that the subjunctive is not voluntative but prospective; why it is less prospective than the second she does not explain. She regards the complete absence of the construction with ἄν from sentences where the "action of the main clause does not depend on any identifiable wish" as significant (pp. 158–59); at first this does appear a decisive finding, but I cannot see that there is an "identifiable wish" in passages where "the action designated by the verb is referred to an obligation" expressed by the impersonal verbal adjectives in -τεον, or by δεῖ, χρή, etc. (p. 155). Isocrates 2, Amigues claims, shows the difference between ἵνα and ὅπως ἄν: τὴν δικαιοσύνην ἀσκοῦμεν . . . οὐχ ἵνα τῶν ἄλλων ἔλαττον ἔχωμεν, ἀλλ᾽ ὅπως ἂν ὡς μετὰ πλείστων ἀγαθῶν τὸν βίον διάγωμεν. She translates, "nous pratiquons la justice, non pour posséder moins que les autres, mais *bien pour obtenir ce résultat:* que nous passions notre vie au milieu de biens aussi nombreux que possible" (p. 150). Here, in fact, is an ἄν that *cannot* be assigned a semantic value contrasting with the bare ὅπως, for as Amigues herself points out (p. 170), Isocrates uses *only* the form with the modal particle.

6. Jussive, Optatival, and Exclamatory Infinitives

Three uses of the independent infinitive are usually considered as a group:

1. The jussive, or imperatival, e.g., Hdt. 3.134.5: σὺ δέ μοι ἐπὶ τὴν Ἑλλάδα <u>στρατεύεσθαι</u>. The jussive infinitive is found with both nominative subject, as here, and accusative subject, e.g., Aristoph. *Av.* 1040–41 <u>χρῆσθαι</u> Νεφελοκοκκυγιᾶς τοῖς αὐτοῖς μέτροισι καὶ σταθμοῖσι καὶ ψηφίσμασι καθάπερ Ὀλοφύξιοι. It is not always clear whether the subject of the infinitive is nominative/vocative or accusative. In the most famous example of the construction, Simon. 167 P ὦ ξεῖν᾽, <u>ἀγγέλλειν</u> Λακεδαιμονίοις . . . , the opening vocative suggests (but does not prove) that the subject of the infinitive, if one had to know for the purpose of adding modifiers in the correct case, was felt as nominative (for the close links between the nominative and the vocative see Wackernagel, *Vorl.* 1.306–10). The manuscripts of Lycurg. *Leocr.* 109 and D.S. 11.33.2 substitute the aorist imperative in quoting the epitaph; imperatival function in the face of infinitival form clearly makes for a *lectio difficilior*. Nevertheless, the vocative does not always exclude an accusative subject (see p. 182).

2. The optatival, e.g., Aristoph. *Ach.* 816–17 Ἑρμᾶ ᾽μπολαῖε, τὰν γυναῖκα τὰν ἐμὰν / οὕτω μ᾽ <u>ἀποδόσθαι</u> τάν τ᾽ ἐμωυτῶ ματέρα.

3. The exclamatory, e.g., Dem. 21.209 τοῦτον δὲ ὑβρίζειν· <u>ἀναπνεῖν</u> δέ.

In all three varieties the verbal notion contained in the infinitive comes under a modal qualification that the reader or listener apprehends from clues of context, genre, gesture, or tone, rather than from formal markers like imperative or optative endings, explicit governing verbs, or fixed combinations, e.g., εἴθε + optative (which indicates future wish).

I am here following a traditional organization of the material (see, e.g., Goodwin, *GMT* §§784–87). But Wackernagel (*Vorl.* 1.266–67) is probably right to insist on separating constructions with subject nominative or vocative from those with subject accusative. The latter quite plainly originate in the ellipsis of governing verbs like δός, εἴη, or εὔχομαι. The former are, in Wackernagel's view, true absolute uses (cf. Schwyzer [*Gramm.* 2.380], who derives both types from ellipsis). Inscriptions may open with formulae like Κλεινίας εἶπε that justify a subject accusative + infinitive, but the omission of such formulae is common (Meisterhans, *Inschrift.*, p. 248; Schwyzer, *Gramm.* 2.382–83). In the case of introductory words like θεοί or ὅδε νόμος, *verba dicendi* or *sentiendi* are perhaps faintly suggested. In the absence of any introductory phrase one cannot say whether the optatival or jussive infinitive was felt to have a warrant in an ellipsis or whether the stone itself, by announcing the genre, as it were, prepared the reader to understand that the verbal action designated by the infinitive was the command or wish of whoever commissioned the inscription.[1] The alternation, "for no obvious reason" (Schwyzer, *Gramm.* 2.382–83), of accusative + infinitive with -τω imperatives found on many inscriptions seems to me evidence against the connection of the infinitive with a governing verb in ellipsis. Such an alternation implies a parallelism, i.e., the modal equivalence of infinitive and imperative, which seems to suggest that the infinitive is intelligible without a governing verb, just as all imperatives are. It is hard to imagine that the putative omitted verb would be followed by both *oratio obliqua* (using the infinitive) and *oratio recta* (using the imperative). The genetic difference between subject nominative/vocative and subject accusative constructions seems to have some correlation with a difference, to be discussed shortly, in the way they are used in our period.[2]

Jussive and optatival infinitive are semantically very close, differing only insofar as the speaker variously estimates the efficacy of his will in bringing about some state of affairs; and both are attested before the classical period. The exclamatory infinitive is different in three respects: it presents a state of affairs that has already come into being, it deplores or is astonished by the state of affairs, and it is a construction for which there is no attestation before Aeschylus.

---

1. We see something a little less grand on *SIG* 1259 (Athens, 4th century B.C.), a short practical letter written on a rolled-up lead plate. The outside directs the bearer to the recipient with two jussive infinitives:

φέρειν ⟨ε⟩ἰς τὸν κέραμ-
ον τὸγ χυτρικόν,
ἀποδοῦναι δὲ Ναυσίαι
ἢ Θρασυκλ(ε)ῖ ἢ θυίωι.

2. But this difference, as well as that between jussive and optatival infinitive, sometimes shrinks to near invisibility. Consider, e.g., Anacreon 357P, where we have first a jussive infinitive with nominative subject (σὺ . . . ἐπακούειν) and then an optatival or jussive infinitive (δέχεσθαι) with subject accusative (τὸν Κλεόβουλον) understood. The tone does not change with the switch in construction. (I assume the retention of the transmitted δέ or δ' at 10; γ', Kan's emendation, turns δέχεσθαι into a complementary infinitive.)

Jussive Infinitive

For Gildersleeve the Greek infinitive was a centaur, a "marvelously mobile noun-verb" whose death was "an enormous, incalculable loss," a mutilation from which the language never recovered. Now Chiron was a great pedagogue, but Gildersleeve had begun his eulogy by speaking of the infinitive as the perfect pupil:

> The infinitive is not a mood, though it has been so accounted by ancient grammarians. A verbal noun, it has learned to represent all the moods, and, as the universal representative, has acquired modal rights. When we first become acquainted with it in Homer, it has learned to represent the indicative, and has taken on, though reluctantly, the negative οὐ. In obedience to the necessities of the indicative, it has developed a future, quite needless in its first estate. In fact, it has all the apparatus for *oratio obliqua* which the Greek handles so lightly, the Roman so heavily. But, as the dative of a verbal noun,[3] its natural affinities are with the imperative, and this imperative infinitive has a vigorous life at the beginning of our record. . . . As prose advances, the imperative infinitive recedes until it finds one last refuge, the conservative pale of legal language. The infinitive of law and decree, of prescription, direction, recipe, the infinitive of Attic decrees and of Xenophon's Hunter's Own Book, is an independent infinitive. No leading verb is necessary. It is simply old-fashioned, like the long imperative in Latin, and suits old-fashioned things like law, old-fashioned spheres like the sphere of venery.[4]

We have, then, in Gildersleeve's account, a picture of the jussive infinitive as an archaism that the developed prose of the fourth century dusted off for use in archaic contexts. This is partly true of the type with subject accusative but is not applicable to the more unruly variety with the subject nominative/vocative. The main puzzles here are (1) whether the second-person nominative/vocative jussive infinitive[5] of tragedy reflects a

---

3. The simple interpretation of all infinitives as formal and functional datives has been long discarded: see Schwyzer, *Gramm.* 1.358ff.; P. Burguière, *Histoire de l'infinitif en grec* (Paris, 1960), pp. 23–24.

4. *Probs.*, pp. 131–32.

5. This monstrously long designation is aesthetically displeasing but not otiose. The second person is most often found as the nominative subject of a jussive infinitive but sometimes as an accusative subject. At Aristoph. *Ach.* 1000–02 we might suppose that the vocative case persists as the unexpressed subject of the infinitive:

> ἀκούετε λεῴ· κατὰ τὰ πάτρια τοὺς Χοᾶς
> πίνειν ὑπὸ τῆς σάλπιγγος . . .

colloquial or high-style usage, (2) why Aristophanes avoids the negative form of the construction, and (3) why, if it truly is a more emphatic form of the imperative (as Kühner-Gerth [2.24] claim) or "has a solemn or formal force" (Smyth §2013), the orators, even the experimentalist Antiphon, found it unsuitable.

The jussive infinitive appears to be a Panhellenic phenomenon. The form with subject accusative is found in Attic, Ionic, Arcadian, Cypriot, Elean, Delphic, and Cretan legal and religious inscriptions. By contrast, the imperatival "potential optative" is restricted to inscriptions in Elean and Arcadian (Wackernagel, *Vorl.* 1.237–38). No literary evidence can be found for the jussive infinitive with second-person nominative/vocative subject in non-Attic dialects other than Homeric and Ionic, and the number of examples in Herodotus is quite large.[6] Nevertheless, there is no chance that Athenian writers regarded the construction as Ionic. Thucydides has only a few examples (see below, pp. 177–78), and Antiphon gave the construction no place whatever in his Ionicizing *Tetralogies*.

The Postpositive Rule

Kluge observed that the jussive infinitive has a strong predilection for frankly conditional sentences or those in which a condition can be easily supplied from the context (*Quaest.*, pp. 12–21). His remarks seem to have been generally ignored, probably because he indulged in considerable exaggeration, for instance, in seeing oracular responses as referred to a condition (p. 18)—oracles are questioned, not regularly presented with hypotheticals.[7] But the frequency of explicit conditions as the protasis to which the jussive infinitive forms the apodosis, when considered together with the structure of some examples that Kluge found recalcitrant, is most suggestive.

Kluge restricted himself to a narrow grammatical category; a simultaneously grammatical and rhetorical analysis is more fruitful. To begin with, a passage like Soph. *El.* 8–9, though not strictly speaking a condition, seems

---

But from other Aristophanic proclamations we see that this is not always so:

> Pax 551–52 ἀκούετε λεώ· τοὺς γεωργοὺς ἀπιέναι
> τὰ γεωργικὰ σκεύη λαβόντας . . .

(Is it possible that in the *Acharnians* the order πίνειν is not strictly parallel to ἀπιέναι in the *Peace* because the former applies to all, the latter to only one part of the population?)

6. Kluge (*Quaest.*, p. 19) lists the following passages (I have added subsection numbers): 1.32.7, 89.2; 3.35.2, 134.5, 155.5; 4.126, 163.3; 5.23.3; 6.86.5; 7.159.7, 209.5; 8.68.1; 9.48.4. All except the last are addressed to the second person.

7. Some oracles do, however, contain a more or less explicit condition, e.g., Hdt. 1.55.2: ἀλλ᾽ ὅταν ἡμίονος βασιλεὺς Μήδοισι γένηται, / καὶ τότε . . . / φεύγειν μηδὲ μένειν, μηδ᾽ αἰδεῖσθαι κακὸς εἶναι.

less anomalous if it is realized that the jussive infinitive is apodotic in the wider sense, i.e., forming a main clause:

> . . . οἵ δ᾿ ἱκάνομεν,
> φάσκειν Μυκήνας τὰς πολυχρύσους ὁρᾶν . . .

And leaving behind the distinction of subordinate and main clause and the often artificial boundaries established by modern punctuation, we come to the underlying rhetorical principle: the jussive infinitive of this specific variety is most often placed in a complex sentence or rhetorical structure in which it serves as climax or final member, or is at least "postpositive," i.e., it does not come first in the complex.[8] Aristoph. *Eq.* 1037–40 contains a jussive infinitive that both follows a mark of punctuation and is contained in a subordinate clause:

> ἔστι γυνή, τέξει δὲ λέονθ᾿ ἱεραῖς ἐν ᾿Αθήναις,
> ὃς περὶ τοῦ δήμου πολλοῖς κώνωψι μαχεῖται
> ὥς τε περὶ σκύμνοισι βεβηκώς· τὸν σὺ φυλάξαι,
> τεῖχος ποιήσας ξύλινον πύργους τε σιδηροῦς.

> φυλάξαι V¹: φύλαξαι RV²ΜΓ²: φύλασσε ΑΓ¹

This passage does, however, satisfy the requirements of the postpositive rule.

The postpositive rule accommodates nearly all the conditional examples collected by Kluge. Soph. OT 461–62 exemplifies the structure:

> . . . κἂν λάβῃς ἐψευσμένον,
> φάσκειν ἔμ᾿ ἤδη μαντικῇ μηδὲν φρονεῖν.

At Hdt. 3.134.5 the jussive infinitive in a true antithesis follows an imperative:

> ῎Ορα νυν, ἐπὶ Σκύθας μὲν τὴν πρώτην ἰέναι ἔασον· . . . σὺ δέ μοι ἐπὶ τὴν ῾Ελλάδα στρατεύεσθαι.

At Thuc. 5.9.7 there is simply the sequence. "First I . . . , then you . . .";

> ἐγὼ μὲν . . . προσπεσοῦμαι δρόμῳ κατὰ μέσον τὸ στράτευμα· σὺ δέ . . . ὕστερον . . . ἐπεκθεῖν καὶ ἐπείγεσθαι ὡς τάχιστα ξυμμεῖξαι.

(The clause beginning ὅταν ἐμὲ ὁρᾷς could, by itself, form a prelude to the jussive infinitive. But I see it as a parenthesis, secondary to the larger

---

8. I realize that the term normally means "not placed first *in a sentence or clause*," but have decided to apologize for the eccentric widening of the term with quotation marks only here.

"I . . . you" structure.) In Aristoph. *Ec.* 1144–46 the positive detailed command in the jussive infinitive follows logically redundant negatived future indicatives:

> οὔκουν ἄπασι δῆτα γενναίως ἐρεῖς
> καὶ μὴ παραλείψεις μηδέν᾽, ἀλλ᾽ ἐλευθέρως
> καλεῖν γέροντα, μειράκιον, παιδίσκον . . .
>
> καλεῖς Cobet: καλεῖν R. Ald.

Soph. *OT* 1459–67, where the jussive infinitive is linked to the preceding structure by a relative clause, also swells from negative to positive command:[9]

> παίδων δὲ τῶν μὲν ἀρσένων μή μοι, Κρέον,
> προθῇ μέριμναν· ἄνδρες εἰσίν, ὥστε μὴ
> σπάνιν ποτὲ σχεῖν, ἔνθ᾽ ἂν ὦσι, τοῦ βίου·
> τοῖν δ᾽ ἀθλίαιν οἰκτραῖν τε παρθένοιν ἐμαῖν,
> οἷν οὔποθ᾽ ἡμὴ χωρὶς ἐστάθη βορᾶς
> τράπεζ᾽ ἄνευ τοῦδ᾽ ἀνδρός, ἀλλ᾽ ὅσων ἐγὼ
> ψαύοιμι, πάντων τῶνδ᾽ ἀεὶ μετειχέτην·
> τοῖν μοι μέλεσθαι· καὶ μάλιστα μὲν χεροῖν
> ψαῦσαί μ᾽ ἔασον κἀποκλαύσασθαι κακά.

This passage contains a jussive infinitive that, though postpositive and emphatic by its position just before the caesura, does not form the climax: an imperative, also referring to Oedipus' daughters, follows soon after the infinitive.

At Soph. *OC* 480–81 the structure is divided between speakers. Oedipus' imperative prompts the jussive infinitive:

> **Οι.** τοῦ τόνδε πλήας θῶ; δίδασκε καὶ τόδε.
> **Χο.** ὕδατος, μελίσσης· μηδὲ προσφέρειν μέθυ.

The Hippocratic corpus is problematic in regard to the postpositive rule. Schulte scolds Kluge for ignoring the corpus, which holds the greatest number of examples of the jussive infinitive.[10] For the most part the canonical order is followed:

> *Aër.* 24 ἀπὸ δὲ τούτων τεκμαιρόμενος, τὰ λοιπὰ ἐνθυμεῖσθαι, καὶ οὐχ ἁμαρτήσῃ.

---

9. For "relative clause" we might substitute "resumptive clause with weakened demonstrative." Whether we read τοῖν or οἷν (see commentators) is not relevant.
10. E. Schulte, *Observationes Hippocrateae Grammaticae* (Berlin, 1914), p. 14.

The participle, whether interpreted as an imperative (= τεκμαίϱον) or a temporal clause (= ὅταν τεκμαίϱῃ), constitutes the first member. But there are exceptions:

> *Mul.* 1.31 οἴνου . . . <u>διδόναι</u> ποτὸν . . . ἢν κύουσαν χολὴ λυπῇ, πτισάνην δίδου . . .

Here we might say with Schulte that there is a single condition explicit or to be supplied throughout, viz. "ὅταν οὕτως ἔχῃ vel si homo in hunc morbum inciderit." Or we might point to a Hippocratic fondness for rearranging common patterns of word order (see K. J. Dover, *Greek Word Order* [Cambridge, 1960], p. 68). Perhaps it is more reasonable to see the Hippocratic corpus as simply so thick with prescriptive expressions, jussive infinitives included, that it is absurd to look for a pattern (see above, pp. 11–12). The postpositive rule, in other words, may apply to the jussive infinitive only in those texts where the construction is an occasional feature.

Outside the Hippocratic corpus, inversions of the canonical order are exceedingly rare. In Hdt. 7.209.5 the jussive infinitive precedes a conditional clause:

> ὦ βασιλεῦ, ἐμοὶ <u>χϱᾶσθαι</u> ὡς ἀνδϱὶ ψεύστῃ, ἢν μὴ ταύτῃ ἐκβῇ τῇ ἐγὼ λέγω.

Dem. 8.38–39 shows an inversion *if* (1) γνῶναι is indeed a jussive infinitive (so Goodwin, *GMT* §784.1), not merely the complement of χϱή in §38 (so Rehdantz ad loc.), and (2) we retain παύσασθε rather than emend to παύσασθαι with Dobree:

> εἰσὶ τοίνυν τινὲς δι τότ᾽ ἐξελέγχειν τὸν παϱιόντ᾽ οἴονται, ἐπειδὰν ἐϱωτήσωσι "τί οὖν χϱὴ ποιεῖν;" οἷς ἐγὼ μὲν τὸ δικαιότατον καὶ ἀληθέστατον τοῦτ᾽ ἀποκϱινοῦμαι, ταῦτα μὴ ποιεῖν ἃ νυνὶ ποιεῖτε, οὐ μὴν ἀλλὰ καὶ καθ᾽ ἕκαστον ἀκϱιβῶς ἐϱῶ. καὶ ὅπως, ὥσπεϱ ἐϱωτῶσι πϱοθύμως, οὕτω καὶ ποιεῖν ἐθελήσουσιν. πϱῶτον μέν, ὦ ἄνδϱες Ἀθηναῖοι, τοῦτο παϱ᾽ ὑμῖν αὐτοῖς βεβαίως <u>γνῶναι</u>, ὅτι τῇ πόλει Φίλιππος πολεμεῖ καὶ τὴν εἰϱήνην λέλυκεν (καὶ παύσασθε πεϱὶ τού-του κατηγοϱοῦντες ἀλλήλων) . . .

To see γνῶναι as complementary we must suppose that Demosthenes meant the audience to imagine the prescription as immediately following on the challenge τί οὖν χϱὴ ποιεῖν; although (1) two long sentences have intervened and (2) ὦ ἄνδϱες Ἀθηναῖοι suggests a nominative, not the accusative subject required by ὑμᾶς. The first contention is easier to accept, since ἀποκϱινοῦμαι and ἐϱωτῶσι keep the question in the air. The second is harder, for it requires a "de-grammaticalization" that I cannot parallel for this particular vocative (but cf. above, p. 166, on ὦ ξεῖνε and below, p. 168, n. 5, on λέῳ).

P. Kiparsky has suggested that the jussive infinitive is an example of "conjunction reduction," i.e., the sequence marked form + conjunction + unmarked form ("Tense and Mood in Indo-European Syntax," *Foundations of Language* 4 [1968]: 51–54; cf. Householder-Nagy, *Trends*, p. 762). Kiparsky's examples are drawn solely from Homer, but within the classical period too some uses of the jussive infinitive fall within the strict use of the term:

> Aristoph. *Ach.* 257–58 πρόβαινε, κἂν τὤχλῳ <u>φυλάττεσθαι</u> σφόδρα
> μή τις λαθών σου περιτράγῃ τὰ χρυσία.

In most instances, however, the jussive infinitive is *not* preceded by an imperative. If Kiparsky's hypothesis is to be retained we must either explain infinitives as detached from the "correct" bipartite sequence or, diluting the term "conjunction reduction" considerably, interpret the clause or sentence that comes before the infinitive as establishing its mood. The first explanation sems most improbable: if the infinitive could be interpreted as an imperative solely because it had once been used after a mood-specific form, there would be no reason to substitute another pattern, i.e., the postpositive pattern. The second is more or less credible, depending on the particular example. Easiest are those with μή in the first part, a word that needs no verb to convey "don't!":

> Aristoph. *Nub.* 850–51 μή νυν τὸ λοιπόν, ἀλλὰ τήνδε μὲν <u>καλεῖν</u>
> ἀλεκτρύαιναν, τουτονὶ δ᾽ ἀλέκτορα.

But when a nonimperative verb form precedes, the jussive infinitive can hardly be called reduced. At Soph. *Ph.* 1079–80 I would rather interpret the construction as follows: the first part stipulates a circumstance—two actions that Neoptolemus and Philoctetes will perform—and by so doing prepares the chorus of sailors to understand the infinitive as designating that action which they are to perform in response:

> . . . νὼ μὲν οὖν ὁρμώμεθον,
> ὑμεῖς δ᾽, ὅταν καλῶμεν, <u>ὁρμᾶσθαι</u> ταχεῖς.

Under this description, the infinitive looks nearly epexegetic. The first part of the complex does not need to establish the imperatival mood explicitly: a future state of affairs (possible or certain) is presented, then a verbal noun. Even though personal endings and number are not attached to the infinitive and a second-person pronoun is not obligatory, the persons addressed understand that in the future state of affairs their part is prescribed by the infinitive.

Only a handful of nominative/vocative jussive infinitives are unprepared by a preceding clause or clauses. (Some inversions that may count as unprepared have already been mentioned: above, on pp. 172–73.) Though I cannot claim to have found every such example, the following discussion probably holds about one-half of the total. Admittedly, we must occasionally make a subjective decision as to what constitutes preparation. For example, the preparatory imperative stands at some distance from the jussive infinitive in Aesch. *PV* 707–12:

> πρῶτον μὲν ἐνθένδ᾽ ἡλίου πρὸς ἀντολὰς
> στρέψασα σαυτὴν στεῖχ᾽ ἀνηρότους γύας·
> Σκύθας δ᾽ ἀφίξῃ νομάδας, οἳ πλεκτὰς στέγας
> πεδάρσιοι ναίουσ᾽ ἐπ᾽ εὐκύκλοις ὄχοις,
> ἑκηβόλοις τόξοισιν ἐξηρτυμένοι·
> οἷς μὴ <u>πελάζειν</u> . . .

But since the intervening clauses merely expatiate on the folk that Io will meet first when she arrives in the unplowed lands, the clause with jussive infinitive warning her not to approach them caps what seems to me a single sequence that follows the imperative without interruption. Others may not read imperative and infinitive here as conjoined forms.

Aside from the examples discussed in the section on inverted order, there are, to my knowledge, only two unprepared jussive infinitives in prose:[11]

Pl. *R.* 508b τοῦτον τοίνυν, ἦν δ᾽ ἐγώ, <u>φάναι</u> με λέγειν τὸν τοῦ ἀγαθοῦ ἔκγονον . . .

And Xen. *Oec.* 3.12:

> πάντως δ᾽, ἔφη, ὦ Κριτόβουλε (φίλοι γὰρ ἐσμεν οἱ παρόντες)
> <u>ἀπαληθεῦσαι</u> πρὸς ἡμᾶς.

ἀπαλήθευσον Stephanus δεῖ R. *Ven.* 513: om. cet.

The latter I classify as unprepared despite πάντως; this is an adverb to which an imperative is but one of several possible sequelae. ἄγε/ἄγετε, on the other hand, is almost invariably followed by an imperative or the semantically kindred hortatory subjunctive of the first person.

There may be an unprepared example at Eur. *Supp.* 45–46 lyr.:

> —ἄνομοι . . . —τέκνα <u>λῦσαι</u>. —φθιμένων
> νεκύων . . .

---

11. I do not count as "prose" slogans like μὴ μνησικακεῖν.

This is, at best, too disjointed to be informative (Murray comments in the apparatus: "aut locus corruptus, aut clamores confusos habes precantium.").

Two examples of unprepared jussive infinitive in the lyrics of the *Antigone* deserve extended comment. Jebb calls the tone of the first solemn; Wecklein thinks the second expresses a childish piety.

> 148–54 ἀλλὰ γὰρ ἁ μεγαλώνυμος ἦλθε Νίκα
> τᾷ πολυαρμάτῳ ἀντιχαρεῖσα Θήβᾳ,
> ἐκ μὲν δὴ πολέμων
> τῶν νῦν θέσθαι λησμοσύναν,
> θεῶν δὲ ναοὺς χοροῖς,
> παννυχίοις πάντας ἐπέλ-
> θωμεν, ὁ Θήβας δ᾽ ἐλελί-
> χθων Βάκχιος ἄρχοι.

θέσθαι L^{ac} rec: θέσθε L^c rec

> 1140–45 καὶ νῦν, ὡς βιαίας ἔχεται
> πάνδαμος πόλις ἐπὶ νόσου,
> μολεῖν καθαρσίῳ ποδὶ Παρνασσίαν
> ὑπὲρ κλίτυν, ἢ στονόεντα πορθμόν.

There is a dramatic as well as a syntactic resemblance: the dramatic action casts both infinitives in an ironic light. In the first (from the second antistrophe of the parodos) the chorus gives the order "forget the war just past"—the subject of the jussive infinitive must be extracted from the dative in the preceding phrase, ἀλλὰ . . . Θήβᾳ. (Since the grammatical subject is diffuse, and not manifestly the first person, Müller's rejection of a jussive infinitive on the ground that an "order to oneself" cannot be found in that construction is unjustified.) Two exhortations follow: "Let us go in nightlong dances to the temples of the gods" (hortatory subjunctive) and "let Bacchus lead" (pure optative). As the tragedy unfolds, the war may be forgotten, but only insofar as it is overwhelmed in the catastrophes that follow. In the first antistrophe of the fifth stasimon, the chorus addresses its jussive infinitive to Bacchus, bidding him to come with his cleansing or healing foot. We could say either that the action promoted by the infinitive is simply not fulfilled or, as Goheen puts it, that "the actual 'cure' takes place through the more terrible and real process of tragic retribution and tragic waste rather than at the hands of a *deus ex machina*" (*The Imagery of Sophocles' Antigone* [Princeton, 1951], p. 43). In context, then, the jussive infinitive that is unprepared is also unjustified. Without the stipulations or hedging of a protasis, a command couched in such syntax seems the mark of a delusion.

Provenience: Subject Nominative/Vocative

The distribution of nominative/vocative jussive infinitives can be marked out more sharply than has been done before. The fullest statement I have seen on the matter exaggerates the frequency of the phenomenon in prose:

> The imperatival infinitive of the second person is relatively most frequent in Homer . . . following whom it is found most often in dramatic dialogue and in Plato, least often in historians . . . and the orators. [Stahl, *Verb.*, p. 599]

On examination, the Platonic examples turn out to be narrowly restricted. All those known to me deal with the protocol of philosophical discussion. Socrates uses the jussive infinitive to indicate when an interlocutor is to ask for a recapitulation of an argument:

> *Ly.* 211a8–b2 πειρῶ τοίνυν, ἦν δ᾽ ἐγώ, ἀπομνημονεῦσαι αὐτὰ ὅτι μάλιστα, ἵνα τούτῳ σαφῶς πάντα εἴπῃς· ἐὰν δέ τι αὐτῶν ἐπιλάθῃ, αὖθίς με <u>ἀνερέσθαι</u> ὅταν ἐντύχῃς πρῶτον

ἀνερέσθαι]ε in ras. B

At *Cra.* 426b the jussive infinitives sanction an interruption:

> ἃ μὲν τοίνυν ἐγὼ ᾔσθημαι περὶ τῶν πρώτων ὀνομάτων πάνυ μοι δοκεῖ ὑβριστικὰ εἶναι καὶ γελοῖα. τούτων οὖν σοι μεταδώσω, ἂν βούλῃ· σὺ δ᾽ ἄν τι ἔχῃς βέλτιόν ποθεν λαβεῖν, <u>πειρᾶσθαι</u> καὶ ἐμοὶ <u>μεταδιδόναι</u>.

At *Sph.* 262e it introduces a method of inquiry:

> Ξε: προσέχωμεν δὴ τὸν νοῦν ἡμῖν αὐτοῖς.
> Θεαι: δεῖ γοῦν.
> Ξε: λέξω τοίνυν σοι λόγον συνθεὶς πρᾶγμα πράξει δι᾽ ὀνόματος καὶ ῥήματος· ὅτου δ᾽ ἂν ὁ λόγος ᾖ, σύ μοι <u>φράζειν</u>.

φράζε ω

In two passages of the *Republic* the jussive infinitive is used to establish the criterion of dialectical success:

> 473a τοῦτο μὲν δὴ μὴ ἀνάγκαζέ με, οἷα τῷ λόγῳ διήλθομεν, τοιαῦτα παντάπασι καὶ τῷ ἔργῳ δεῖν γιγνόμενα ⟨ἂν⟩ ἀποφαίνειν· ἀλλ᾽, ἐὰν οἷοί τε γενώμεθα εὑρεῖν ὡς ἂν ἐγγύτατα τῶν εἰρημένων πόλις οἰκήσειεν, φάναι ἡμᾶς ἐξηυρηκέναι ὡς δυνατὰ ταῦτα γίγνεσθαι ἃ σὺ ἐπιτάττεις.

508b τοῦτον τοίνυν, ἦν δ᾽ ἐγώ, φάναι με λέγειν τὸν τοῦ ἀγαθοῦ
ἔκγονον, ὃν τἀγαθὸν ἐγέννησεν ἀνάλογον ἑαυτῷ, ὅτιπερ αὐτὸ
ἐν τῷ νοητῷ τόπῳ πρός τε νοῦν καὶ τὰ νοούμενα, τοῦτο τοῦτον
ἐν τῷ ὁρατῷ πρός τε ὄψιν καὶ τὰ ὁρώμενα.

At *Sph.* 218a, perhaps the weakest example, the jussive infinitive assigns
responsibility for the length of the discussion. Since the question of
impatience is only tangential to dialectic method,[12] the jussive infinitive is
perhaps playfully formal:

ἂν δ᾽ ἄρα τι τῷ μήκει πονῶν ἄχθῃ, μὴ ἐμὲ <u>αἰτιᾶσθαι</u> τούτων, ἀλλὰ
τούσδε τοὺς σοὺς ἑταίρους.

Considering how often the imperative is used in dialogue, Plato's restriction is remarkable. Xenophon may have put a substantial rather than
methodological jussive infinitive into the mouth of his Socrates at *Oec.*
3.12 (already quoted above, on p. 174). Since the infinitive would be an
unprepared construction, it is very probable either that Xenophon in fact
wrote ἀπαληθεῦσον or ἀπαληθεῦσαι δεῖ or that he blundered, intending
to suggest a solemn plea but instead manifesting his weakening grip on
Attic idiom.

Among historians, only Herodotus can be said to use the second-person
jussive infinitive with any frequency. Kluge (*Quaest.*, p. 10) lists thirteen
instances.[13] On reading through Kluge's list, though, one sees that it is a
construction held in reserve for moments of special weight in his narrative.[14] Thucydides has two examples,[15] if the manuscript readings are
allowed to stand:

1.35.5 καὶ ναυτικῆς καὶ οὐκ ἠπειρώτιδος τῆς ξυμμαχίας διδομένης
οὐχ ὁμοία ἡ ἀλλοτρίωσις, ἀλλὰ μάλιστα μέν, εἰ δύνασθε,
μηδένα ἄλλον <u>ἐᾶν</u> κεκτῆσθαι ναῦς, εἰ δὲ μή, ὅστις ἐχυρώτα-
τος, τοῦτον φίλον <u>ἔχειν</u>.

post μὲν add. δεῖ Sitzler

---

12. Daniel Kinney suggests that the issue of patience takes on considerable importance
once Plato rejects brevity as a philosophical virtue and comes to insist on the need for
leisurely dialectic. According to this explanation the passage becomes strong evidence for my
theory of Platonic usage.
13. See list in n. 6, above.
14. The infinitive at 3.155.5, but no other, looks like a relatively casual command.
15. A third example, at 5.9, has already been quoted above (p. 170). The list offered by
Cyranka (*Orat. Thuc.*, p. 45) is incomplete. There may be a third-person usage at 6.34.9: see
Dover ad loc.

6.17.1 καὶ νῦν μὴ πεφόβησθε αὐτήν, ἀλλ᾽ ἕως ἐγώ τε ἔτι ἀκμάζω μετ᾽ αὐτῆς καὶ ὁ Νικίας εὐτυχὴς δοκεῖ εἶναι, <u>ἀποχρήσασθαι</u> τῇ ἑκατέρου ἡμῶν ὠφελίᾳ.

πεφόβησθε Reiske: πεφοβῆσθαι codd. (ex — εισαι c): ἀποχρήσασθε f: ἀποχρήσασθαι Μ: ἀποχρήσεσθαι c: ἀποχρήσεσθε cet.

Xenophon seems to have abstained entirely from the construction within his historical writings. Thus, it occurs very rarely in historiography. Of course only speeches and dialogue are natural environments for imperatives; still, the number of opportunities presented by military commands and diplomatic urgings is exceedingly large.

Much the same can be said for the orators, who are forever exhorting their audiences to take some action or adopt some attitude. Yet there are, to my knowledge, only two possible examples of the usage in the orators; Dem. 8.39 and [Dem.] 47.70, listed by Stahl (*Verb.*, p. 600):

ἀλλ᾽ ὑπὲρ σεαυτοῦ καὶ τῆς οἰκίας ἀφοσιωσάμενος ὡς ῥᾷστα τὴν συμφορὰν <u>φέρειν</u>, ἄλλῃ δὲ εἴ πῃ βούλει, τιμωροῦ.

If we have a jussive infinitive here, the postpositive rule is preserved by the aorist participle. The whole passage recounts legal opinions and advice given by οἱ ἐξηγηταί and is prefaced by ἡμεῖς τοίνυν σοι τὰ μὲν νόμιμα ἐξηγησόμεθα, τὰ δὲ σύμφορα παραινέσομεν. The first item includes a verb that can be understood as complementary or as a stand-in for the third-person imperative: πρῶτον μὲν ἐπενεγκεῖν δόρυ . . . εἴ τις προσ-ήκων ἐστιν τῆς ἀνθρώπου (47.69). This is followed by τάδε δὲ συμβου-λευόμέν σοι, which is easily taken as governing three infinitives, of which φέρειν is the last. τιμωροῦ is the only imperative in the passage: I am tempted to consider it a sign that the exegetes, having completed their professional advice, are now speaking as laymen. They have explained to the speaker that he has no standing in the matter according to religious law and outlined the strategic disadvantages of prosecuting the murderers. "Make the best of it," they say, concluding their expert opinion. "Any other means of revenge you wish to employ," they say "man to man," "lies outside our field of competence."

Of course, since the putative jussive infinitive lies within a direct quotation of exegetes, whose language may have been in some respects exceptional, this passage cannot serve as evidence for oratorical usage per se.[16]

Assuming, as always, that the chronological disparity between most of

---

16. No jussive infinitives of any type are listed in Rehdantz, *Gramm. u. lex.* Index s.v. Infinitiv.

our poetic and prosaic texts has not utterly misled us, we may find the cause for oratorical abstention from the construction in the postpositive rule. The infinitive command regularly follows the exclusion of other courses of action, whether the exclusion is expressed by antithesis or through the implication that circumstances have been adequately considered in the introductory section. The infinitive thereby takes on a peremptory tone unacceptable to "Attic urbanity" in general and oratorical practice in particular. Plato, I imagine, felt that Socrates could adopt this tone while dictating rules of dialectic, for they had a special structural importance exempting them from the high standards of etiquette maintained (though often ironically) throughout the dialogues. To converse with Socrates was to accept in advance not his substantive opinions but his method. No orator, it seems, could make a similar demand on a jury or assembly.

Those commentators and grammarians who address the question of nuance are unanimous in attributing greater weight and emphasis to the jussive infinitive (of all varieties) than to the imperative (e.g., K-G 2.23–24).[17] I believe it is a mistake to see the same stylistic coloring in both subject nominative/vocative and subject accusative constructions. The former does not invariably suggest the majesty of law or the solemnity of prayer. Aristophanes does, it is true, deploy the construction in an absurd high-style oracle (quoted above, on p. 170). (Note the article for the demonstrative in the fourth line and the use of single τε to join words: both are archaic features.) And MacDowell is right to say that Philocleon "is giving a solemn instruction" at Aristoph. *V.* 385–86:

---

17. There are several specific theories on the difference in meaning between regular imperatives and jussive infinitives, none of them adequate to explain all the examples. Schulte (*Observationes Hippocrateae Grammaticae*, p. 27) thinks the second-person jussive infinitive is used for universal, rather than particular, prescriptions pertinent to a specific condition, hence its frequency in Hesiod's *Erga* and the Hippocratic corpus. A similar argument for semantic specialization is made by Carla Schick, "Una questione di sintassi storica: l'infinito imperativale e i varî modi di esprimere il commando in greco arcaico," *RAL.* ser. 8a, 10 (1955): 410–21. Several scholars argue that to promote actions more distant in time the infinitive, rather than the imperative, is used (see B. D. Delbrück, *De Infinitivo Graeco* [Halle, 1863]; C. Gaedicke [ref. in Wackernagel, *Vorl.* 1.267—Wackernagel is not convinced]; M. X. Hebold, *De Infinitivi Syntaxi Euripidea* [Halle, 1881], p. 13; R. Wagner, *Der Gebrauch des imperativischen Infinitivs im Griechischen* [Prog. Schwerin, 1891]; C. Hentze, "Der imperativische infinitiv im den homerischen gedichten," *BB* 27 [1902]: 106–37). A. Moreschini-Quattordio, "L'uso dell' infinitivo e dell' imperativo in Omero e nella tradizione epigrafica," *SCO* 20–21 (1970–71): 347–58. H. Amman proposes a variation: the jussive infinitive anticipates a spatial separation of the speaker and his interlocutor. The speaker knows in advance that he will not have a part in the action. This accounts for the solicitous and insistent tone of passages with the infinitive ("Die ältesten Formen des Prohibitivsatzes im Griechischen und Lateinischen," *IF* 45 [1927]: 330–31).

δράσω τοίνυν ὑμῖν πίσυνος, καὶ—μανθάνετ᾽;—ἤν τι πάθω᾽ γώ,
ἀνελόντες καὶ κατακλαύσαντες <u>θεῖναί</u> μ᾽ ὑπὸ τοῖσι δρυφάκτοις.

It is possible that the formality of a herald's proclamation is to be recognized at *Ec.* 1144–46 (quoted above, on p. 171). If so, the diminutives μειράκιον and παιδίσκον, colloquial features par excellence, mark a lowering of the style.

But a colloquial usage appears probable in at least eight Aristophanic passages:

Ach. 257–58   πρόβαινε, κἂν τὤχλῳ <u>φυλάττεσθαι</u> σφόδρα
μή τις λαθών σου περιτράγῃ τὰ χρυσία.
(*σφόδρα* is in the usual comic position: LSJ s.v. I plan to discuss this style marker in detail elsewhere.)

Nub. 849–51   ἄμφω ταὐτό; καταγέλαστος εἶ.
μή νῦν τὸ λοιπόν, ἀλλὰ τήνδε μὲν <u>καλεῖν</u>
ἀλεκτρύαιναν, τουτονὶ δ᾽ ἀλέκτορα.

Nub. 1079–81   μοιχὸς γὰρ ἦν τύχης ἀλούς, τάδ᾽ ἀντερεῖς πρὸς αὐτόν,
ὡς οὐδὲν ἠδίκηκας· εἶτ᾽ εἰς τὸν Δί᾽ ἐπανενεγκεῖν,
κἀκεῖνος ὡς ἥττων ἔρωτος ἐστὶ καὶ γυναικῶν·

Pax. 1153   ὧν ἔνεγκ᾽, ὦ παῖ, τρί᾽ ἡμῖν ἓν δὲ <u>δοῦναι</u> τῷ πατρί.

Lys. 535–37 anap. καὶ τουτονγὶ τὸν καλαθίσκον.
κᾆτα <u>ξαίνειν</u> ξυζωσάμενος
κυάμους τρώγων·

Th. 157–58   ὅταν σατύρους τοίνυν ποῇς, <u>καλεῖν</u> ἐμέ,
ἵνα συμποιῶ σοὔπισθεν ἐστυκὼς ἐγώ.

(The presence of *τοίνυν* makes a sarcastically high-blown introduction to an obscene joke unlikely: see Denniston, *Part.*, pp. 568–69.)

Ra. 130–33 **Δι.**   τί δρῶ;
Ηρ. ἀφιεμένην τὴν λαμπάδ᾽ ἐντεῦθεν θεῶ,
κἄπειτ᾽ ἐπειδὰν φῶσιν οἱ θεώμενοι
"εἶνται," τόθ᾽ <u>εἶναι</u> καὶ σὺ σαυτόν.

Ra. 169 **Δι.** ἐὰν δὲ μηῦρω;
Εα.   τότ᾽ ἔμ᾽ <u>ἄγειν.</u>
Δι.   καλῶς λέγεις.

In none of these is there a hint of parody of poetic, hieratic, or formal language. A colloquial jussive infinitive thus seems most probable. Therefore one should not automatically attribute elevation to every nominative/vocative jussive infinitive in tragedy.[18]

We have already seen (p. 175) that Sophocles ventured two unprepared uses of the construction in lyrics. Another deviation from colloquial usage (as ascertained from Aristophanes) and Attic prose is the willingness of tragedy and Ionic prose to employ it in prohibitions: see Smyth §203d.[19] The only possible exception is best explained without recourse to the jussive infinitive (Aristoph. *Nub.* 433: see Dover ad loc.). *Nub.* 849–51 (quoted above) shows how Aristophanes circumvents this restriction. I conjecture that this phenomenon can be traced to the affinity of the jussive infinitive for conditional clauses, a tendency especially marked in Aristophanes. A negative apodosis regularly takes οὐ, but οὐ rarely stands with the infinitive outside of indirect statment.[20] To avoid the collision of two grammatical rules the natural language abstains from using the construction in prohibitions. True, Attic prose tolerates an occasional prohibition as an apodosis, e.g., Pl. *Ap.* 20e4 μὴ θορυβήσητε, μηδ' ἐὰν δόξω τι ὑμῖν μέγα λέγειν. Perhaps, where function was unambiguously consistent with the form, the rule assigning negatives did not pertain. We might also consider the possibility that Attic writers sensed the jussive infinitive as epexegetic and therefore as much a statement of fact, which one would deny with οὐ, as a command, which one would reject with μή. The choice of negatives, then, would lead to an impasse that Attic speakers and prose writers would rather avoid.

Provenience: Subject Accusative

We have so far been concerned with nominative/vocative jussive infinitives. The form construed with the subject in the accusative case shows a far more limited distribution. It is the lapidary construction par excellence, and its appearances in literature never seem very far in tone from the stonecutter's chisel. Aristophanes mimics the style of official proclamations:

---

18. Schick ("Una questione di sintassi storica," p. 420) also considers the possibility that the jussive infinitive occurred in the spoken language. She does not, however, differentiate among lyric, tragic, and prose uses, and she is silent on comic uses.

19. The rule is not absolute: Pl. *Sph.* 218a (quoted above, on p. 177) is one exception. W. Dittmar has no negative examples from Menander, which is some evidence that the construction had no place in fourth-century natural language (*Sprachliche Untersuchungen zu Aristophanes und Menander* [Leipzig, 1933], p. 93).

20. οὐ sometimes negatives a complementary infinitive with χρή and (less clearly) accompanies an infinitive, though it is felt with or repeats an οὐ used with the introductory verb (Smyth §§2714, 2721, 2738b).

Av. 448–50 ἀκούετε λεῷ· τοὺς ὁπλίτας νυνμενὶ
ἀνελομένους θῶπλ᾿ ἀπιέναι πάλιν οἴκαδε,
σκοπεῖν δ᾿ ὅ τι ἂν προγράφωμεν ἐν τοῖς πινακίοις.

We see from this passage that the second person of ἀκούετε and the vocative λεῷ do not always require a nominative/vocative subject for the infinitive (cf. above, p. 166). Cf. Dem. 21.51 (an oracle, perhaps genuine):

αὐδῶ ᾿Ερεχθείδῃσιν, ὅσοι Πανδίονος ἄστυ
ναίετε καὶ πατρίοισι νόμοις ἰθύνεθ᾿ ἑορτάς,
μεμνῆσθαι Βάκχοιο, καὶ εὐρυχόρους κατ᾿ ἀγυιὰς
ἱστάναι ὡραίων Βρομίῳ χάριν ἄμμιγα πάντας,
καὶ κνισᾶν βωμοῖσι κάρη στεφάνοις πυκάσαντας.

Orators weave this form of the jussive infinitive into their narrative:

Andoc. 1.81 . . . ἔσοξε μὴ μνησικακεῖν ἀλλήλοις τῶν γεγενημένων.
δόξαντα δὲ ὑμῖν ταῦτα, εἵλεσθε ἄνδρας εἴκοσι· τούτους
δὲ ἐπιμελεῖσθαι τῆς πόλεως, ἕως ἄλλοι νόμοι τεθεῖεν·
τέως δὲ χρῆσθαι τοῖς Σόλωνος νόμοις καὶ τοῖς Δράκον-
τος θεσμοῖς.

This passage stands between verbatim readings of the decrees of Patrocleides and Teisamenus. It slides from an accusative absolute that represents the ἔδοξε of the normal prescript into a series of jussive infinitives. One of these, χρῆσθαι, anticipates the wording of §83. ἐπιμελεῖσθαι in §81 is followed by ἐπιμελείσθω in §84 (the two verb forms do not refer to the same thing), which recalls the alternation of jussive infinitive and third-person imperative commonly found on inscriptions (see above, p. 167).[21]

Thucydides and Xenophon use this construction to record treaties (many examples are listed in K-G 2.23). Herodotus, to my knowledge, entirely avoids it, presumably because it smacks of the chronicle. It is at home in Plato's *Laws*. The association of the construction with the most formal types of language seems to have been very close indeed. I have not seen a single certain example in a casual command.

Optatival Infinitive

The optatival infinitive with subject accusative (if the subject can be ascertained: see above, p. 166) has an even narrower range. Regardless of genre, it characteristically follows an explicit invocation of divinity:

---

21. As quoted in §77, the Decree of Patrocleides, to which the accusative absolute refers, starts with Πατροκλείδης εἶπεν, omitting ἔδοξε τῇ βουλῇ κτλ.

Pind. *P.* 1.67–68   Ζεῦ τέλει᾽, αἰεὶ δὲ τοιαύταν ᾽Αμένα παρ᾽ ὕδωρ
αἶσαν ἀστοῖς καὶ βασιλεῦσιν <u>διακρί-
νειν</u> ἔτυμον λόγον ἀνθρώπων.

Hdt. 5.105.2 ὦ Ζεῦ, <u>ἐκγενέσθαι</u> μοι ᾽Αθηναίους τείσασθαι.[22]

Aesch. *Sept.* 253 θεοὶ πολῖται, μή με δουλείας <u>τυχεῖν</u>.

Aristoph. *Ach.* 816–17 ῾Ερμᾶ ᾽μπολαῖε, τὰν γυναῖκα τὰν ἐμὰν
οὕτω μ᾽ <u>ἀποδόσθαι</u> τάν τ᾽ ἐμωυτῷ ματέρα.
(The Doricism is no high-style parody: the speaker is a Megarian.)

I have seen no clear examples of the optatival infinitive in Attic prose.
Stahl (*Verb.*, p. 600) ends his list with Pl. *Ion.* 530a, where Socrates opens
the dialogue with the words τὸν ῎Ιωνα χαίρειν. But I cannot believe that
this is a substitute for χαίροι. The overwhelming preponderance of greet-
ings and leave-takings show the imperative, either in the simple form
(χαῖρε, χαίρετον, χαίρετε) or added to a participial form of χαίρω, e.g.,
Soph. *Tr.* 819 ἑρπέτω χαίρουσα. Participial χαίρω + optative is exceedingly rare, and perhaps unattested altogether in Attic (LSJ s.v. χαίρω
IV.3). χαίρειν as the opening of a letter is surely imperatival. So I would
classify the *Ion* passage as a playfully formal subject accusative jussive
infinitive. "Playfully formal" does not, however, imply a nonce witticism.
Theoc. 14.1 opens with χαίρειν πολλὰ τὸν ἄνδρα Θυώνιχον. Since the
poem has many colloquial touches, I am tempted to think that this
expression was current in educated speech of the fourth and third centuries. Dover comments on τὸν ἄνδρα: "possibly we are meant to imagine
that there is a momentary delay in Aischinas's recollection of the name of
the man he recognizes by sight." If this interpretation is correct, and
χαίρειν + accusative was the sort of expression one would utter to a man
one did not know very well, it follows that the expression was not rare.

Exclamatory Infinitive

We have, so far, been considering constructions well attested before the
fifth century, particularly in epic. The exclamatory infinitive, however, is
unknown until 458, when it appears twice in the *Oresteia*:

---

22. Strictly speaking, there is no personal subject here, only the "nonperson" of ἐκγίγνεται
in infinitive form (on the "nonperson" see Benveniste, "Structures des relations de personne
dans le verbe," *Prob.*, pp. 225–36).

Ag. 1662–64 ἀλλὰ τούσδ᾽ ἐμοὶ ματαίαν γλῶσσαν ὧδ᾽ †ἀπανθίσαι†
κἀκβαλεῖν ἔπη τοιαῦτα δαίμονος περωμένους,
σώφρονος γνώμης δ᾽ ἁμαρτεῖν τὸν κρατοῦντα ⟨   ⟩.

Eum. 837–39 = 870–72 ἐμὲ παθεῖν τάδε,
φεῦ,
ἐμὲ παλαιόφρονα κατά τε γᾶν οἰκεῖν,
ἀτίετον μύσος·
φεῦ·

P. T. Stevens (*Colloq. Eur.*, p. 61) comments: "The infinitive without article . . . is found in Aristophanes only in *V.* 835 and perhaps *Nub.* 819, as compared with seven examples of the articular infinitive; moreover, in general the article tends to be more rarely used in poetic as contrasted with prosaic and colloquial language, so that the articular infinitive in exclamations, not found in tragedy apart from E. and S. *Ph.* 232, may have been regarded as more colloquial." If I understand Stevens correctly, he conceives of the anarthrous form as a modification of the colloquial construction with the article rather than as an item in the natural language. But Demosthenes uses the anarthrous type (see below), and without warrant in the natural language Aeschylus would have had to count heavily on delivery or gesture to make the meaning of the line clear. It seems easier to suppose that both forms were extant, and that we see here a manifestation of the general preference for anarthrous expression in poetry and a specific disinclination to risk confusion with the prosaic nominative/accusative articular infinitive.

Fraenkel (ad *Ag.* 1662) observes that in the anarthrous examples of the exclamatory infinitive "there is always a pronoun or pronoun-adjective at the head of the sentence." I think the reason for this may have been to facilitate emphatic, indignant delivery. ἐμέ, τούσδε, and forms of τοιοῦτος and the like are, in these constructions, words one would spit out, pointing mentally or physically to the person or things so as to suggest, even before the infinitive, amazement and outrage. The principle, I suggest, is really the same in exclamatory infinitives with the article: some word is bound to rush to the head of the sentence to leave the mood (in the nontechnical sense of the word) of the infinitive in no doubt. The right attack on the τό *indignantis* itself was sufficient at Aristoph. *Ra.* 530–31, where the contemptuous adjectives follow the infinitive:[23]

23. Cf. Burguière (*Histoire de l'infinitif en grec*), pp. 44, 110–11 on the affective force of the rhythmic position that τό occupies in tragedy.

> τὸ δὲ προσδοκῆσαί σ᾽ οὐκ ἀνόητον καὶ κενὸν
> ὡς δοῦλος ὢν καὶ θνητὸς ᾽Αλκμήνης ἔσει;

Other preparations of the exclamatory infinitive are φεῦ, as in Soph. Ph. 234–35,

> ὦ φίλτατον φώνημα· φεῦ τὸ καὶ λαβεῖν
> πρόσφθεγμα τοιοῦδ᾽ ἀνδρὸς ἐν χρόνῳ μακρῷ,

or a genitive of cause, as in Eur. Alc. 832–33,

> . . . ἀλλὰ σοῦ τὸ μὴ φράσαι,
> κακοῦ τοσούτου δώμασιν προκειμένου.

(Dale ad loc., in a fine discussion of these genitives, says that the infinitives in passages like this may be considered epexegetic.)

The few prose examples support Stevens's claim that the exclamatory infinitive, at least with the article, is colloquial. Plato has one sure instance, put in the mouth of the plain-talking Eryximachus in the conversational opening of the *Symposium*:

> 177b4–c2 . . . ἀλλ᾽ ἔγωγε ἤδη τινὶ ἐνέτυχον βιβλίῳ ἀνδρὸς σοφοῦ, ἐν
> ᾧ ἐνῆσαν ἅλες ἔπαινον θαυμάσιον ἔχοντες πρὸς
> ὠφελίαν, καὶ ἄλλα τοιαῦτα συχνὰ ἴδοις ἂν ἐγκεκω-
> μιασμένα—τὸ οὖν τοιούτων μὲν πέρι πολλὴν σπουδὴν
> ποιήσασθαι, ῎Ερωτα δὲ μηδένα πω ἀνθρώπων τετολ-
> μηκέναι εἰς ταυτηνὶ τὴν ἡμέραν ἀξίως ὑμνῆσαι.

The two instances in Demosthenes (both anarthrous) are, as Dover observes (ad Aristoph. *Nub.* 819), representations of "other people's thoughts and words":

> 21.209 . . . ἀλλ᾽ οὐκ ἂν εὐθέως εἴποιεν "τὸν δὲ βάσκανον, τὸν δ᾽
> ὄλεθρον, τοῦτον δ᾽ ὑβρίζειν, ἀναπνεῖν δέ;"

> 25.91 ἐπειδὰν οὖν τις ὑμῶν ἐφ᾽ οἷς οὗτος ἀσελγαίνει λυπηθεὶς εἴπῃ
> "τοῦτον δὲ ταῦτα ποιεῖν, καὶ ταῦτ᾽ ὀφείλοντα τῷ δημοσίῳ"

In the first passage the infinitive appears only after the subject is blackened by the words βάσκανον and ὄλεθρον. The second establishes the tone by the participle in the introductory sentence.

To my knowledge, no orator presents an exclamatory infinitive as his own utterance. The closest examples are purely epexegetic and follow explicit notices of the speaker's attitude, i.e., one does not imagine the orator's voice trembling with emotion as he pronounces the infinitive:

Antiphon 1.28 θαυμάζω δὲ ἔγωγε τῆς τόλμης τοῦ ἀδελφοῦ καὶ τῆς
διανοίας, τὸ διομόσθαι ὑπὲρ τῆς μητρὸς εὖ εἰδέναι
μὴ πεποιηκυῖαν ταῦτα.

Hyp. *Epit.* 3 ἄξιόν ἐστιν ἐπαινεῖν τὴν πόλιν ἡμῶν τῆς προαιρέσεως
ἕνεκεν, τὸ προελέσθαι.[24]

It could be that orations as actually delivered employed the exclamatory
infinitive, but *logographoi* avoided writing them into a text for fear that
clients and readers would botch the delivery. Demosthenes ventured the
construction in 21, a forensic speech written for himself. The dubious
authenticity of 25 denies us the right to say he would trust a client.
Demostheness allowed this infinitive only in reporting another's speech,
not as his own words; *a fortiori,* the exclamatory infinitive had no place in
epideictic oratory, say, in Hyperides' *Epitaphios.*

---

24. Riddell (*Plat. Id.* §85) perhaps goes too far in saying, "The speaker justifies the
warmth with which he has spoken by subjoining a studiedly dispassionate statement on the
case [employing an infinitive]."

Some Conclusions

From the individual discussions of the differentiae a few generalizations on provenience are possible. They are offered with the caveat that uncertainties of transmission and classification throw an uneven haze over the terrain.

1. The differentiae I have examined quite sharply distinguish "serious" poetry, i.e., epinicians and tragedy, from comic verse and prose. Versification was seldom sufficient excuse to introduce the differentiae. To a degree this vindicates Aristotle's rejection of distinctions between literary works based on the presence or absence of meter. Empedocles, Aristotle's example of a metrical writer, we are not to regard as fundamentally a poet (cf. above, pp. 2–3), does, in fact, make very scanty use of the differentiae: I have found only the poetic plural of a common sort, e.g., μεγάροισι at 124 Wright (137 D-K).4, the terminal accusative (see above, p. 73), and an unlikely "omitted ἄν" (p. 148). Parmenides, the other reasonably well preserved philosophical writer of metrical texts, is also uninterested in the differentiae: I find the poetic plural δώματα at B1.9, possible local datives (see above, p. 96), a possibly poetic use of the ablatival genitive (see above, p. 100), and a terminal accusative (see above, p. 73).

2. Nevertheless, a small number of features found in "serious" poetry, e.g., certain "poetic" plurals and the jussive infinitive with nominative/ vocative subject, also appear in fifth-century colloquial speech but barely ever in *Kunstprosa* of the fifth and fourth centuries. I join those who think that *Kunstprosa* did sometimes employ the potential optative without ἄν, but otherwise I have seen very little in respect of the differentiae that discredits the traditional doctrines on the syntax of Attic prose. Greek can be perfectly supple without recourse to a small body of deviant items; and the syntax of everyday Greek held little to offend fastidious prose authors.[1]

---

1. One possible exception is the use of ἄν with the imperfect or aorist to express repeated action. The distribution was determined by R. Seaton, "The Iterative Use of ἄν with the Imper[fect] and Aor[ist] Indic[ative]," *CR* 3 (1889): 343–45. See also Stevens, *Colloq. Eur.*, p. 60.

3. The differentiae do not mark the lyrics of tragedy off from dialogue as strongly as grammarians generally suppose. There is no syntactical feature exclusive to the lyrics; a notably strong predominance of lyric occurrences is to be seen only in the deployment of the potential optative with ἄν. This fact of distribution is of considerable significance, given the great differences between lyric and dialogue in other aspects: singing vs. speaking, large metrical differences, lexicon, more frequent omission of the article in the former, and the Doric ᾱ for η. To these linguistic contrasts we may add differences in theme and imaginative presentation.[2] Further, the lyrics of Aristophanes are not much thicker with the differentiae than his dialogue.[3] In tragedy and comedy the distributional pattern recalls the use of Ionic -σσ- for Attic -ττ-: lyrics and dialogue in tragedy show the Ionic form, lyrics and dialogue in comedy show the Attic form. Both this morphological feature and the differentiae are exceptions to the general approximation of comic to tragic lyric (see Schwyzer, *Gramm.* 1.111). We may conclude that the poets gave priority to the enveloping genre, not to metrical or other considerations arising from the "subgenre," in determining whether the differentiae were appropriate. The common descent of tragic and comic lyric from earlier choral song, for instance, did not prevent their divergence in the aspect of syntax.

4. The differentiae are not used to distinguish the general speech habits or temporary emotional states of speakers. Admittedly, any deviation from the normal attracts the audience's attention, and the audience will not totally separate the form of an expression from its content. But it should be clear from the investigation of the differentiae that not one of them has a strong association with a particular class, age, or gender of speaker. There is reason to assign a certain nuance to the jussive infinitive and to εἰ clauses with bare subjunctives, but that is all. Here, too, we have an indication that the principal determinant in the purely linguistic practice of an author is the genre of the work as a whole, not the smaller units within the work, whether formal or thematic.[4] Uniformity of linguistic usage stands in marked contrast to the extreme rhetorical variations from character to character. In every sort of artistic expression there is an economy of means; the role of the syntactical differentiae examined in this book seldom extends beyond the characterization of language as generic.

2. See H. Friis Johansen, *General Reflection in Tragic Rhesis* (Copenhagen, 1959), pp. 12, 165–68.

3. See appendix 1c (pp. 57–59) on poetic plurals, p. 98 on local datives, p. 73 on the terminal accusative.

4. Cf. Stevens, *Colloq. Eur.,* p. 65: "only fifty colloquialisms are given to characters of humble status, such as attendants, retainers, guards, and the like, and in passages of dialogue between a servant and a main character colloquial expressions are as likely to be given to a king or a queen as to a servant." See also Ussher's commentary on Euripides' *Cyclops,* pp. 65, 207, and G. Sifakis, "Children in Greek Tragedy," *BICS* 26 (1979): 69, 71–72.

Two remarks on the origin of the differentiae. Virtually every feature I have discussed is a patent archaism, but an archaism of a diffuse sort, never a borrowing from a specific passage, work, or even genre of earlier literature. I conjecture that the poets saw an aesthetic advantage in linguistic features that recalled the language of earlier poets without suggesting prefabrication of the utterance in its entirety, or even that the modern craftsman held a particular creation of the past before him as he worked. Of course, the same sense of fresh creation from old linguistic material could be attributed to the use of any word familiar from earlier literature. But the syntactical differentiae, like morphological or prosodic features, are by their nature elements of language less likely to remind the audience of particular passages from archaic literature.

Attic, the native dialect of the writers most prominent in this study, was the repository of many archaisms of syntax. The dialect retained features abandoned not only by other dialects of Greek before the classical age but even by the Homeric art language (see Schwyzer, "Synt. Arch." passim). It is not easy to say whether features like the so-called genitive of agent, which coexist in tragedy and colloquial Attic, were ever perceived as archaic.[5] In any case, I have seen no sign that the Attic poets cultivated what we know to be archaisms of their everyday speech, or that they sought archaisms of specifically Attic provenience no longer in colloquial use in their time. Actually, the subtle deviations from the normal (i.e., comic) use of the dual by the tragic poets show just the reverse.[6] Athenians were notably chauvinistic about their ancient land and its autochthonous inhabitants, but they looked to Panhellenic sources, not to the antiquities of their own dialect, to heighten their poetry. (I note a phonological analogue: the lyric vocalism $\bar{a}$ for η is an imported element, not Old Attic, as Mahlow had argued. This is amply demonstrated by Björck, *Das Alpha Impurum.*)

The patent archaizing represented by the differentiae may explain the great reluctance of prose writers to include them among the poetic devices suitable for use in their medium. Rhythm, figures, and the acoustic strategies of poetry seemed to them (I conjecture) elements latent in routine contemporary language, and in this respect not part of poetry's exclusive domain, though poetry exploited them more often. Some of the early prose writers did not scruple, however, to borrow poetic words (see above, pp. 1–2), and it may be objected that many of those words would have been perceived as archaic and should, on my theory, have been rejected as well. To this I can respond only that a lexical archaism was a

---

5. See above, p. 101.
6. See above, pp. 59–60, and Cuny, *Nombre Duel* passim.

temptation less easily resisted because a particular word is a discrete item, and therefore can be regarded as an outright borrowing from poetry, something in quotation marks, so to speak. Quotation marks cannot enclose syntactical deviations like unexpressed ἄν's.

Condensation and Precision

Several of the differentiae examined in this book are syntactically less explicit and shorter than their pedestrian gloss: the terminal accusative, local dative, potential optative and dependent subjunctive without ἄν, and absolute infinitive. We may call this quality "condensation." Since condensation is so conspicuous in poetic syntax, it seems likely that poets appreciated some aesthetic quality in it. (I admit from the outset that it is but a hypothesis that the Greeks who deployed these constructions thought of them as aesthetically similar.)

A cynic could argue that alternate forms composed of fewer syllables than the semantically corresponding pedestrian gloss are merely handy tools in the production of metrical language. True, of course, but the technical skill of the major poets of the classical period should preclude our thinking that a quandary in scansion often induced them to settle for a metrical expedient that they found displeasing for any reason. If we knew more of the mediocrities and failures of Greek literature we might see instances of prosodic desperation, pieces of Greek that had to be ugly to scan.[7]

According to one view, forcibly expressed by G. Björck, poetry and colloquial language differ from *Kunstprosa* in their inclination to indefiniteness and their aversion to "an excess of parts of speech which convey little emotion, such as prepositions, prefixes, articles, and pronouns" (*Alpha Imp.*, p. 305).[8] Lack of precision, it is claimed, frees the imagination: exactly this makes a poetic utterance more pregnant with meaning than a prosaic equivalent.[9] This theory has considerable intuitive appeal: the poetic *afflatus* is beyond fussy detail, and the audience joins the poet in vigorous imaginative activity. Or, we might say, poetry is radically ambigu-

---

7. A notable instance of desperation is Critias' resort to mixed elegiac and iambic meters in his poem to Alcibiades, 4 West. But this is a consequence of the metrical shape of Alcibiades' name, and a joke. (Cf. the allegation of distorted quantities at Aristot. *Poet.* 1458b5–10.

8. Cf. K-G 1.443 Anmerk. 1; P. T. Stevens ad Eur. *Andr.* 3.

9. Björck's example (p. 304) is Aesch. *Ag.* 12 νυκτίπλαγκτος, which may be less gravid than he supposes: see Fraenkel ad. loc.

ous, and imprecision promotes ambiguity; further, all men are susceptible to poetry, and imprecision encourages them to think as poets do.[10]

Leaving aside the merit of these generalizations, can we say that the condensations of poetic syntax were valued for their imprecision? I think not. There are very few instances in which the syntax of the condensed form would not have been immediately clear to an audience experienced in Greek poetry; or, better, in which an audience would have wavered if challenged to produce the pedestrian gloss. Possible exceptions are (1) absolute infinitives that straddle the line between jussive and optatival functions (but it is significant that two sorts of *Kunstprosa,* Attic and Ionic, do not treat this infinitive alike: see above, p. 183) and (2) some main-clause optatives without ἄν that might—according to a theory I distrust—hover between potential and cupitive function (see above, pp. 137–38).

Further, we may grant that *Kunstprosa* is more explicit than poetry in respect to the differentiae under discussion and the other features mentioned by Björck, and still deny that poetry is a less precise means of linguistic expression. We do not call English more precise than Chinese because the former, but not the latter, requires a mark of plurality with nouns, even after numbers: "five table*s*" vs. "five table." Many attributes of language are redundant in most contexts. A mechanically reproduced ἄν, for example, is not needed to clarify the syntactical role of a subordinate clause in the subjunctive; therefore the absence of the particle in poetry cannot be said to deprive a sentence of syntactical precision. Similarly, the absence of a preposition with an accusative designating the goal of motion does not make a sentence in poetry semantically obscure unless the hearer is conscious of some uncertainty of meaning (say, whether or not the motion is hostile) that a preposition would resolve. This is not to deny that some of the linguistic means employed by Greek prose, especially the definite article, significantly promoted the precision of discourse *in certain contexts*; nor is it to deny that a *general* association of these elements with discursive prose, particularly philosophical and scientific, caused their absence from poetry to strike *some* Greeks as a symptom of a lack of ἀκρίβεια.[11]

10. William Empson comments on a Chinese poem, "Swiftly the years, beyond recall. / Solemn the stillness of this spring morning": "These lines are what we should normally call poetry only by virtue of their compactness; two statements are made as if they were connected, and the reader is forced to consider their relation for himself. . . . This, I think, is the essential fact about the poetical use of language" (*Seven Types of Ambiguity,* 3d. ed. [Norfolk, Ct., 1953], p. 25).

11. I would associate myself with N. E. Collinge, "Ambiguity in Literature: Some Guidelines," *Arethusa* 2 (1969): 19: "as the identity of a language resides in its grammar, so the constraints at that level are the strongest" and (pp. 22–23) "If no signal is visible, it is injudicious, and probably wrong, to infer an ambiguity."

Is condensation a sort of emblem carried by poetry to assert its universality, even in the midst of speaking of the particular? Even if the condensed forms are not significantly imprecise in their utilization in context, could their form suggest the "concrete universal?"[12] Here too I am skeptical. First, it should be remembered that both the phenomena mentioned by Björck and my syntactical differentiae are possibilities exploited by poetry, not obligatory features; only the absence of the article is a poetic trait so common that one cannot go ten lines without noticing it. The most common of the syntactical differentiae—the terminal accusative—occurs in only some one-fifth of the possible locations. The logical, *affektschwach* elements are in a majority.

The second obstacle is considerably more serious. If the notion of the emblem is not a mere fantasy of critics, those differentiae that suggest it ought to appear most often in passages of poetry that are most explicitly general, for instance, in aphoristic lines in epinicians, in appeals to general principle in tragic *rhesis,* and especially in the lyrics of tragedy. The tragic chorus employs *paradeigmata* because it assumes, or states, that the specifics of myth, though distant from the dramatic here and now, might reveal the shape and meaning of the action that it observes on the stage and seeks to understand. The article is indeed comparatively less frequent in lyric passages, and the nominal construction has at least a weak association with aphorisms (see below, pp. 195–201); but literary tradition is certainly at work here—lyric and hexameter (the meter par excellence of proverbs) are probably older than iambic trimeter, and the definite article is young and associated with Ionia. The differentiae, however, do not significantly congregate in lyric, even though they too are more archaic than the pedestrian glosses. (Cf. above, pp. 143–64, on the bare subjunctive protasis, the single differentia associated to some degree with generalization.)

Abstraction and Defamiliarization

"Abstract" often implies "unspecific," "rejecting the practical detail," even "unreal." I think that it can be applied to the syntactical differentiae in another, more fruitful sense: "self-consciously part of language" and "self-consciously a specific part of language."

The theory of the pedestrian gloss suggests at least the slight awareness that a particular expression is alien from routine language. Now, to some

---

12. See W. K. Wimsatt, "The Structure of the 'Concrete Universal' in Literature," in *Criticism,*[3] ed. M. Shorer, J. Miles, G. McKenzie (New York, 1958), pp. 393–403.

extent, the audience of Greek poetry hears every part of the poem as unroutine: meter accomplishes this by constantly calling attention to a repeated pattern of long and short syllables. If a prose writer incautiously falls into meter, his audience is distracted from his topic and attends to the formal character of his language (cf. Introduction, n. 41). *Any* poetic feature draws the listener away from routine language, and thereby makes language remarkable, but the syntactical differentiae do this, in my view, with particular strength for several reasons:

1. Lexical substitutions are "infinitely extendable."[13] The differentiae are simpler: for each one the pedestrian gloss is a single expression. Drawing a metaphor from music, we may say that the pedestrian gloss beats against the differentia and produces a familiar harmonic. Further, the differentiae are, compared with poetic words, relatively few, and all but the exclamatory infinitive (see above, pp. 183–86) enjoy literary pedigrees. In a sense, poetry that antedates our period established a norm that stands beside everyday classical Greek.

2. The pedestrian gloss is more crucial to the comprehension of a syntactical differentia than to the comprehension of a nonstandard lexical item. It is well known that strange lexicon disrupts the sense of meaningfulness far less than strange syntax.[14]

3. The syntactical differentia suggests the principle of lexical substitution more readily than lexical substitution can suggest the principle of syntactical substitution. Deviant syntax must be realized through lexicon, whereas a lexical item that is realized through routine syntax leaves the issue of syntactical synonyms submerged. μολεῖν in standard syntactical dress might be more noticeable as different from routine words for "come," and might elicit some consciousness of synonyms. But ὅπως μόλῃ might elicit consciousness of the same synonyms as existing in two realizations, one with and one without ἄν.

4. Precisely because they are sporadic rather than systematic features (like meter or dialect), the differentiae heighten the sense of unpredictability in language. To notice that language is unpredictable is to be highly conscious of the code as something different from the message. The sporadic distribution prevents the familiarity of the differentiae adduced in (1) from falling into monotony.[15]

The condensed differentiae are endowed with an additional power—to

---

13. Roger Fowler, "Linguistic Theory and the Study of Literature," in *Essays on Style and Language,* ed. R. Fowler (London, 1966), p. 16.

14. The standard example of the former is Lewis Carroll's "Jabberwocky."

15. On the "higher irregularity" see M. A. K. Halliday, "The Linguistic Study of Literary Texts," in *Proceedings of the Ninth International Congress of Linguists,* ed. H. G. Lunt (The Hague, 1964), p. 305.

make poetry conspicuous *qua* deviant language. Assuming that they are legitimized by literary tradition as acceptable alternates to their respective pedestrian glosses, their appearance suggests an elasticity of length that both accommodates and causes the abstract pattern of meter. Once we dismiss the idea of linguistic forms produced under the threat of metrical breakdown, we can appreciate the condensations as a virtue, not a weakness; they are examples of poetic language as a plastic medium capable of changes that do not sacrifice meaning. The differentiae are, in my view, pregnant with nothing but the pedestrian gloss; but even that makes an interesting conception.

Appendix A. Nominal Constructions

The term *nominal construction* refers to clauses lacking a copulative verb, e.g., ἕτοιμος ὁ ἀνήρ. The copula that is "missing," or better, "not expressed,"[1] is ἐστί or εἰσί, the zero-tense, zero-mood, zero-person verb form. Closely related to nominal constructions, but not usually regarded as examples of the type, are clauses where the verb, if expressed, would be εἶναι, εἴη, or εἶεν when these verbs could stand as representations in *oratio obliqua* of ἐστί or εἰσί. In the remarks that follow I shall call attention to any examples of this kind that are included in my lists of nominal vs. verbal constructions.

By virtue of its relative simplicity as compared with the form using the copula, the nominal construction resembles several items of genre-conditioned syntax, e.g., the terminal accusative. But the nominal construction shows only a general tendency to congregate with special frequency in certain genres. Therefore I offer here only some general remarks and a few specific illustrations bearing on the possible genre conditioning of the construction.

Alone among scholars who have examined the problem, Benveniste argues that a semantic differentiation is the sole determinant of the choice between nominal or verbal expression: nominal constructions are used, he claims, for what the speaker regards as timeless, general truths, the verbal form for assertions that he regards as tied to a particular time.[2] But even C. Guiraud, a scholar always at pains to defend the semantic distinctiveness of the nominal form, allows for a multiplicity of other factors, including genre.[3] He writes (*Phrase nom.*, p. 79): "The absence of the verb

1. Benveniste, *Prob.*, p. 157.
2. Ibid., pp. 151–67. Benveniste writes as though a palpable *cordon* separated nominal from verbal constructions. In practice, however, an ἐστί (less often γίγνεται *vel sim*) is often sitting just before the clause one is examining, and in many cases reasonable scholars disagree as to whether that verb persisted in the Greek ear long enough to enter the clause and serve as its copula.
3. Some of these are conveniently listed by K. J. Dover in his review of Guiraud's book (*CR* 77 [1963]: 308): (1) mechanical analogy, formulae, and the influence of familiar expres-

'to be' is more frequent in the choruses, and more irregular as well." And (p. 88): "In the choruses, for reasons of expressivity, and in oracles, for reasons of efficiency, the verb 'to be' is freely omitted." And (p. 158):

> The nonverbal expression unquestionably predominates in the gnomic authors Hesiod and Theognis. It has become "a law of the genre." From there the construction can be transferred to certain reports and descriptions. Conversely, Herodotus, a historian and geographer, uses mainly the expression with the verb "to be." This type of expression sometimes spills over into an area which traditionally fell into the expression without the verb, viz. particular judgments. Pindar, *as a matter of personal taste* [my emphasis] . . . multiplies the nonverbal expressions in his descriptions. Imitating Pindaric lyric, the tragedians equally multiplied the nonverbal constructions in their choruses.

The individual predilections of Pindar are subsumed, if we follow Guiraud's account, into the generic characteristics of tragedy. In the case of Herodotus, a general tendency of his dialect joins with the subject matter of his genre to make him abstemious in the use of nominal constructions, and thus a figure who stands apart from the rest of the "common literary patrimony": "We can explain the rarity of sentences lacking a verb as a trait of 'modernism' peculiar to Ionic. But we can also see in that fact a consequence of the historical and geographical genre, which multiplies descriptions and, consequently clauses, with ἐστί and εἰσί" (*Phrase nom.*, p. 159).[4]

We can take Guiraud's many qualifications as evidence *a fortiori* that genre combines with a large number of nonsemantic factors that influence the distribution of the nominal construction. In an attempt to gauge the relative importance of genre, I have conducted a brief survey of a few specific words and phrases in several authors, genres, and subgenres, giving special attention to prose authors. In part I simply marshal the

---

sions. (2) Metrical convenience. (3) Speed and economy of expression. (4) Individual preference. (5) Rules of genre. (6) Liking for variety. (7) Indifference and arbitrariness. We may add some categories investigated by Lasso de la Vega, "Orac. nom.": main clause vs. subordinate clause, interrogatives, exclamations, expressions with deictics. I am in strong agreement with Guiraud in regarding meter as the least important determinant (*Phrase nom.*, pp. 158–59).

4. Herodotus is a great nuisance for Guiraud. He candidly admits (p. 153) that Herodotean usage with οἰχός and χρεόν defy his *a priori* principles. Herodotus' descriptions of animals in Book 2 are distressingly nominal, and Guiraud offers (p. 158) what seems to me a desperate speculation: "it is not forbidden to suppose" that Herodotus was in that one spot imitating the style of the *Odyssey*.

pertinent findings of previous discussions; in a few cases I offer supplementary canvasses of my own.

Verbals in -τεο

C. E. Bishop's study is particularly useful for our purpose, as he offers statistics "by department." He reports that the grand total of "verbalia recorded between Theognis and Dinarchus, inclusive, is 1831. Speaking generally, the copula is expressed with about one in five of those verbals, the number of expressed copulae being 358" ("Verbals in -*TEO*," p. 249).[5] Bishop refines this statistic as follows: In tragedy the copula is "omitted" six times more often than it is expressed, in comedy twice as often, whereas in Herodotus the copula is expressed six times more often than not, in Thucydides about one-third times more often.[6] Taken *en masse*, orators show "omission" 130 times, expression 101 times, but Lysias, Lycurgus, and Dinarchus express the copula more often than not in a ratio of about 5:12, and Andocides and Isaeus show equal proportions of expression and "omission" (pp. 250–51).

Bishop finds that Plato's usage in the *Gorgias* is at variance from the rest of his writings. In that dialogue the nominal construction occurs about twice as often as the form with copula; elsewhere Plato shows the nominal construction about ten times more often. A survey of Plato's employment of ῥᾴδιον + infinitive shows a disparity between general and temporary habit similar to what Bishop finds: of 73 instances I have found only 11 with ἐστί, and 4 with εἶναι in *oratio obliqua*; 3 of the former and 3 of the latter appear in the *Cratylus,* and there is only 1 instance in the dialogue of ῥᾴδιον in the nominal construction.[7] These two examples of single-dialogue eccentricity are, in my opinion, nothing more than short-term

---

5. Bishop's figures for nonexpression of the copula are too high in my judgment. Conscious of the problem in defining "the limits beyond which an easily supplied copula should be considered omitted, and when not," he mentions Pl. *Lg.* 724b ἐστὶν ῥητέα τε καὶ ἀκουστέα as an example of "copula omitted" with the second verbal ("Verbals in -*TEO*," p. 249). I think that τε καί is too strong a bond to allow taking ῥητέα and ἀκουστέα as syntactically autonomous. Bishop also includes in his figures some passages with past-tense copulae (p. 251).

6. Bishop combines the two historians, which yields a ratio of 2:1 in favor of the expressed copula; my impression is that Thucydides did not find in Herodotus' general abstention from nominal constructions a genre tendency that he was to follow. Lasso de la Vega ("Orac. nom.," pp. 332–33) thinks that in this respect the practices of Heraclitus, Democritus, and Gorgias are pertinent. These very different notions of influence are easily explained: Bishop and Lasso de la Vega were looking at different things. The latter, for instance, also searched for -τέον in Thucydides, but as it happens there is only one in his sample, in the second book.

7. Including *Men.* 94e6, where Butterman conjectured ῥᾷον for the transmitted ῥᾴδιον as an instance of copula expressed, and also *Prot.* 328a7, where I see the εἶναι as carried over from a5. The total count of ῥᾴδιον + infinitive includes examples with oblique (i.e., nonzero) tenses and moods.

preferences, no different from words or phrases writers of any language favor for a short period.

Bishop's statistics for Xenophon show a near equality of the alternate forms in the totals for four works, the *Memorabilia,* the *Anabasis,* the *Cyropaedia,* and the *Hellenica.* But in the remainder of the Xenophontine corpus the nominal construction predominates in a ratio of about 4:1. The figures for the first four works named substantiate fairly well Bishop's claim that "as he approaches the more strictly historic style . . . Xenophon assumes the historiographer's mode, and the copula appears more frequently" ("Verbals in -*TEO,*" p. 250). The *Memorabilia* has 35 examples of verbals without copula, 10 with, the *Hellenica* 5 and 15, the *Anabasis* 8 and 14, respectively. It seems reasonable to regard the *Memorabilia* and, to a lesser extent, the *Cyropaedia,* as less historical than anecdotal, and so stylistically further from what Xenophon might have regarded as historiography per se than the *Anabasis,* which shows about the same ratio as Thucydides, and the *Hellenica,* which lies approximately between Thucydides and Herodotus.

Another indication of the role of nonsemantic factors in the choice of nominal construction is the differing treatment of plural verbalia. Bishop (p. 129) contrasts the exact balance of the plural with and without copula, 18 apiece, to the ratio of about one instance with as against 4 without in his total sample. To some extent this is epiphenomenal: Thucydides and Aristophanes, writers more favorable than many others to expression of the copula, account for 19 of the 36 plural verbals that Bishop counted.[8]

ῥᾴδιον + infinitive
In seven passages Euripides cast the syntagma ῥᾴδιον + infinitive in a nominal construction; only once is the copula expressed.[9] This strong preference for the nominal construction, together with the abundance of the word ῥᾴδιον in prose authors, makes possible some further genre and subgenre comparisons. I have already mentioned the distribution of nominal vs. verbal forms with ῥᾴδιον in Plato. My inspection of oratorical usage also shows a weaker predominance of the nominal construction. Taken as

---

8. Bishop (p. 127) reports 9 examples in Aristophanes (6 with copula) and 10 in Thucydides (6 with copula).

9. With ἐστί: *Hec.* 755. Nominal construction: *Alc.* 1053, *Ba.* 461, *Hec.* 664, 1247, *HF* 88, *IA* 1370, *Or.* 712. Three times ῥᾴδιον qualifies a noun or pronoun (*Ba* 1139, *Med.* 1375 [nisi ῥᾴδιοι legitur], *Tr.* 1057); each time the copula is omitted. (I note that Guiraud, *Phrase nom.,* p. 22, errs in reporting that Wilhelm Wilke, *De ellipsi copulae εἶναι in fabulis Euripideis* [Breslau, 1877], p. 7, found no instances of ῥᾴδιον with copula. In fact, Wilke mentions two instances, *Hec.* 755 and *Or.* 712–13, where he read τρόπαι᾽ ἦν, not the zero-tense copula even if that is what Euripides did write.)

a whole, the Demosthenic corpus holds 34 instances of ῥᾴδιον. Not of interest are 3 attestations with ἦν and one passage where the adjective merely qualifies πρᾶγμα in an appositional clause.[10] Of the 30 remaining instances, only 4 are attended by the present-tense indicative, third-person copula. Three of these appear in speeches marked as spurious by Rennie in his *OCT*.[11] This leaves a single instance at 27.32, in the very early speech against Aphobus. The nominal construction is, therefore, virtually obligatory in Demosthenic speeches, both forensic and symbouleutic.

The picture in Lysias is not as clear. The Lysianic corpus contains 19 occurrences of ῥᾴδιον + complementary infinitive.[12] Discarding 2 examples with ἦν (4.11, 16.7), and 2 with εἶναι in *oratio obliqua*, there are in the remainder 13 nominal constructions and 2 with ἐστί (6.7, 31.20). In the first, the oath immediately preceding suggests an unusually strong emphasis:

ὥστε μὰ τὸν Δία οὐ ῥᾴδιόν ἐστιν ὑμῖν αὐτῷ οὐδὲν χαρισαμένοις παρὰ τὸ δίκαιον λαθεῖν τοὺς Ἕλληνας.

It may have mattered that the complementary infinitive is quite abnormal in meaning something other than "perceive," "understand," or "explain." Moreover, oaths with μά are attested only four times in the Lysianic corpus, three times in this very speech and once in 8. The other example of the syntagma with copula occurs in a speech that is unusual because it was composed for delivery before the *boule*. But I can see no reason why that body would be better disposed to the verbal form than would heliastic jurors.[13]

Unfortunately, there are only two examples of ῥᾴδιον + complementary infinitive in Aristophanes: *Av.* 644, where φράζειν is easily supplied from the preceding words, and *Th.* 68. These are both nominal constructions occurring in nonparatragic lines, but they are too few to indicate the colloquialism of the construction.

10. I have not included 19.34 in the count, where the adjective goes with εἶναι.

11. 42.17,22; 43.81.

12. Including 24.11, deleted by Scheide. The complements in Lysias (as in the other orators) are normally words that mean "perceive," "understand," or "express" and pertain to the jury or speaker. An instance like 25.16 is unusual, for the meaning of the infinitive is not related to the litigant's argument per se.

13. Both 6 and 31 (especially the former) exhibit stylistic features that set them apart from practices in 12, the Lysianic "yardstick" (see Dover, *Lysias,* pp. 82, 88). If, as Dover suggests, the style of 6 was adjusted to suit the "personality and style of the person who was going to deliver it," the author (Lysias or whoever) may have permitted this feature, normally excluded from forensic oratory, as a colloquialism. The problem, as I point out in the next paragraph, is that the colloquialism of ῥᾴδιον with copula cannot be proved.

Isocrates' practice suggests that genre was considerably less important than other determinants. Of the 41 examples of the syntagma, 24 are in nominal construction, 12 have ἐστί, and five are with εἶναι.[14] I discern no pattern in the distribution of the two types among the various classes of the Isocratean corpus.

οἷός τε

It has already been noted that Herodotus shows a higher precentage of the nominal construction with verbals than Thucydides, and a much higher percentage than other Attic writers. We see something similar in the case of οἷός/οἷόν/οἷη τε. He wrote that syntagma with ἐστί or εἰσί 14 times, once in *oratio obliqua* with εἶναι, and once with εἶναι, but never in the nominal construction.[15] In Euripides the combination is nearly always found in nominal construction.[16] Again we are deprived of useful evidence from Aristophanes: there are only 2 examples of οἷός τε, both with copula, at *Nub.* 1402 and *Eq.* 737. In Demosthenes I have counted 30 examples of οἷός τε, most of which occur after ὡς. Of the 3 present-tense indicative examples, all are in nominal construction. Once more the data are too slender to permit a conclusion.

Plato wrote οἷός τε 45 times.[17] As in the Demosthenic corpus, many examples are barred from the nominal construction by requiring nonpresent, nonindicative, or non-third-person forms of the copula. Of the survivors, four are nominal constructions, five have the copula. If there is any significance to the distribution of these nine examples in respect of style, I have failed to perceive it. All that can be concluded is that Euripides and the Attic prose authors examined permitted themselves a choice between nominal and verbal expression with οἷός τε that Herodotus did not. Again, genre does not appear to be decisive.

ἀνάγκη + infinitive

Lasso de la Vega ("Orac. nom.," pp. 320–25, 334) presents the following statistics for nominal vs. verbal construction, broken down to show the

---

14. Complements in Isocrates unusual for being unrelated to the business of persuading the jury: 4.57, 5.92.

15. Both narrative and speeches are represented, the latter in somewhat greater numbers. Mere pedantry would insist on categorizing 7.16γ3 as nominal: εἰ δέ τοι οὕτω δεδόκηται γίνεσθαι καὶ οὐκ οἷά τε αὐτὸ παρατρέψαι. I have not, however, been so lax as to include several examples with the first and second persons or one with εἶναι in *oratio obliqua*.

16. Wilke ap. Guiraud, *Phrase nom.*, p. 22.

17. Here I have counted only the nominative singular. *Spuria* and *Epistulae* are also excluded from the count.

distribution in main and subordinate clauses, in a variety of authors and genres:[18]

| | *Nominal* | | *With copula* | |
	main	*subordinate*	*main*	*subordinate*
Plato, *Symposium*	38	5	3	1
Thucydides 2	19	5	—	1
Demosthenes 4, 6, 9, 18	25	5	12	5
Lysias 1, 7, 10, *Eroticus* apud Pl. *Phdr.* 231a–34c	17	6	5	1
Isocrates 4	29	1	13	3
Sophocles, *OT*	15	2	—	—
Aristophanes, *Lys.*	16	—	1	—
Lysias 2, 33	9	1	—	—
Plato, *Menex.*	10	2	—	—

This compilation shows that the orators do not maintain intergenre consistency: Isocrates wrote the verbal rather often in the epideictic speech examined by Lasso de la Vega, whereas the two Lysianic speeches of that subgenre and Plato in his parody of epideictic did not. However, the figures given by Lasso de la Vega for the *Symposium* may be a misleading indicator of Plato's personal preference, for in the *Phaedrus* and the first five books of the *Laws* I have found not one example of ἀνάγκη + infinitive with the copula.[19]

18. Lasso de la Vega's statistics are all for the third-person singular. Like Bishop, he counts as nominal constructions many passages where a copula lies just before the phrase in question (see "Orac. nom.," p. 317). I am made uncomfortable as well by his inclusion of the *Eroticus*, his omission of Lysias 12, and the statistics from the *Symposium* and *Lysistrata* taken as stylistically uniform units. Still, his work is of great value for its discrimination of sentence types and the comparison of principal and subordinate clauses.

19. There are 30 examples. I admit the possibility that at *Lg.* 671b2 ἀνάγκη, which stands alone in reply, picks up an implied ἐστί from ὑπεθέμεθα . . . ἀναγκαῖον εἶναι just before.

Appendix B. The Differentiae in Satyr Drama

Assembled here are all instances of the differentiae I have found in four plays securely identified as satyric: Aeschylus' *Dictyulci* and *Isthmiastai*,[1] Sophocles' *Ichneutae,* and Euripides' *Cyclops.* I have also examined the satyric *Sisyphus* attributed to Critias by Sextus Empiricus (Critias B25 D-K),[2] but have seen none of the differentiae therein.

Optatival infinitive: Soph. *Ichn.* 74 τυχεῖν[3]

Omission of ἄν with subjunctive in protasis: Soph. *Ichn.* 145 εἰ δέ που δέῃ

Poetic plurals: Eur. *Cyclops* 23 δόμοις, 33 δόμους, 280 ἁρπαγὰς, 597 οἴκους (Canter, for the transmitted οἴνους), 536 δόμοισι, 679 δόμων[4]

Terminal accusatives: Aesch. *Dictyulci* 806 ἴξῃ . . . χέρας,[5] Eur. *Cyclops* 43 lyr. νίσῃ σκοπέλους, 92–93 γνάθμον ἀφιγμένοι

"Genitive of agent": Eur. *Cyclops* 24 ἑνὸς ληφθέντες[6]

Satyr drama, the *Cyclops* above all, exhibits a number of formal marks associated with comedy: the deictic iota,[7] diminutives, violations of Porson's law, toleration of anapests in trimeter past the first foot, etc. The presence of syntactical features common in tragedy per se, even in the *Cyclops,* shows how strongly satyr drama juxtaposed the low and the high.

1. See R. G. Ussher, "Aeschylus' *Isthmiastai* as Satyr Drama," *Phoenix* 31 (1977): 287–99.

2. D. Sutton points to the diminutive χωρίον at l. 39 as strong evidence that the play was satyric ("Critias and Atheism," *CQ* 31 [1981]: 35–36). Euripidean authorship is ably defended by D. Panchenko, "Euripid ili Kritii?" *Vestnik drevnei istorii* 151 (1980): 144–62.

3. Pearson (*The Fragments of Sophocles,* ad loc.) terms the infinitive "exclamatory."

4. We might also include all plural words in the *Cyclops* that designate Polyphemus' one eye (so Ussher ad 20–22).

5. Conceivably the accusative is felt with ἐς in the line before.

6. See Ussher ad loc.

7. *Cyclops* 169, and perhaps much earlier in the history of the genre at Aesch. *Isthmiastai* 88, where Lloyd-Jones reads τουτ[ὶ]. In general, however, "concessions to comedy" appear to have been far less conspicuous in satyr drama before the *Cyclops:* see R. G. Ussher, "Sophocles' *Ichneutai* as a Satyr Play," *Hermathena* 118 (1974): 130–38.

Appendix C. The Differentiae in Fourth-Century Tragedy

The remnants are meager, the textual tradition weak. Consequently, it would be imprudent to make any generalization on the fate of the differentiae in the fourth century, except to say that they did not utterly disappear. My survey produces the following (text and numeration from Snell, *Tragicorum Graecorum Fragmenta*, vol. 4):

60 Astydamas II fr. 8.3 καλεῖν—jussive infinitive.
70 Carcinus II fr. 1 ἀσκεῖν, εὐτυχεῖν—possibly jussive infinitives, but preceding lines may have held a governing verb.
    fr. 5.2 βουλεύμασιν—poetic plural from a fifth-century perspective, but cf. Pl. *R.* 334a.
71 Chaeremon fr. 14.17 λειμῶσι—illative dative.
    fr. 20 σχολῇ βαδίζων ὁ χρόνος ἀφικνεῖται τ⟨ὸ π⟩ᾶν (ταν Grotius ἐκφανεῖ τὸ πᾶν Meineke)—terminal accusative.
72 Theodectes fr. 13.1 δόμους—poetic plural
88 Diogenes Sinop. fr. 5.2 δόμων—poetic plural.

Principal Texts and Commentaries

The entry for each author or collection opens with the edition whose text, critical apparatus, and numeration I normally display.

Aeschines: ed. Friedrich Blass. Edition of 1908, corr. Ulrich Schindel. Stuttgart, 1978.

Aeschylus: ed. Denys Page. Oxford, 1972.

Agamemnon: Eduard Fraenkel. Oxford, 1950. J. D. Denniston and Denys Page. Oxford, 1957.

Choephoroi: Arthur Sidgwick. 2d ed. Oxford, 1884.

Persae: H. D. Broadhead. Cambridge, 1960. Petrus Groeneboom. Göttingen, 1960 (translated into German from the Dutch original).

Septem: Petrus Groeneboom. Groningen, 1938.

Fragments: ed. H. W. Smyth and Hugh Lloyd-Jones (Loeb Classical Library: Aeschylus, vol. 2), 2d ed. Cambridge, Mass., 1963. H. J. Mette. Berlin, 1959.

Index Aeschyleus: Gabriel Italie. 2d ed., rev. S. L. Radt. Leiden, 1964.

Andocides: ed. Friedrich Blass and Karl Fuhr. Leipzig, 1913.

On the Mysteries: Douglas MacDowell. Oxford, 1962.

De pace: Umberto Albini. Florence, 1964.

De reditu: Umberto Albini. Florence, 1961.

Antiphon: ed. Friedrich Blass and Theodor Thalheim. Leipzig, 1914.

Tetralogies: Fernanda Decleva Caizzi. Milan, 1969.

Index Antiphonteus: F. L. Van Cleef. Ithaca, 1895.

Aristophanes: ed. Victor Coulon. Paris, 1923–30. ed. (with commentary) Jan van Leeuwen. Leiden, 1893–1906.

Clouds: K. J. Dover. Oxford, 1968.

Ecclesiazusae: R. G. Ussher. Oxford, 1973.

Lysistrata: Ulrich von Wilamowitz-Möllendorf. Berlin, 1927.

Ranae: W. B. Stanford. 2d ed. London, 1963.

Vespae: Douglas MacDowell. Oxford, 1971.

Index Aristophaneus: O. J. Todd. Cambridge, 1932.

A Complete Concordance to the Comedies and Fragments of Aristophanes: Henry Dunbar. Oxford, 1883.

Aristotle: *Poetica*: ed. Rudolf Kassel. Oxford, 1965. comm. D. W. Lucas. Oxford, 1968.

Politica: ed. W. D. Ross. Oxford, 1957.

Rhetorica: ed. W. D. Ross. Oxford, 1959.

Bacchylides: ed. Bruno Snell and Herwig Maehler. Leipzig, 1964.

Comicorum Atticorum Fragmenta: ed. Theodor Kock. Leipzig, 1880–88.

Demosthenes: ed. S. H. Butcher, William Rennie. Oxford, 1903–1931.

Index Demosthenicus: Siegmund Preuss. Leipzig, 1892.

Empedocles: ed. M. R. Wright. New Haven, 1981.

Euripides: ed. Gilbert Murray. Oxford, 1902–1910.

Alcestis: A. M. Dale. Oxford, 1954.

Andromache: P. T. Stevens. Oxford, 1971.

Bacchae: E. R. Dodds. 2d ed. Oxford, 1960.

Cyclops: R. G. Ussher. Rome, 1978.

Electra: J. D. Denniston. Oxford, 1939.

Helen: Richard Kannicht. Heidelberg, 1969.

Hercules Furens: Ulrich von Wilamowitz-Möllendorf. 2d ed. Berlin, 1895.

Hippolytus: W. S. Barrett. Oxford, 1964.

Medea: Denys Page. Oxford, 1938.

Orestes: Vincenzo di Benedetto. Florence, 1965.

Supplices: Christopher Collard. Groningen, 1975.

Troades: K. H. Lee. London, 1976.

A Concordance to Euripides: J. T. Allen and Gabriel Italie. Berkeley and Los Angeles, 1954.

Herodotus: ed. Karl Hude. Oxford, 1908. ed. (with commentary) Heinrich Stein. Various eds. Berlin, 1877–1883.

A Lexicon to Herodotus: J. E. Powell. Cambridge, 1938.

Homer: ed. D. B. Monro and T. W. Allen. Oxford, 1902–1908.

Iliad: Walter Leaf. 2d ed. London, 1900–1902.

Isaeus: ed. Pierre Roussel. Paris, 1922. ed (with commentary) William Wyse. Cambridge, 1904.

Index to the Speeches of Isaeus: W. A. Coligher and W. S. Maguiness. Cambridge, 1961.

Isocrates: ed. Georges Mathieu and Émile Brémond. Paris, 1950–56.

Index Isocrateus: Siegmund Preuss. Leipzig, 1904.

Lyric Poets: *Poetarum Lesbiorum Fragmenta*. Edgar Lobel and Denys Page. Oxford, 1955.

Poetae Melici Graeci. ed. Denys Page. Oxford, 1962.

Iambi et Elegi Graeci: ed. Martin L. West. Oxford, 1971–72.

Poetarum elegiacorum testimonia et fragmenta: ed. Bruno Gentili and Carlo Prato. Leipzig, 1979.

Lysias: ed. Karl Hude. Oxford, 1912.

Index Lysiacus: D. H. Holmes. Bonn, 1895.

Pindar: ed. Bruno Snell and Herwig Maehler. Epinicians: Leipzig, 1971.

Fragments: 3d ed. Leipzig, 1964.

Lexicon to Pindar: W. J. Slater. Berlin, 1969.

Plato: ed. John Burnet. Oxford, 1900–1907.

Gorgias: E. R. Dodds. Oxford, 1959.

A Word Index to Plato: Leonard Brandwood. Leeds, 1976.

Sophocles: ed. A. C. Pearson. Oxford, 1924. ed. (with commentary) R. C. Jebb. Cambridge, 1883–96.

Ajax: J. C. Kamerbeek. 2d ed. Leiden, 1963.

Antigone: Gerhard Müller. Heidelberg, 1967. J. C. Kamerbeek. Leiden, 1978.

Electra: J. C. Kamerbeek. Leiden, 1974.

Oedipus Rex: J. C. Kamerbeek, Leiden, 1967.

Trachiniae: J. C. Kamerbeek. Leiden, 1959.

Fragments: ed. A. C. Pearson. Cambridge, 1917.

Lexicon Sophocleum (= *Lex. Soph.*): F. T. Ellendt. 2d ed., rev. H. F. Genthe. Berlin, 1872.

Thucydides: ed. H. S. Jones. Ed. with ap. crit. rev. J. E. Powell. Oxford, 1942.

Commentaries: K. W. Krüger. 2d ed. Berlin, 1859–60. Julius Steup and Johannes Classen. 3d–5th eds. Berlin, 1908–1922. A. W. Gomme, Antony Andrewes, K. J. Dover. Oxford, 1956–81.

Tragicorum Graecorum Fragmenta: ed. August Nauck. 2d ed., rev. Bruno Snell. Hildesheim, 1964. ed. Denys Page (Greek Literary Papyri, vol. 3 [Loeb Classical Library]), Cambridge, 1942.

Xenophon: ed. E. C. Marchant. Oxford, 1900–1920.

Lexicon Xenophanteum: F. W. Sturz. Leipzig, 1801–1804.

Index Locorum

General Index